A SELECTED BIBLIOGRAPHY
ON VALUES, ETHICS, AND ESTHETICS

Harvard University, Laboratory of Social Relations, Cambridge, Mass.

and

Center for Advanced Study in the Behavioral Sciences, Stanford, Cal.

A Selected Bibliography on

Values, Ethics, and Esthetics

in the Behavioral Sciences and Philosophy, 1920-1958

by

Ethel M. Albert
Clyde Kluckhohn

with the assistance of

Robert LeVine
Warren Seulowitz
Miriam Gallaher

THE FREE PRESS OF GLENCOE, ILLINOIS

CONTENTS

Preface and Acknowledgments .... vii–xviii

Abbreviations for References Used in the
  Bibliography 1–2

Guide to the Bibliography 3–41

The Bibliography

  I. Anthropology 43–86

  II. Psychology, Social and Educational
     Psychology, Psychiatry and Psycho-
     analysis 87–136

  III. Sociology 137–180

  IV. Political Science, Public Administration
     and Government 181–201

  V. Economics 202–224

  VI. Philosophy 225–299

  VII. Related Sources Outside the Behavioral
     Sciences and Philosophy

     A. Humanities, History, Law and
       Theology 300–311

     B. Physical Sciences, Biology and
       Mathematics 312–322

Alphabetical Index of Authors 323–339

Appendix 340–342

PREFACE

A historical account will clarify as much as anything what this bibliography attempts and what it does not. For some time before their participation in the Comparative Study of Values in Five Cultures Project of the Laboratory of Social Relations, Harvard University (1949-1955), * the compilers had been accumulating bibliographies on values. Though fragmentary, the references were useful to colleagues on the project, behavioral scientists who had little acquaintance with either the philosophical literature on values or the numerous but scattered publications of behavioral scientists, some of which appeared in volumes or periodicals not frequently read by anthropologists, psychologists, and sociologists. As a first step, Dr. Victor Ayoub, who had had undergraduate training in philosophy, prepared a brief working bibliography of important books, chiefly in philosophy. With his list were collated the references in the files of Kluckhohn and Albert. It soon became clear that the collection would be much more serviceable if it were enlarged. With the help of Victor Ayoub and John Waggoner and of numerous colleagues at Harvard and at other universities who had also been collecting values bibliography, a duplicated draft was produced during the

---

* Supported by the Rockefeller Foundation through its Division of Social Sciences.

summer of 1954 of "A Selected Values Bibliography for the Comparative Study of Values."

Reactions to this document convinced us that extended, systematic search and some editing were required to produce a satisfactory research instrument. Mr. Robert LeVine during 1954-55 and Mr. Warren Seulowitz during 1955-57 at Harvard University, and Miss Miriam Gallaher during 1958 at the Center for Advanced Study in the Behavioral Sciences gave much time to library research and to consultation and correspondence with informed scholars in the United States and abroad. Both authors have been Fellows at the Center for Advanced Study in the Behavioral Sciences, where the final draft of the bibliography was prepared.

The very magnitude of the task as it developed is to us an indication of its probable utility. Interest in the field of values and its ramifications has grown considerably during the past few decades and continues to grow. The major trend in the recent study of values is, moreover, increasingly interdisciplinary in character. Yet, with the partial exception of the philosophical journals, there has been no "obvious" place in which to publish on the subject. Although there has been a great amount of research on values, it has been less cumulative than is desirable, and acquaintance with the ideas and research results in one's own or other disciplines has often been inadequate.

The great quantity and variety of literature on values and the dispersal of its sources are the formidable conditions that inspired and yet rendered problematic the assembling of this values bibliography. It has perforce been considered the sufficient goal of the bibliography to collect a fair and representative sample of what has been written on values in recent years in the behavioral sciences and philosophy and to arrange some two-thousand entries selected in as orderly and useful a way as the present state of the subject permits.

A decision had to be made as to how "values" would be conceived for the purposes of the bibliography. It is a notoriously vague and ambiguous term, differently defined by each writer. The authors have expressed their own views elsewhere, * but authoritative definition for general use is not the task of bibliography. If a writer has chosen to call his subject "values," his decision was respected and the work included when it fell within the defined objectives of the bibliography in other respects. Acceptance of a variety of meanings of the term has produced an ill-assorted assemblage in parts of the bibliography. Some concepts bearing a different name have been omitted though closely

---

* Kluckhohn, Clyde, Values and Value-Orientations in the Theory of Action, Toward a General Theory of Action, (Parsons, Talcott; Shils, Edward, and Tolman, E. C., eds.), Cambridge: Harvard University Press: 388-433 (1951). Albert, Ethel M., The Classification of Values: A Method and Illustration, American Anthropologist 58: 221-248 (1956).

related to values while others, possibly with a poorer title, have been included. We are fully at ease with only one exclusion, that of current value theory in economics, where "value" is unequivocally defined as "price." The literature on public opinion, attitudes, prejudice, communication, decision-making, as well as law and jurisprudence, religion, theology and the history of morals, though unequivocally germane to the study of values in the behavioral sciences, would require separate bibliographical ventures. Only a small sample of the work done in these fields was included, the deficiency to some degree compensated by the inclusion, wherever possible, of bibliographical sources for them. The section on esthetics does not list more than a fraction of the numerous publications on myths and the various arts which are source material for the study of esthetic values in non-literate cultures. Obviously, merely a reference to value in passing or a presumed or possible relevance to values did not justify inclusion of a work in the bibliography.

Almost all of the entries are in English and chiefly of American provenience. A few references are given in French, German and other European languages, with English translations where these were found. In fine, it was assumed that the bibliography would be used chiefly by American scholars, a fair assumption in view of the results of the bibliography search, that by far the greatest interest in values for the time covered is in the United States.

While in philosophy, values inquiry in some form goes back to the beginning of its history, in the behavioral sciences, the 1920's and 1930's appeared to be the time of the real stirring of interest in the descriptive (i. e., non-philosophical) study of values. Full and systematic library search covered the period 1935-spring 1958, but the immediately preceding period was well enough represented to suggest 1920 as a good starting-point for the bibliography. Here, however, as with most decisions that had to be made, certain exceptions were recognized as more important than the decisions as such. The classical tradition of philosophy, it was felt, had to be covered. This was done through the inclusion of anthologies, some written well before 1920. Where the significant writings of individuals within the 1920-1958 time period extended back in time some years before it, they were, of course, included in the listing (e.g., the works of Alfred Kroeber in anthropology). Early works of historical interest were also included (e.g., Washington Matthews's study of American Indian ethics in 1899 as one of the first of its kind). Where work produced prior to 1920 continues to be influential (e.g., G. E. Moore's Principia Ethica, 1903, which is now more influential in philosophy than it was at the time of its first publication), or a work provides background or information relevant to the more recent study of values, it was included despite the fact that publication pre-dated 1920. Some 4% of the total entries are of this kind. * At the other end of the temporal span, where information was obtained about works in progress or in press that seemed of importance for the study of values, the titles were included, and these take up some 1% of the total number of entries.

Two considerations chiefly determined the decision as to which of the six to seven thousand titles that had been accumulated in the course of the search would be included in the final draft and which excluded. First, it was patently impractical to attempt an exhaustive listing. The result would be both too unwieldly and too detailed to be of any real use. Experience with the bibliography in manuscript form suggested the present number as convenient and sufficiently comprehensive for ordinary research purposes. The attempt to restrict the number of entries by using a criterion of quality failed, as did the attempt to indicate judgments of different quality among the entries included. To the surprise of the compilers, there was little agreement between them as to which writings were so good that inclusion was imperative, which so poor that exclusion was obvious. It may be that qualitative judgments must vary with the particular research interests of

---

* A bibliography of the periodical literature on values in philosophy (in English, French and German), for the period 1867-1937, has been assembled, without annotation, in: David Rynin, Supervisor (1937) Index to Philosophical Periodical Literature, Berkeley, Calif., vol. V, 307-333. Available in the Howison Library, Dwinelle Hall, University of California at Berkeley.

each investigator. At all events, neither inclusion nor exclusion represents our opinion of the quality of a publication. It is altogether possible that significant and relevant works have failed to come to the attention of the compilers or have, in the process of repeated reshufflings, been inadvertently omitted. If this has occurred, it can only cause us lively regrets. In examining our titles, we found ourselves decreasingly concerned with deciding which papers or books were in some sense significant and increasingly concerned with identifying the principal approaches actually in use in the study of values. The second principle, then, for deciding what titles to include was that of mapping the various areas of values inquiry in the behavioral sciences and philosophy. Further, it was decided to follow through with related references from outside the immediate field of values. So, for example, consideration of value relativity and universals tends to involve the investigator in questions of cultural relativity and universals, and titles on the latter are included in the bibliography. The entries on decision-making, choice and utility in relation to values are supported by references to the statistical and mathematical sources of the models used. What was sacrificed for the sake of following value concepts through to their theoretical origins or extensions in other fields were chiefly titles of a kind already abundantly represented in the bibliography, e.g., philosophical analyses of various ethical terms, descriptions of the values of groups of schoolchildren. Entries not directly on values but included as relevant to the subject are marked distinctively. These constitute about 6-1/2% of the total number of entries. In the same spirit, room was made for works on values by physical scientists, biologists, mathematicians, theologians, lawyers, and others outside the behavioral sciences and philosophy, when these seemed intrinsically interesting as value theory or value philosophy, or when they bore directly on themes treated by behavioral scientists, e.g., evolutionism in relation to ethics or the relation of facts and values in scientific inquiry.

Persistent trial and error persuaded the compilers that by far the most manageable and ultimately most useful way of classifying the entries was by alphabetical order according to author within the disciplinary specialty of each. Professional affiliation as anthropologist, socio- logist, economist, etc., was checked in: Jacques Cattell, Editor (1956) American Men of Science: A Biographical Directory, New York, R. R. Bowker Co., vol. III. Also used were the Directory of American Scholars (eighth ed.) and, for scholars from outside the United States, the Index Generalis (Paris). Individuals noted as being in more than one discipline in the directory were for the most part listed under the first-named specialty and cross-referred to the other. Where it was not possible to ascertain an author's professional affiliation in any of the directories or lists of members of learned societies, the entry was made in the category suggested by the subject matter. There are certain residual irregularities of classification of a small number of authors. An alphabetical index of authors is provided.

An approximation to a subject index for the bibliography is the "Guide to the Bibliography," in which several score topics are listed, together with the numbers of the relevant entries. The choice of topics was inductively determined, and the Guide is no more a systematic or logical system of concepts than is the field of values it attempts to chart. Whereas the body of the bibliography reveals the range of subjects treated within each discipline, the Guide brings together for each topic the work done on it in the various behavioral sciences and philosophy. The interdisciplinary spread is of more than casual magnitude for a large number of research interests, as inspection of the Guide will show.

Most of the entries have been annotated, though not where the title seemed adequate to suggest the content. Some of the annotations, though superfluous for those conversant with a given field, will, it is hoped, be helpful to those from other disciplines. Thus, a remark on an anthropological source that may convey no new information to an anthropologist may do so for a psychiatrist or philosopher.

We have been mindful throughout of the interdisciplinary character of the bibliography. Individuals interested in a particular subject may find the bibliography listing less than exhaustive on that subject. Such individuals, it is assumed, will already have a firm command of the material and can use this bibliography to check that their own is as complete as it need be. Of somewhat greater potential utility is the information made easily available on what is being done on a given subject in disciplines other than the researcher's. The bibliography may also suggest related subjects in the same or other disciplines that can profitably be considered in designing or executing values research. For those interested in the overall characteristics of the field of values, reading straight through the bibliography, while likely to prove a strange, even "surrealistic" experience, may provide a challenge to systematization. If so, the future of the study of values may be more satisfactory than the past mirrored in the present collection.

If the values bibliography should, in spite of its many limitations and defects, prove useful, it will in no small measure be due to the assistance given by many persons. We acknowledge with gratitude our debt to Dr. Ralph W. Tyler, Director of the Center for Advanced Study in the Behavioral Sciences (supported by a grant from the Ford Foundation), for a subsidy which made possible the publication of the manuscript. We also express our gratitude for the privilege of working at the Center and for research assistance on this bibliography provided to us there.

During the five years of compilation, we have been provided with titles for our bibliography by many, including some (indicated by *) who have been participants with us in the Comparative Study of Values in Five Cultures Project. For this help we gratefully acknowledge our debt to Gordon W. Allport, Victor Ayoub,* Jerome S. Bruner, Robert Butts, William F. Dukes, Munro S. Edmonson,* Felix M. Keesing, John Ladd,* George Mills,* Charles W. Morris, Kaspar Naegele,* Thomas F. O'Dea,* Talcott Parsons,* Sheldon P. Peterfreund, Father John Rock, David Schneider, Niel Smelser and Otto von Mering*. For suggestions and helpful comments, the authors are indebted to Abraham Edel, Charles B. Fahs and the late Robert Redfield. For making available the facilities of the Values Study as its coordinator and for his encouragement, thanks are due to Evon Z. Vogt. We are very much obliged for suggestions and references to the following who were Fellows at the Center for Advanced Study in the Behavioral Sciences in 1957-58: David Easton, Heinz Eulau, Milton Friedman, David Mandelbaum, Melvin Reder, Milton Singer, Robert Solow and George Stigler, and to Kenneth Arrow, a Fellow during 1956-57. Mr. Ivan Johnson, Librarian of the Center for Advanced Study in the Behavioral Sciences, was most helpful in dealing with questions of form for the bibliography. Mrs. Barbara Anderson gallantly undertook the task of checking the accuracy of several thousand entries prior to final typing. To Mrs.

Clarissa Schnebli, Mrs. June Barnes, the late Miss Betty
Edwards and Mrs. Mary Tye, goes not the least part of
our gratitude for their patient and efficient performance of
the painstaking clerical and typing work needed to trans-
form a sheaf of reference cards into a presentable manuscript.

ABBREVIATIONS FOR REFERENCES USED IN THE
BIBLIOGRAPHY

Abbreviation	Word	Abbreviation	Word
Acad.	Academy	Med.	Medical, Medicine
Amer.	American		
Anthrop.	Anthropological, Anthropology	Natl.	National
		Pers.	Personality
Appl.	Applied	Phen.	Phenomenological
Archaeol.	Archaeology	Phil.	Philosophical, Philosophy
Assn.	Association		
Brit.	British	Pol.	Political, Politics
Bull.	Bulletin	Proc.	Proceedings of the ...
Comp.	Comparative		
Econ.	Economics, Economy	Psycho-Anal.	Psycho-Analysis, Psycho-Analytic
Ed.	Edition, Editor	Psychol.	Psychological, Psychology
Educ.	Education	Publ. Opin.	Public Opinion
Ethnol.	Ethnology	Quart.	Quarterly
Genl.	General	Res.	Research
Inst.	Institute	Rev.	Review, Revue
Internatl.	International	Rev. ed.	Revised edition
J.	Journal of ...		
Measmt.	Measurement	Sci.	Science, Scientific

Abbreviation	Word	Abbreviation	Word
Soc.	Social, Society	Trans. by	Translated by ...
Sociol.	Sociological, Sociology	Univ.	University, Universities
Stud.	Studies	U.S.G.P.O.	United States Government Printing Office
S.W.	Southwestern		
Symp.	Symposium		
Trans.	Transactions	Vol.	Volume

BRIEF FORMS FOR REFERENCES

Harvard Values Study: "Comparative Study of Values in Five Cultures" Project, Laboratory of Social Relations, Harvard University.

Peabody Museum, Harvard: Papers of the Peabody Museum of Harvard University.

Res. Stud. Washington: Research Studies of the State College of Washington.

Symp. Sci. Phil. Relig.: Symposia of the Congress on Science, Philosophy and Religion, Edited by Lyman Bryson and Louis Finkelstein, et al. New York: Harper.

Note: + before an entry in the bibliography designates a work that is relevant to, but not directly concerned with, values.

GUIDE TO THE BIBLIOGRAPHY

OUTLINE

I. Definition, Classification and Theory for Values Research.

II. Topical Studies.

    1. Administration and Values.

    2. Authoritarianism and Authority.

    3. Change and Persistence in Personal and Social Values.

    4. Change, Conflict and Persistence of Values in Culture Contact.

    5. Children's and Adolescents' Values.

    6. Choice and Preference.

    7. Communication, Information, Public Opinion and Propaganda in Relation to Values.

    8. Conflict, Deviance, Disorganization and Crises Involving Values.

    9. Cross-Cultural Comparisons of Values.

    10. Culture and Personality; National Character.

    11. Decision-Making.

    12. Democracy.

13. Economic Theory, Economic Organization and Values; Economic Values and Goals.

14. Free Will, Determinism and Indeterminacy.

15. Freedom and Liberty.

16. Game Theory in Relation to Values.

17. Ideology.

18. International Relations and Values.

19. Kinship, Family and Marriage in Relation to Values.

20. Language, Symbols and Signs in Relation to Values.

21. Law, Justice, Jurisprudence and the Judicial Process.

22. Mental Health, Adjustment and Therapy in Relation to Values.

23. Moral Judgments.

24. Morals in Business and Government.

25. Pattern, Consistency and Integration in Relation to Values.

26. Perception and Values.

27. Personality, Character and Values.

28. Planning and Values.

29. Policy.

30. Political Behavior and Values.

31. Political Philosophy, Political Theory and Values.

32. Power.

33. Psychoanalysis and Values.

34. Reason and Cognition in Ethics and Value Theory.

35. Relativism, Cultural and Ethical.

36. Religion and Values.

37. Sanctions, Conscience and Punishment.

38. Sex, Morals and Values.

39. Social Control, Norms, Taboos and Conformity.

40. Social Stratification and Values.

41. Social System, Structure and Organization in Relation to Values.

42. Social Welfare in Economic Theory.

43. Socialization, Learning, Child Development and Education.

44. Students' Values.

45. Universals, Descriptive and Ethical.

46. Utility Theory.

47. Work, Vocational and Occupational Values.

III. Area Studies.

1. Africa.

2. American Indians.

3. Asia: China, India and Ceylon, Japan, Near East.

4. Europe and European-based Communities in Africa, Latin America, Australia and New Zealand.

5. Oceania.

6. United States: General and Ethnic Groups.

IV. Methods of Values Inquiry.

1. Content Analysis.

2. Comparative Methods and Studies of Variation.

3. Experimental, Interview and Quantitative Methods: General, Questionnaires, Scales and Inventories, Tests.

4. Interdisciplinary Approaches.

5. Mathematical, Statistical and Formal Models.

6. Philosophical Methods.

V. Values and Science.

1. Biological Bases of Values.

2. Ethics and the Behavioral Sciences.

3. Facts and Values.

4. Science as an Ethic.

5. Science of Values and of Ethics and Normative Science.

6. Scientific Esthetics.

7. Scientific Theory, Action and Values.

8. Value Judgments and Neutrality in Scientific Inquiry.

9. Value Theories Developed from Behavioral Science Theories.

10. Value Theory and Scientific Knowledge: Methodological Issues.

VI. Philosophical Value and Ethical Theories.

1. Contextualism.

2. Deontology.

3. Evolutionism.

4. Existentialism.

5. General Theory of Value.

6. Humanism.

7. Idealism and Personalism.

8. Intuitionism.

9. Logical Empiricism and Positivism.

10. Materialism.

11. Phenomenology.

-7-

12. Philosophical Analysis, Metaethics and Linguistic Approaches to Values and Ethics.

13. Pragmatism.

14. Self-Realization Theories.

15. Theological Value and Ethical Theories.

16. Utilitarianism.

17. Readers, Anthologies and Surveys in Moral Philosophy and Ethical Theory.

VII. Logico-Linguistic Analyses.

1. Analyses of Moral and Value Judgments.

2. Analyses of Value Terms; Definability or Indefinability of Value Terms.

3. Cognitivism.

4. Emotivism.

5. Ethics ("Value") and Morals ("Obligation") Distinguished.

6. Objectivity and Subjectivity in Value Judgments.

VIII. Esthetics and Studies of Art, Humor, Literature and Music.

I.   DEFINITION, CLASSIFICATION AND THEORY FOR
     VALUES RESEARCH.

     (Anthrop.) 36, 56, 76-77, 80, 89, 92, 96, 120, 122, 132-
     133, 142, 158-160, 166, 177, 187, 207, 214-217, 235,
     240, 249, 255, 261, 269, 282, 293-294; (Psychol.) 314-
     315, 320, 341, 346, 363, 373, 389, 392, 395, 417, 433,
     442, 447, 471, 479, 481, 484, 494-495, 501, 532, 541,
     551, 561, 564, 567, 568, 569, 576, 581, 587, 592, 596,
     606-607, 608, 616; (Sociol.) 634, 644, 647-648, 664, 674,
     677-678, 682, 688-689, 696, 703-705, 715, 732, 733, 779,
     807, 812, 814, 825-826, 830-831, 858, 863, 869, 875,
     904-905, 917; (Pol. Sci.) 942, 999-1000, 1062; (Econ.)
     1066, 1069, 1096, 1171, 1195, 1211, 1225; (Phil.) 1241-
     1242, 1262, 1264, 1274, 1276, 1316, 1363, 1400, 1537,
     1561, 1597, 1619-1621, 1625, 1668, 1674, 1734, 1752,
     1783-1784; (Other) 1969, 1970. See also: V. Values and
     Science; VI. Philosophical Value and Ethical Theories,
     especially 5, General Theory of Value.

---

* Successive numbers separated by commas refer to works of
  different authors, those separated by dashes of the same
  author.

II.   TOPICAL STUDIES.

  1. Administration and Values. (Anthrop.) 63-65, 130, 131,
      134, 135, 137, 275; (Psychol.) 425; (Sociol.) 652, 844-
      845; (Pol. Sci.) 924-925, 955, 963, 971, 982, 1010, 1036,
      1038-1039, 1052; (Econ.) 1073, 1130, 1174, 1220; (Other)
      1858. See Also: II. 24, Morals in Business and Govern-
      ment.

  2. Authoritarianism and Authority. (Anthrop.) 58, 168;
      (Psychol.) 307, 457, 566; (Sociol.) 652, 704, 722, 760,
      918; (Pol. Sci.) 1033; (Phil.) 1275, 1394, 1638; (Other)
      1874.

  3. Change and Persistence in Personal and Social Values.
      (Psychol.) 318, 367, 451, 458, 553, 620, 623, 628, 632;
      (Sociol.) 669, 685, 687, 689, 707, 712, 715, 762, 767-
      768, 781, 810, 821, 832, 835, 839, 889, 893, 894, 899;
      (Econ.) 1149, 1223; (Phil.) 1334, 1636; (Other) 1920.

  4. Change, Conflict and Persistence of Values in Culture
      Contact. (Anthrop.) 3, 8, 9, 20, 27, 33, 39, 48, 52, 55,
      60, 68, 76, 105, 126-127, 131, 135, 148, 153, 175, 210,
      230, 235, 238, 251-252, 254, 274-275, 283; (Psychol.)
      362, 369, 481, 483, 487; (Sociol.) 649-650, 708, 710, 719,

737, 780, 853, 857, 874, 885, 888; (Pol. Sci.) 926, 1027, 1045; (Econ.) 1090, 1134, 1170, 1229; (Phil.) 1637, 1785; (Other) 1858. See also: II. 13, Economic Theory; II. 31, Political Philosophy.

5. Children's and Adolescents' Values. (Anthrop.) 97, 225, 267; (Psychol.) 304, 327, 366, 370, 397-398, 412, 434-437, 440, 446, 457, 468, 485, 496, 499, 505, 542, 560, 610, 611, 629; (Sociol.) 843. See also: II. 43, Socialization; II. 44, Students' Values.

6. Choice and Preference. (Psychol.) 375, 428, 462, 547-548, 554, 600; (Sociol.) 711; (Pol. Sci.) 1021, 1039-1040; (Econ.) 1065-1066, 1085, 1088-1089, 1113, 1117, 1156; (Phil.) 1233, 1366, 1532, 1544, 1621, 1642, 1675-1676, 1763, 1767; (Other) 1845, 1959, 1983, 1985, 1987. See also: II. 11, Decision-Making; II. 14, Free Will and Determinism; II. 16, Game Theory; II. 46, Utility Theory; VI. Philosophy.

7. Communication, Information, Public Opinion and Propaganda in Relation to Values. (Anthrop.) 17, 26, 75; (Psychol.) 445, 478, 521, 569, 583; (Sociol.) 656-657, 680, 756, 761, 858, 861; (Pol. Sci.) 923, 941, 983, 1041,

1049; (Econ.) 1134, 1220; (Phil.) 1302; (Other) 1852, 1980, 1991. See also: II. 17, Ideology; II. 20, Language, Symbols and Signs.

8. Conflict, Deviance, Disorganization and Crises Involving Values. (Anthrop.) 26, 85, 124, 126, 179, 186, 194, 242, 275; (Psychol.) 304, 322, 332, 333, 334, 335, 418, 424, 444, 459, 460, 486, 498, 518, 520, 531, 589, 603, 625, 633; (Sociol.) 637, 639, 659, 661, 662, 687, 690, 693, 729, 736, 750, 754, 758, 769, 775, 800, 802, 803, 805, 816, 820, 827, 836, 854, 871, 876, 878, 879, 898, 901, 913; (Pol. Sci.) 1146; (Econ.) 1128, 1142; (Phil.) 1292, 1347, 1409, 1438, 1499, 1500-1502, 1574, 1578, 1605, 1768-1769; (Other) 1904, 1917, 1931, 1932, 1949-1950, 1953, 1978. See also: II. 4, Change ... in Culture Contact; II. 37, Sanctions.

9. Cross-Cultural Comparisons of Values. (Anthrop.) 3, 9, 20-21, 26, 43, 85, 94, 97, 118, 120, 121, 124, 127, 141, 151, 180-181, 194-195, 198-199, 210, 239-240, 274, 285-287, 297; (Psychol.) 329, 434-435, 446, 457, 483, 490, 496, 499, 516, 549; (Sociol.) 671, 693, 717, 770, 774, 819, 867, 887-888, 889, 891, 903, 916; (Econ.) 1129; (Phil.) 1241, 1408-1409, 1489, 1570, 1609-1610, 1622,

1625-1626, 1645.

10. Culture and Personality; National Character. (Anthrop.)
12, 18, 19, 20, 22-23, 39-40, 44, 58, 66, 93, 97, 99,
105, 106-108, 119, 124, 145, 152, 188, 200, 202, 204,
250, 278, 288, 297; (Psychol.) 310, 325-326, 347, 377,
469, 500; (Sociol.) 716, 724, 757, 819, 839-840, 867;
(Pol. Sci.) 923, 1056; (Phil.) 1732, 1786; (Other) 1847,
1852, 1893.

11. Decision-Making. (Anthrop.) 134; (Psychol.) 358, 361,
364, 375, 381, 425, 445, 461, 484, 554, 579; (Sociol.)
657, 761, 782, 783, 849, 881; (Pol. Sci.) 938, 953-954,
997, 1038-1039, 1043-1044; (Econ.) 1073, 1101, 1121,
1193, 1198, 1220; (Phil.) 1230-1231, 1290, 1319, 1322,
1324-1325, 1342-1343, 1464, 1513, 1562, 1632; (Other)
1921, 1945, 1958, 1978-1979, 1983. See also: I. 6,
Choice and Preference; II. 14, Free Will and Determinism; II. 16, Game Theory; II. 46, Utility Theory.

12. Democracy. (Anthrop.) 198-199, 213; (Psychol.) 475;
(Sociol.) 657, 761, 781, 783, 867; (Pol. Sci.) 925, 927,
938-939, 946, 958, 959, 966, 967, 968, 969, 979, 988,
991-992, 1006, 1020, 1028-1029, 1032, 1033, 1045, 1047,

1048, 1054; (Econ.) 1089, 1141, 1186; (Phil.) 1527. See also: II. 31, Political Philosophy.

13. Economic Theory, Economic Organization and Values; Economic Values and Goals. (Anthrop.) 36, 53, 73-74, 76, 96, 116, 180, 279; (Psychol.) 328, 339, 348, 421, 461; (Sociol.) 673, 676, 712, 763, 793, 796, 806, 904-905, 916; (Econ.) 1064, 1068-1069, 1080, 1083-1085, 1094, 1095, 1096, 1098, 1100, 1102, 1104, 1106, 1108, 1123, 1125-1126, 1129, 1138, 1159, 1161, 1169, 1171, 1172, 1180, 1185, 1190, 1205, 1207, 1215, 1216, 1219, 1225; (Phil.) 1335, 1482, 1544, 1752; (Other) 1838, 1914, 1937, 1987. See also: II. 4, Change ... in Culture Contact; II. 29, Policy; II. 42, Social Welfare in Economic Theory.

14. Free Will, Determinism and Indeterminacy. (Psychol.) 491; (Phil.) 1255, 1276, 1304, 1341, 1369, 1379, 1432, 1441, 1453, 1486, 1488, 1653, 1726, 1775, 1777, 1789, 1796, 1810; (Other) 1835, 1979. See also: II. 11, Decision-Making; VI. 4, Existentialism.

15. Freedom and Liberty. (Anthrop.) 63, 168-169, 187; (Psychol.) 408, 581; (Sociol.) 637, 658, 674, 776-777, 797, 820, 834, 861, 864, 877; (Pol. Sci.) 973, 979, 989,

996; (Econ.) 1087, 1107, 1128, 1141-1143, 1199; (Phil.) 1275, 1326, 1390, 1394, 1489, 1514-1516, 1542, 1573, 1637, 1641, 1687, 1766; (Other) 1830, 1853, 1860, 1869, 1874. See also: VI. 4, Existentialism.

16. Game Theory in Relation to Values. (Anthrop.) 17; (Sociol.) 661; (Pol. Sci.) 1037, 1040, 1042; (Econ.) 1220; (Phil.) 1291; (Other) 1922, 1958, 1984, 1987. See also: II. 11, Decision-Making.

17. Ideology. (Psychol.) 327, 525; (Sociol.) 650, 652, 735, 759, 767, 799, 827, 882, 889, 909; (Pol. Sci.) 968, 1054; (Econ.) 1161, 1194; (Phil.) 1647; (Other) 1952. See also: II. 31, Political Philosophy.

18. International Relations and Values. (Sociol.) 758; (Pol. Sci.) 923, 942, 987, 989, 993, 1016-1017, 1025, 1031, 1044, 1061-1062; (Econ.) 1160, 1170, 1201, 1217; (Phil.) 1577, 1580, 1643, 1645. See also: II. 4, Change and Persistence of Values in Culture Contact; II. 7, Communication, etc.

19. Kinship, Family and Marriage in Relation to Values. (Anthrop.) 43, 52, 80, 87, 238; (Psychol.) 388, 402, 440; (Sociol.) 635, 645, 662, 668, 673, 691, 715, 749, 764,

766, 827, 835, 856, 862, 880, 885, 911, 916, 919; (Pol. Sci.) 1026.

20. Language, Symbols and Signs in Relation to Values. (Anthrop.) 32, 34, 104, 120, 150, 169-170, 298; (Psychol.) 305, 340, 358, 410, 419, 502, 536, 539, 545-546, 556, 567, 588, 627; (Sociol.) 635, 702, 722, 737, 916; (Pol. Sci.) 983, 1001, 1031-1032; (Phil.) 1273, 1316-1317, 1337, 1445, 1451, 1521, 1623-1624, 1708; (Other) 1848-1851, 1877, 1878-1879, 1937, 1991. See also: II. 7, Communication; IV. 1, Content Analysis; VII. Logico-Linguistic Analyses; VIII. Esthetics.

21. Law, Justice, Jurisprudence and the Judicial Process. (Anthrop.) 5, 11, 51, 67, 91, 118, 121, 125, 179, 180, 186, 229, 243, 256, 270, 274, 281; (Sociol.) 639, 706, 890; (Pol. Sci.) 921, 932, 947, 948, 957, 984, 987, 989, 1024; (Econ.) 1122, 1142; (Phil.) 1258, 1544, 1588-1589, 1601, 1609, 1638, 1649, 1651, 1815; (Other) 1831, 1854, 1855, 1856, 1861, 1863, 1867, 1891, 1894, 1904, 1905, 1906, 1919.

22. Mental Health, Adjustment and Therapy in Relation to Values. (Anthrop.) 88, 105, 211; (Psychol.) 313, 319,

321, 365, 366, 423, 454, 492, 557, 578, 585, 615, 625;
(Sociol.) 639; (Pol. Sci.) 998; (Phil.) 1827; (Other) 1878.
See also: II. 27, Personality; II. 33, Psychoanalysis and
Values.

23. Moral Judgments. (Psychol.) 304, 324, 335, 435, 485,
490, 505, 512, 542; (Sociol.) 691, 764, 769, 856, 895,
897; (Phil.) 1334. See also: II. 27, Personality; VII. 1,
Analyses of Moral and Value Judgments.

24. Morals in Business and Government. (Sociol.) 884; (Pol.
Sci.) 925, 944, 962, 1009, 1014, 1023, 1060; (Econ.) 1074,
1166, 1189, 1209. See also: II. 1, Administration.

25. Pattern, Consistency and Integration in Relation to Values.
(Anthrop.) 1-2, 12, 21-22, 53, 56, 86, 88-89, 136-139,
142, 168, 196, 207, 217, 236, 241, 271, 277, 288;
(Psychol.) 320, 326, 328, 362, 393, 398, 405, 455, 462,
465, 477, 479; (Sociol.) 636, 683, 716, 753, 799, 812,
826-827, 830-831, 844, 847, 862, 883, 890, 894, 910,
915; (Econ.) 1159; (Phil.) 1241-1243, 1354-1356, 1376,
1378, 1393, 1395, 1425-1426, 1449, 1483, 1510, 1669,
1674, 1811, 1817; (Other) 1896, 1919, 1986.

26. Perception and Values. (Psychol.) 311, 339-340, 341-342, 348, 384, 426, 452, 465, 466, 467, 503, 513, 545-546, 572, 582, 588, 597, 612, 624; (Sociol.) 708; (Phil.) 1550; (Other) 1873, 1879, 1960.

27. Personality, Character and Values. (Anthrop.) 263; (Psychol.) 306, 370, 373, 383, 409, 413, 439, 450, 453, 455, 477, 497, 501, 502, 509-510, 534, 557, 572, 576, 580, 584, 592, 593, 594, 599, 609, 614, 615, 633; (Sociol.) 713, 722, 803, 831; (Phil.) 1280, 1341, 1345, 1384, 1473, 1572, 1593, 1618. See also: II. 10, Culture and Personality; II. 43, Socialization.

28. Planning and Values. (Anthrop.) 13; (Psychol.) 368, 616; (Sociol.) 672, 736; (Pol. Sci.) 1013; (Econ.) 1072, 1076, 1126, 1130, 1152, 1164, 1181, 1200, 1227.

29. Policy. (Psychol.) 484; (Sociol.) 640, 782, 804, 860; (Pol. Sci.) 924, 928, 935, 937, 938, 949, 961, 1002, 1017, 1039; (Econ.) 1071, 1078, 1099, 1107, 1173, 1177, 1184, 1186, 1193, 1199, 1200, 1201, 1203, 1208, 1213-1214, 1217; (Phil.) 1520, 1562. See also: II. 13, Economic Theory; II. 18, International Relations; II. 31, Political Philosophy; V. 7, Scientific Theory, Action and Values.

30. Political Behavior and Values. (Psychol.) 394, 421, 422, 521, 523, 584; (Sociol.) 657, 676, 760, 783, 867, 890; (Pol. Sci.) 954, 995, 1026, 1037, 1040, 1042-1043, 1063; (Econ.) 1123.

31. Political Philosophy, Political Theory and Values. (Anthrop.) 66, 246; (Psychol.) 524; (Sociol.) 689, 821, 877; (Pol. Sci.) 930, 931, 932, 934, 937, 940, 945, 948, 956, 960, 968, 972, 974, 975, 978, 981, 989-990, 994, 996, 1003, 1005, 1007, 1012, 1018, 1019, 1020, 1024, 1034, 1035, 1041, 1049-1050, 1057; (Econ.) 1092, 1119, 1120, 1128, 1147, 1150, 1152, 1173, 1218, 1221; (Phil.) 1314-1315, 1339, 1411, 1416, 1496, 1510, 1526, 1587, 1600, 1720, 1722, 1745, 1748, 1758-1759; (Other) 1839, 1865, 1981. See also: II. 2, Authority; II. 11, Decision-Making; II. 12, Democracy; II. 15, Freedom and Liberty; II. 17, Ideology; II. 24, Morals and Government; II. 29, Policy; II. 30, Political Behavior and Values; II. 32, Power.

32. Power. (Psychol.) 522; (Sociol.) 653; (Pol. Sci.) 932, 956, 970, 979, 996, 1000, 1011, 1018, 1024, 1039, 1058; (Phil.) 1526, 1579, 1759; (Other) 1830.

33. Psychoanalysis and Values. (Anthrop.) 108, 164, 297; (Psychol.) 307, 308, 322, 337, 378-379, 383, 390, 393-394, 396-400, 401-405, 407, 408-411, 417-418, 443, 444, 455-456, 468, 473, 517, 518, 523-526, 527-528, 544, 555, 559, 578, 622; (Sociol.) 726, 837; (Pol. Sci.) 998; (Phil.) 1271, 1401, 1507, 1558, 1825; (Other) 1901.

34. Reason and Cognition in Ethics and Value Theory. (Anthrop.) 25, 157; (Psychol.) 358, 373, 474; (Sociol.) 651, 723, 752, 883; (Pol. Sci.) 1004, 1006, 1007, 1021, 1028, 1039-1040; (Econ.) 1101, 1157; (Phil.) 1237, 1260, 1292, 1342, 1345, 1349, 1364, 1366, 1377, 1398, 1411, 1466-1467, 1523, 1536, 1558, 1632, 1642, 1675, 1692, 1733, 1750, 1755, 1768, 1790-1792, 1822. See also: II. 11, Decision-Making; V. 3, Facts and Values.

35. Relativism, Cultural and Ethical. (Anthrop.) 6, 14, 21, 48, 68, 77, 110-114, 140, 143, 146, 157, 162, 290, 294; (Psychol.) 320, 344, 404, 407, 474, 631; (Sociol.) 667, 721, 726-727, 732, 745, 799, 863, 883; (Pol. Sci.) 929, 985, 1006, 1007, 1022, 1028, 1051, 1055; (Econ.) 1106, 1146; (Phil.) 1244-1245, 1258, 1259, 1274, 1309, 1344, 1370, 1490, 1520, 1522, 1546, 1651, 1741, 1781, 1782, 1801; (Other) 1833, 1836, 1870, 1912, 1939-1941, 1966,

1988. See also: II. 45, Universals, Descriptive and Ethical; V. Values and Science; VI. 9, Logical Empiricism and Positivism; VI. 13, Pragmatism; VII. 6, Objectivity and Subjectivity in Value Judgments.

36. Religion and Values. (Anthrop.) 52, 62, 71-72, 76, 83, 111, 126, 219, 230, 237, 259; (Psychol.) 313, 356, 357, 395, 405, 410, 421, 427, 560, 578, 629; (Sociol.) 650, 713, 763, 777, 800, 822, 823, 852, 890, 904, 913; (Phil.) 1239, 1258, 1270, 1450-1452, 1466, 1569, 1596, 1637, 1752, 1825; (Other) 1842, 1877, 1884, 1944. See also: VI. 15, Theological Value and Ethical Theories.

37. Sanctions, Conscience and Punishment. (Anthrop.) 75-76, 119, 195, 219, 246; (Psychol.) 322, 333, 404, 459, 468, 544, 602; (Sociol.) 671, 722; (Phil.) 1258, 1261, 1406, 1483, 1631; (Other) 1843, 1852.

38. Sex, Morals and Values. (Anthrop.) 194, 212, 244, 246; (Psychol.) 401, 432, 458, 560; (Sociol.) 668-669, 671, 715, 717, 749, 764, 827, 856, 886; (Phil.) 1334.

39. Social Control, Norms, Taboos and Conformity. (Anthrop.) 45, 57, 82, 103, 129, 136, 226, 244, 246, 265; (Psychol.) 309-310, 338, 387, 402, 416, 462, 560, 568, 577, 581,

605, 626; (Sociol.) 658, 662, 731, 769, 781, 813, 828, 878, 911; (Pol. Sci.) 1008; (Econ.) 1100; (Phil.) 1287, 1594, 1811; (Other) 1844, 1881, 1894, 1906. See also: II. 39, Law and Justice; II. 43, Socialization.

40. Social Stratification and Values. (Anthrop.) 37, 52, 154, 180, 242; (Psychol.) 347, 353, 521-522, 565; (Sociol.) 653, 692, 720, 722, 755, 765, 770, 792, 801, 816, 827, 839, 846, 893, 894.

41. Social System, Structure and Organization in Relation to Values. (Anthrop.) 1-2, 9, 17, 27, 44, 47, 75, 94, 220, 226, 254, 291, 300; (Psychol.) 330, 386, 463, 465, 547-548, 560, 582, 589; (Sociol.) 636, 664, 678, 683, 703-706, 709-710, 713, 718, 753, 757, 785, 805, 806, 811-812, 815, 820, 825-831, 845, 855, 879, 881, 892, 895, 899-900, 905, 912, 914; (Pol. Sci.) 921; (Econ.) 1220; (Phil.) 1261, 1428, 1547, 1593-1594, 1618, 1682, 1720; (Other) 1987. See also: II. 13, Economic Theory; II. 19, Kinship; II. 30, Political Behavior and Values; II. 40, Social Stratification.

42. Social Welfare in Economic Theory. (Psychol.) 375; (Sociol.) 809; (Pol. Sci.) 928, 940; (Econ.) 1066, 1076-

1077, 1082, 1089, 1095, 1096-1099, 1103, 1110, 1111, 1124, 1130, 1132, 1135, 1151, 1153-1154, 1155, 1160, 1167, 1178-1179, 1182, 1192, 1196.

43. Socialization, Learning, Child Development and Education. (Anthrop.) 13, 33, 49, 78, 93, 98, 109, 184, 194-195, 208, 209, 210, 212, 264, 297; (Psychol.) 323, 329, 331, 354, 355, 373, 378-379, 382, 402, 415, 434-437, 438, 468, 483, 508, 519, 530, 535, 538, 575, 622-623; (Sociol.) 692, 828, 852, 893; (Other) 1853, 1907.

44. Students' Values. (Anthrop.) 26, 55; (Psychol.) 318, 324, 372, 374, 421, 422, 427, 431, 451, 516, 549, 552-553, 574, 591, 601, 605, 613, 620, 627, 630; (Sociol.) 848, 852, 856, 876, 878, 882, 899; (Pol. Sci.) 933; (Other) 1842. See also: II. 5, Children's and Adolescents' Values.

45. Universals, Descriptive and Ethical. (Anthrop.) 2, 30, 42, 47, 96, 111, 140, 143-145, 157, 171, 176-177, 206, 234, 261, 263, 295, 301; (Psychol.) 344, 418, 474, 501, 506, 523, 536, 559, 568, 585, 596, 615; (Sociol.) 698, 776, 815, 868, 896, 910; (Pol. Sci.) 1058-1059; (Phil.) 1270, 1276, 1308, 1312, 1320, 1328, 1344, 1416, 1425-1426, 1480, 1577, 1580, 1600, 1608, 1643, 1649, 1676, 1765;

(Other) 1888, 1911, 1933, 1960, 1966-1968, 1991. See also: II. 35, Relativism; VI. Philosophical Value and Ethical Theories.

46. Utility Theory. (Psychol.) 360; (Sociol.) 808; (Econ.) 1115, 1124, 1157, 1206; (Phil.) 1291, 1343; (Other) 1924, 1982-1983, 1985. See also: II. 11, Decision-Making; VI. 16, Utilitarianism.

47. Work, Vocational and Occupational Values. (Anthrop.) 84, 123; (Psychol.) 319, 353, 372, 385, 462, 574, 590, 601; (Sociol.) 638, 652, 700, 792, 793, 847-848; (Econ.) 1071, 1118, 1197, 1201, 1228.

III. AREA STUDIES (Place and other names as used by authors).

1. Africa. (Anthrop.) 48, 67, 79; (Psychol.) 369; (Pol. Sci.) 1010; (Phil.) 1580. Specific Areas. (Anthrop. if not otherwise indicated) Abaluyia 289; Akan 5; Ashanti 38; Azande 69; Bacongo 9; Bantu 218, 243; (Phil.) 1570; (Other) 1909; Barotse 91; Bemba 238; Bushong 280; Cewa 229; Dogon 100-102; East Africa 51; Fang 9; Fon 203; Gold Coast (Pol. Sci.) 926; Kumu 27; Lele 50; Lovedu 156; Mende 178; Ngoni 232; Northern Rhodesia 225; Nuer 70-72, 125; Nyakyusa 299-300; Ruanda 190; Shilluk 174; Shona 121;

-24-

South Africa (Sociol.) 676; Tallensi 80; Thonga (Psychol.) 362; Tiv 32; Tonga 45; Tswana 244; Urundi (Phil.) 1246.

2. American Indians (North, Central, South). (Anthrop.) 35, 118, 148, 193, 210, 274; (Psychol.) 378, 435, 538. Specific Areas (Anthrop. if not otherwise indicated) Apache 212, 215; Arapaho (Sociol.) 737; Atsugewi 84; Aztec 222; Cheyenne 179; Colombia 242; Crow 181; (Phil.) 1570; Guatemala 268; (Sociol.) 891; Havasupai 259; Hopi 58, 93, 271-275; (Phil.) 1294; Hupa-Yurok 94; Kaska 122-123; Labrador 257; Mandan-Hidatsa 33; Navaho 3, 43, 49, 85, 116, 136, 138, 148-150, 182, 185, 205, 230, 237, 239-240, 258, 281, 283, 287, 288; (Psychol.) 483; (Sociol.) 774, 918; (Phil.) 1242, 1537; Ojibwa 105; Omaha 78; Plains 20; Pueblos 49, 93; Saora 62; Shoshoni 181; Tarahumara 82, 303; Tepoztlan 172; Tlingit 209; Tolowa-Tututni 53; Wintu 167; Zuni 3, 20-21, 24, 43, 85, 93, 173, 184, 239, 256, 278, 287, 288; (Psychol.) 354, (Sociol.) 774, (Phil.) 1247.

3. Asia. (Anthrop.) 202; (Pol. Sci.) 1010, 1027; (Phil.) 1489, 1609-1610, 1622, 1637, 1645; (Other) 1860. China (Anthrop.) 126-127, 128; (Psychol.) 490, 549; (Sociol.) 819; (Econ.) 1137; (Phil.) 1408-1409, 1580, 1596, 1625, 1829; (Other) 1872, 1916-1917. India and Ceylon (Anthrop.) 52,

59, 60, 83, 115, 189, 247, 251-254, 264; (Psychol.) 347, 549; (Sociol.) 819, 851, 874, 879, 885; (Pol. Sci.) 931, 1045; (Econ.) 1148, 1181, 1200, 1229; (Phil.) 1240, 1272, 1443-1444, 1580, 1583, 1625, 1636, 1643, 1644, 1697-1698, 1786; (Other) 1864, 1875, 1880, 1884, 1895-1896, 1900, 1903. Japan (Anthrop.) 23, 26, 66, 97, 98, 106, 108, 129, 208, 220, 267, 549; (Sociol.) 649-650; (Phil.) 1625, 1780, 1794; (Other) 1847, 1868. Near East (Psychol.) 516, 549; (Sociol.) 650, 708; (Other) 1876.

4. Europe and European-based communities in Africa, The Americas, Australia and New Zealand (for United States - see III. 6). (Anthrop.) 94, 202; (Psychol.) 334; (Sociol.) 735, 785; (Pol. Sci.) 935; (Other) 1844, 1881. Austria (Phil.) 1372; Australia (Sociol.) 675; Canada (Sociol.) 719, 780, 843; Eastern Europe (Anthrop.) 302; (Sociol.) 736, 889; England (Anthrop.) 99, (Sociol.) 867; France (Anthrop.) 204, (Sociol.) 867; (Pol. Sci.) 1026, (Phil.) 1684; Germany (Psychol.) 408, 496, (Phil.) 1351; Italy (Psychol.) 422, (Phil.) 1313, 1417; Latin America and West Indies (Anthrop.) 44, (Sociol.) 891, 893, (Pol. Sci.) 1054, (Phil.) 1704, 1709, (Other) 1905; New Zealand (Psychol.) 434, 437, 499; Norway (Psychol.) 549, 560, (Sociol.) 763, 816, (Phil.)

1625, 1654; Poland (Sociol.) 888; Russia (Anthrop.) 248,
(Psychol.) 325-326, 583, (Sociol.) 693, 716, 719, 736,
756, 903, (Pol. Sci.) 955, (Phil.) 1253; Spain (Anthrop.)
221, (Pol. Sci.) 1056, (Phil.) 1580; Sweden (Sociol.) 717,
858. See also: VI. Philosophical Value and Ethical
Theories.

5. Oceania. (Anthrop.) 21, 119. Specific Areas (Anthrop. if
not otherwise indicated) Bali 17-18, 19, (Psychol.) 377;
East Indies (Pol. Sci.) 933; Gahuku-Gama 231; Hawaii 61;
Iatmul 12; Ifaluk 37; Ifugao 11; Indonesia 270, 279, (Other)
1832; Java 86, 87; Maori 73, (Psychol.) 329, 536; Philip-
pines (Pol. Sci.) 933; Samoa 134; Tikopia 74-75; Trobriand
165, 186, (Phil.) 1570; Yap 246.

6. United States. (Anthrop.) 8, 26, 54-55, 85, 90, 94-95,
97, 127, 153-154, 169, 197, 224, 239, 240, 250, 260, 262,
278, 284, 285, 287, 288, 291; (Psychol.) 314-315, 353,
420, 434-435, 446, 483, 496, 516, 521-522, 533, 549,
569, 623; (Sociol.) 659, 684, 690, 693, 717, 733, 743, 748,
771, 774, 801, 817, 829, 832, 839-840, 842, 867, 903,
909, 912-913, 918; (Pol. Sci.) 933, 992, 1027; (Econ.)
1149, 1187-1888; (Phil.) 1520, 1625, 1732; (Other) 1837,
1852, 1857, 1859, 1871, 1890, 1893, 1908. (See also:

Psychology, Sociology, Philosophy, _passim_.) Ethnic
groups. Italians (Sociol.) 880; Japanese (Anthrop.) 39-
40, 210, (Psychol.) 481; Jews (Psychol.) 380, (Sociol.)
857, 880; Mennonites (Psychol.) 457; Mormons (Anthrop.)
239, 285, 287, 288, (Psychol.) 382, (Sociol.) 774, 802,
824; Negroes (Anthrop.) 223, (Psychol.) 374, 446, 550,
589, (Sociol.) 720, 749, 850, 854, 856, (Econ.) 1168,
(Phil.) 1438; Poles (Sociol.) 888; Spanish-Speaking Peoples (Anthrop.) 57, 85, 240, 287, (Sociol.) 774, 853, (Pol.
Sci.) 1056.

IV.   METHODS OF VALUES INQUIRY.

1.   Content Analysis. (Anthrop.) 23, 57, 61, 95, 222, 224,
248, 258; (Psychol.) 420, 617-619; (Sociol.) 635, 685, 762,
785, 819, 847, 903; (Pol. Sci.) 1001; (Phil.) 1242, 1294,
1417, 1537, 1570. See also: VII. Logico-Linguistic
Analyses.

2.   Comparative Methods and Studies of Variation. (Anthrop.)
76, 90, 96; (Psychol.) 304, 328-329, 338, 349, 353, 388,
397-398, 431, 432, 469, 513, 550, 583, 589, 601, 603,
629; (Sociol.) 652, 692, 707, 772, 802, 815, 862, 868,
886, 887-888, 911; (Pol. Sci.) 933, 1001; (Phil.) 1334.
See also: II. 9, Cross-Cultural Comparisons; II. 40,

Social Stratification.

3. Experimental, Interview and Quantitative Methods.

    (Anthrop.) 181, 200, 230, 288, 292; (Psychol.) 307, 309-
    310, 339-340, 348, 353, 354, 370, 373, 388, 396, 406,
    419, 421, 441, 442, 452, 462, 467, 493, 495, 499, 513,
    516, 539, 540, 542, 543, 546, 547-548, 549, 556, 566,
    567, 572, 584, 588, 589, 600, 603-604, 610, 611, 624,
    626, 632; (Sociol.) 635, 636, 642, 657, 671, 679, 681,
    695-697, 699, 700, 742, 757, 760, 774, 783, 845, 852,
    856, 876-877, 881, 895, 911; (Pol. Sci.) 923, 933, 942,
    1031-1032; (Econ.) 1159; (Phil.) 1343, 1540, 1625-1626.
    Questionnaires (Anthrop.) 43, 267; (Psychol.) 349, 422,
    475, 512, 580, 601; (Sociol.) 691, 764, 878, 899; (Phil.)
    1625; (Other) 1842. Scales and Inventories (Psychol.) 307,
    314-315, 316, 318-319, 334, 345, 359, 371, 372, 374,
    380, 385, 414, 431, 432, 449, 464, 490, 498, 502, 504,
    545, 550, 566, 570, 571, 574, 580, 591, 594-595, 599,
    612, 613, 614, 620, 627, 630; (Sociol.) 679, 741, 880;
    (Phil.) 1342, 1626; (Other) 1959. Tests (Anthrop.) 122,
    200, 248, 259, 267, 283, 297; (Psychol.) 304, 319, 327,
    336, 396-398, 429-430, 434-437, 457, 476, 483, 485, 582,
    597, 621. See also: IV. 5, Mathematical Methods.

4. Interdisciplinary Approaches. (Anthrop.) 1-2, 9, 17, 34, 36, 41, 55, 76, 94, 96, 104, 108, 134, 139, 145, 152, 154, 164, 165, 206, 220, 230, 240, 245, 248, 256, 261-262, 263, 283, 285, 287, 297; (Psychol.) 328-329, 343, 361, 362, 375, 378, 381, 461, 479, 483, 484, 526, 529, 544, 556, 559, 565, 573, 575; (Sociol.) 638, 645, 649, 658, 671, 677-678, 682, 755, 758, 760, 783, 806, 831, 877, 878, 887-888, 902, 907-908, 915; (Pol. Sci.) 936, 938, 940, 942, 948, 954, 957, 985, 993, 995-996, 998, 1000, 1012, 1026, 1038, 1050; (Econ.) 1088, 1090, 1095, 1100, 1117, 1130, 1134, 1138, 1145, 1149, 1156, 1168-1169, 1171, 1193, 1197, 1203, 1211, 1216, 1223, 1229; (Phil.) 1241, 1244-1247, 1252, 1262, 1273-1276, 1280, 1294, 1299, 1323, 1333, 1343, 1344-1345, 1354, 1361, 1363, 1370, 1378-1379, 1394-1395, 1400, 1401, 1417, 1425-1426, 1438, 1460, 1468, 1473, 1478, 1480, 1493, 1507, 1521, 1523, 1534, 1537, 1547, 1548, 1558, 1568-1570, 1578-1580, 1582, 1584, 1625-1626, 1665, 1670-1671, 1674, 1682, 1735, 1763, 1804, 1825; (Other) 1857, 1894, 1914. See also: II. 10, Culture and Personality; II. 21, Law; II. 41, Social System; II. 43, Socialization; V. 2, Ethics and the Behavioral Sciences; VIII. Esthetics.

5. Mathematical, Statistical and Formal Models. (Psychol.)
360-361, 375, 579; (Sociol.) 808, 849; (Pol. Sci.) 1037,
1040, 1042-1043; (Econ.) 1065-1066, 1113, 1115, 1124,
1157, 1198, 1206, 1213, 1220; (Phil.) 1231, 1252, 1290-
1291, 1322-1325, 1342-1343, 1656, 1779; (Other) 1920,
1921, 1922, 1924, 1945, 1958, 1959, 1978, 1979, 1982,
1983, 1984, 1985, 1987.

6. Philosophical Methods. See VI. Philosophical Value and
Ethical Theories, especially 7, Idealism; 9, Logical Empiricism and Positivism; 11, Phenomenology; 12, Philosophical Analysis and Linguistic Approaches; 13, Pragmatism; and VII. Logico-Linguistic Analyses.

V. VALUES AND SCIENCE.

1. Biological Bases of Values. (Anthrop.) 7, 164; (Psychol.)
501, 596, 616; (Phil.) 1353, 1483, 1538, 1623, 1701, 1710,
1733; (Other) 1925, 1935, 1943-1944, 1946, 1947, 1975-
1976, 1977, 1988, 1991. See also: VI. 3, Evolutionism.

2. Ethics and the Behavioral Sciences. (Anthrop.) 46, 56,
60, 146, 201; (Psychol.) 350, 352, 442, 480, 525, 528,
537; (Sociol.) 706, 726, 747, 798, 908; (Pol. Sci.) 936,
951-952, 964-965, 977, 980, 995, 1005, 1015; (Econ.)

1067, 1081, 1086, 1091, 1095, 1096-1099, 1105, 1109, 1112, 1116, 1119, 1123, 1127, 1131-1132, 1133, 1136, 1144, 1158, 1163, 1164, 1165, 1167, 1172, 1176, 1184, 1204, 1211; (Phil.) 1297, 1314-1315, 1339, 1401, 1430, 1568, 1581, 1582, 1597, 1602, 1607, 1707, 1723, 1745; (Other) 1883. See also: V. 9, Value Theories Derived from Behavioral Science Theories.

3. Facts and Values. (Anthrop.) 126, 140, 192; (Psychol.) 305, 320, 358, 364, 373, 470-472, 474, 598; (Sociol.) 705, 738-740, 742, 779, 784, 865-866, 906; (Pol. Sci.) 951, 957, 960, 986, 1000, 1030, 1035, 1053; (Econ.) 1140, 1145, 1162, 1168-1169, 1175, 1180, 1193; (Phil.) 1244-1245, 1280, 1348, 1391, 1399, 1458, 1471, 1528, 1530, 1676, 1728, 1729, 1802, 1826; (Other) 1897, 1932, 1938, 1956. See also: II. 35, Relativism; VII. 3, Cognitivism; VII. 4, Emotivism.

4. Science as an Ethic. (Anthrop.) 117; (Sociol.) 686, 859, 866; (Phil.) 1344; (Other) 1926-1928, 1929-1930, 1933, 1938, 1965, 1967.

5. Science of Values and of Ethics and Normative Science. (Anthrop.) 163; (Psychol.) 312, 351, 357, 448, 511, 527,

556, 576, 602; (Sociol.) 660, 704, 738, 747, 784, 863;
(Econ.) 1226; (Phil.) 1230, 1261, 1276, 1321-1323, 1329,
1340, 1352-1354, 1373, 1377, 1391, 1396, 1405, 1427,
1439, 1447, 1468-1469, 1475, 1592, 1603, 1621, 1736,
1740, 1802; (Other) 1930, 1943, 1957, 1961, 1967-1968,
1988.

6. Scientific Esthetics. (Psychol.) 336, 359, 474, 540, 543;
(Phil.) 1266, 1350-1351, 1493, 1538, 1540, 1629, 1656;
(Other) 1892.

7. Scientific Theory, Action and Values. (Anthrop.) 15-16,
25, 46, 63-65, 81, 130, 187, 198-199, 201, 213, 266,
276-277, 296; (Psychol.) 367, 433, 454, 481-482, 488,
489, 552, 558, 562-563, 581, 602; (Sociol.) 637, 640-641,
645, 647, 670, 674, 689, 721, 729, 744, 746, 750, 787,
789, 794, 804, 841-842, 854, 860, 866, 920; (Pol. Sci.)
935, 949, 963, 999, 1002; (Econ.) 1079, 1093, 1095,
1100, 1140, 1143, 1158, 1193, 1224; (Phil.) 1274, 1309,
1389-1390, 1432, 1442, 1475, 1484, 1485, 1496, 1507-
1508, 1536, 1563, 1600, 1639, 1642, 1665, 1740, 1742,
1775, 1790, 1821, 1827; (Other) 1929-1930, 1931, 1940,
1949-1950, 1974, 1981, 1989.

8. Value Judgments and Neutrality in Scientific Inquiry.
    (Anthrop.) 6, 10, 24, 31, 46, 104, 112, 173, 201, 207,
    233, 235, 249, 261, 266, 269, 272-273, 290; (Psychol.)
    305, 308, 330, 337, 350, 352, 399-400, 413, 423, 454,
    480, 507, 562, 569, 578; (Sociol.) 643, 644, 646, 651,
    654, 659, 663, 666-668, 670, 704-706, 714, 734, 759,
    777-778, 791, 798, 823, 833, 838, 865, 870, 906, 907-
    908; (Pol. Sci.) 922, 929, 936, 943, 950, 964-965, 976-
    977, 1018, 1046, 1051, 1053; (Econ.) 1070, 1075, 1106,
    1111, 1114, 1135, 1139, 1145, 1170, 1183, 1191, 1194,
    1210, 1212, 1222; (Phil.) 1412, 1448, 1524, 1587, 1653,
    1666, 1712; (Other) 1932, 1942, 1954, 1966, 1971, 1972,
    1973, 1990.

9. Value Theories Developed from Behavioral Science
    Theories. (Anthrop.) 14, 42, 48, 56, 147, 164, 241;
    (Psychol.) 342-344, 365, 390, 391, 409-411, 418, 443,
    447, 455-456, 523-526, 529, 531, 551, 585, 586-587, 631;
    (Sociol.) 662, 711, 730, 738-739, 813, 837, 842, 864,
    869, 872, 883, 910; (Econ.) 1223; (Phil.) 1290-1291,
    1299, 1323, 1460, 1468, 1534. See also: V. 2, Ethics and
    the Behavioral Sciences; VI. 3, Evolutionism.

10. Value Theory and Scientific Knowledge: Methodological Issues. (Psychol.) 441, 448, 482, 511, 552, 581; (Sociol.) 655, 726, 784, 786-787, 795, 800, 902, 917; (Econ.) 1123; (Phil.) 1243-1245, 1262, 1287, 1297, 1308, 1309, 1314, 1361, 1367, 1378-1379, 1429-1430, 1439, 1463, 1471, 1473, 1474, 1478, 1487, 1496, 1503, 1507, 1517, 1534, 1543, 1551, 1553, 1598, 1618, 1629, 1642, 1646-1647, 1650, 1666, 1706, 1717, 1740, 1749, 1750, 1763, 1778, 1826, 1827.

VI. PHILOSOPHICAL VALUE AND ETHICAL THEORIES.

1. Contextualism. (Phil.) 1243, 1455, 1668-1674.

2. Deontology (Ethics of Right or Obligation). (Phil.) 1306, 1311-1312, 1314-1315, 1418-1422, 1627, 1693-1694, 1713-1714. See also: VI. 8, Intuitionism.

3. Evolutionism. (Anthrop.) 4, 7, 28, 41, 155, 163, 191-192, 227-228, 235, 293-294, 295-296; (Psychol.) 401-405, 542; (Sociol.) 665, 725-728, 751-752, 873, 917; (Pol. Sci.) 972; (Phil.) 1249-1251, 1270, 1273-1274, 1353, 1421, 1569-1570, 1574, 1703; (Other) 1843, 1934, 1935-1936, 1947-1948, 1949-1950, 1951-1952, 1953, 1955, 1962, 1963, 1964, 1977, 1988. See also: V. 1, Biological Bases

of Values; VI. 13, Pragmatism.

4. Existentialism. (Psychol.) 625; (Phil.) 1267, 1278, 1281, 1333, 1453, 1476-1477, 1500-1503, 1565, 1585, 1604, 1628, 1735, 1787-1788, 1810; (Other) 1846.

5. General Theory of Value. (Psychol.) 376, 471; (Econ.) 1085, 1202; (Phil.) 1298, 1354, 1357, 1372, 1466, 1482, 1529, 1597, 1655, 1661-1662, 1665, 1672, 1679-1680, 1684, 1702, 1724-1725, 1731, 1756, 1760, 1797-1798, 1819.

6. Humanism. (Econ.) 1138; (Phil.) 1367, 1502, 1542, 1558, 1629, 1754, 1824, 1827-1828; (Other) 1900, 1902, 1907, 1973. See also: VI. 13, Pragmatism.

7. Idealism and Personalism. (Phil.) 1279, 1282-1285, 1288, 1301, 1316-1317, 1407, 1437, 1630, 1640, 1655, 1715, 1730-1731, 1793, 1817-1820.

8. Intuitionism. (Phil.) 1299, 1312, 1314-1315, 1484, 1541, 1597, 1611-1612, 1753.

9. Logical Empiricism and Positivism. (Psychol.) 399; (Sociol.) 686, 703-706, 777; (Econ.) 1175; (Phil.) 1261, 1279, 1392, 1397, 1478, 1740, 1790, 1816, 1822; (Other)

1926, 1939-1942. See also: VII. 4, Emotivism.

10. Materialism (including Marxism). (Psychol.) 456, 514; (Sociol.) 735, 877; (Pol. Sci.) 934, 968, 1020; (Econ.) 1076, 1120, 1150, 1152, 1185, 1221; (Phil.) 1264, 1384, 1748.

11. Phenomenology. (Psychol.) 471; (Phil.) 1333, 1391, 1472, 1477, 1495, 1524, 1584, 1597, 1683, 1738-1739, 1742, 1762, 1813; (Other) 1870.

12. Philosophical Analysis, Metaethics and Linguistic Approaches to Values and Ethics. (Anthrop.) 165; (Pol. Sci.) 957; (Phil.) 1277, 1279, 1292-1297, 1303-1306, 1361, 1366, 1383, 1385, 1402, 1456-1458, 1462, 1464, 1484, 1491, 1492, 1535, 1611-1612, 1652, 1659, 1677, 1695, 1719, 1721, 1726, 1727, 1746-1747, 1761, 1768-1772, 1773-1774, 1800, 1816, 1825. See also: VII. Logico-Linguistic Analyses.

13. Pragmatism (including Experimentalism and Scientific Humanism). (Sociol.) 786-791; (Econ.) 1067-1070; (Phil.) 1230, 1243-1245, 1279, 1289-1291, 1321-1322, 1323-1324, 1325, 1352-1359, 1373-1379, 1427-1430, 1438-1440, 1446-1447, 1468-1471, 1497-1499, 1504-1506,

1514-1516, 1553-1556, 1559-1560, 1561-1563, 1591-1594, 1619-1625, 1626, 1631-1632, 1657, 1660-1665, 1667, 1679-1680, 1703, 1705-1706, 1716-1718, 1795, 1815; (Other) 1957. See also: VII. 3, Cognitivism.

14. Self-Realization Theories. (Phil.) 1284, 1312, 1401, 1419, 1483, 1512, 1798.

15. Theological Value and Ethical Theories. (Sociol.) 872; (Econ.) 1190-1191; (Phil.) 1232-1233, 1258, 1436, 1450-1452, 1454, 1500-1502, 1549, 1585, 1586-1589, 1601-1602, 1788; (Other) 1836, 1838, 1846, 1870, 1886, 1887. See also: VI. 7, Idealism and Personalism.

16. Utilitarianism. (Anthrop.) 294; (Econ.) 1173; (Phil.) 1306, 1421, 1492, 1570, 1750, 1753, 1765. See also: II. 13, Economic Theory; II. 46, Utility Theory.

17. Readers, Anthologies and Surveys in Moral Philosophy and Ethical Theory. (Phil.) 1248, 1303, 1310, 1327, 1383, 1400, 1415, 1481, 1529, 1533, 1599, 1699, 1707, 1744, 1747, 1757, 1759.

VII. LOGICO-LINGUISTIC ANALYSES.

1. Analyses of Moral and Value Judgments. (Sociol.) 788;
    (Pol. Sci.) 983; (Phil.) 1236, 1238, 1243, 1254, 1258,
    1265, 1306, 1318, 1353, 1357-1358, 1371, 1383, 1389,
    1398-1399, 1403, 1410, 1416, 1422, 1457, 1460, 1464,
    1465, 1504, 1511, 1517-1518, 1527, 1528, 1544, 1559,
    1571, 1584, 1606, 1652, 1673, 1690, 1705, 1721, 1727,
    1751, 1770, 1776, 1797-1798, 1808, 1816; (Other) 1867.
    See also: II. 23, Moral Judgments.

2. Analyses of Value Terms; Definability or Indefinability of
    Value Terms ("Naturalism" and "Non-Naturalism").
    (Anthrop.) 86, 167; (Psychol.) 442; (Phil.) 1234-1235,
    1249, 1252, 1259, 1268, 1302, 1307, 1308, 1332, 1346,
    1349, 1360, 1361, 1368, 1386-1388, 1389, 1403, 1413-
    1414, 1420, 1448, 1455, 1457, 1472, 1507, 1519, 1532,
    1537, 1539, 1552, 1556, 1575, 1579, 1611-1612, 1613,
    1661, 1668, 1678, 1692, 1727, 1737, 1749, 1752, 1762,
    1804, 1814, 1817, 1820, 1823, 1827.

3. Cognitivism (Value Judgments as Verifiable Statements).
    (Anthrop.) 68; (Psychol.) 342, 515, 598; (Sociol.) 790;
    (Phil.) 1293, 1358, 1374-1375, 1401, 1470, 1479, 1524,
    1548, 1554, 1559, 1648, 1651, 1658-1659, 1701, 1708,

1727-1728, 1765, 1791, 1826; (Other) 1929. See also:
V. 3, Facts and Values; V. 5, Science as an Ethic.

4. Emotivism (Value Judgments as Expressions of Emotion).
(Phil.) 1245, 1256-1257, 1296, 1382, 1397, 1423-1424,
1459, 1523, 1604, 1659, 1677, 1688-1691, 1700, 1701,
1768-1769. See also: V. 3, Facts and Values.

5. Ethics ("Value") and Morals ("Obligation") Distinguished.
(Phil.) 1271, 1314-1315, 1422, 1523, 1544, 1560, 1640,
1655, 1693, 1702, 1713, 1749, 1804, 1812, 1815.

6. Objectivity and Subjectivity in Value Judgments. (Psychol.)
474; (Sociol.) 721; (Phil.) 1295, 1300, 1404, 1435, 1467,
1474, 1520, 1540, 1650, 1654, 1675, 1722; (Other) 1937,
1939, 1988. See also: II. 35, Relativism.

VIII. ESTHETICS AND STUDIES OF ART, HUMOR,
LITERATURE AND MUSIC.

(Anthrop.) 29, 35, 57, 61, 100, 161, 181, 182, 183, 205,
245, 258; (Psychol.) 317, 336, 359, 473, 474, 497, 536,
540, 543, 566, 573, 580; (Sociol.) 635, 685, 701-702, 718,
762, 785, 815, 855, 892, 903, 917; (Phil.) 1250-1251,
1253, 1265, 1266, 1269, 1285, 1286, 1316, 1330, 1331,
1336-1338, 1350-1351, 1356, 1362, 1365, 1380-1381, 1385,

1393, 1423-1424, 1431, 1433, 1434, 1446, 1449, 1452,

1454, 1461, 1466, 1482, 1491, 1493, 1494, 1506, 1509,

1514, 1519, 1521, 1525, 1531, 1538, 1540, 1545, 1546,

1549, 1550, 1554, 1564, 1566, 1567, 1576, 1586, 1590,

1595, 1615-1617, 1624, 1629, 1633-1635, 1656, 1660,

1664, 1669, 1681, 1686, 1688, 1690-1691, 1696, 1711,

1716, 1718, 1730-1731, 1752, 1755, 1760, 1764, 1770-

1772, 1773-1774, 1789, 1803, 1805, 1806, 1807, 1818-

1819, 1829; (Other) 1834, 1840-1841, 1848-1851, 1862,

1866, 1873, 1882, 1889, 1892, 1898, 1899, 1901, 1910,

1913, 1915, 1918.

THE BIBLIOGRAPHY

I. ANTHROPOLOGY

1. Aberle, David F. (1950) Shared Values in Complex societies. Amer. Sociol. Rev. 15: 495-502. --
Analysis of value-integration in societies with
complex role systems.

2.+___, Cohen, Albert K. , Davis, Arthur K. , Levy,
Marion J. , Jr. and Sutton, Francis X. (1950)
The Functional Prerequisites of a Society.
Ethics 60: 100-111. --Universal social struc-
tural imperatives.

3. Adair, John and Vogt, Even Z. (1949) Navaho and Zuni
Veterans; A Study of Contrasting Modes of Cultural Change. Amer. Anthrop. 51: 547-561. --
Contrasting reactions to World War II demand
for military service related to cultural value
differences.

── Albert, Ethel M. See Philosophy.

4. Allier, R. (1929) The Mind of the Savage. Trans. by F.
Rothwell. New York: Harcourt. --An argument
against the notion of "primitive mentality,"
based on the view that both moral regression
and moral progress occur in history.

5. Allott, A. N. (1953) Customary Law of the Akan Peoples.
African Stud. 12: 26-30.

6. American Anthropological Association, Executive Board
(1947) Statement on Human Rights. Amer.
Anthrop. 49: 539-543. --Declaration of respect
for cultural diversity submitted to United
Nations Commission on Human Rights.

*The space below the rule is provided for the reader's conven-
ience in making notations or additions to the bibliography.*

7. Ashley Montagu, M. F. (1950) On Being Human. New York: Schuman. --Biological and social evidence for the view that cooperation, not conflict, is the value dictated by the natural law of life.

8. Bailey, Wilfrid C. (1952) Cotton Center, Texas, and the Late Agricultural Settlement of the Texas Panhandle and New Mexico. Texas J. Sci. 4: 482-486. --Reports minimal change in values in a situation of marked contrast and change.

9. + Balandier, Georges (1955) Sociologie actuelle de l' Afrique noire; Dynamiques des changements sociaux en Afrique Centrale. Paris: Presses Universitaires de France. --See especially: Parts One (3-70) and Three (285-504), comprehensive analysis of a nativistic movement in the "colonial situation" of French West Africa, using rural and urban populations of Congolese and Fang; includes analysis of effects of culture contact on Europeans in Africa.

10. Barnett, Homer G. (1948) On Science and Human Rights. Amer. Anthrop. 50: 352-355. --Criticism of the value commitment of the statement on human rights by the American Anthropological Association (see 6).

11. Barton, R. F. (1919) Ifugao Law. Berkeley: Univ. of California Press (University of California Publications in Archaeol. and Ethnol. 15).

12. Bateson, Gregory (1936) Naven. Cambridge: Cambridge Univ. Press. --Functional analysis of a ceremony of the Iatmul of New Guinea in terms of ethos (values) and eidos (cognitive patterns); ideal personality types described.

13. ___ (1942) Social Planning and the Concept of "Deutero-Learning." Symp. Sci. Phil. Relig. 2: 81-97. Also in: Theodore M. Newcomb and Eugene

Hartley, eds. Readings in Social Psychology.
New York: Holt, 1947. 121-128. --Learning
theory for the study of the internalization of
cultural values.

14. ___ (1943) Human Dignity and the Varieties of Civilization. Symp. Sci. Phil. Relig. 3: 245-251.

15. ___ (1943) The Science of Decency. Phil. Sci. 10:
140-142. --Applied scientists promote in people
the qualities they assume they possess; for optimal results, applications should be based on
mathematical-relational thinking.

16. ___ (1946) From One Social Scientist to Another.
Amer. Sci. 34: 1-6. --Behavioral science as
a means to social control and implementation of
values.

17. ___ (1949) Bali; The Value System of a Steady State.
IN: Meyer Fortes, ed. Social Structure. London: Oxford Univ. Press. 35-53. --Balinese
values in terms of communication theory and
theory of games applied to social organization.

18. ___ and Mead, Margaret (1942) The Balinese Character; A Photographic Analysis. New York:
New York Acad. Sci.

—— Beaglehole, Ernest. See Psychology.

—— Bellah, Robert N. See Sociology.

19. Belo, J. (1948) The Balinese Temper. IN: Douglas G.
Haring, ed. Personal Character and Cultural
Milieu. Syracuse: Syracuse Univ. Press.
109-134.

20. Benedict, Ruth (1928) Psychological Types in the Cultures of the Southwest. Proc. 23rd. Internatl.
Congress of Americanists: 572-581. --Report

of persistent differences in values between Pueblo and Plains Indians, despite prolonged contact.

21. +___ (1934) Patterns of Culture. New York: Houghton, Mifflin. --Exposition and illustration of cultural relativism.

22. ___ (1938) Continuities and Discontinuities in Cultural Conditioning. Psychiatry 1: 161-167. Also in: Clyde Kluckhohn, Henry Murray and David Schneider, eds. Personality in Nature, Society, and Culture. New York: Knopf, 1953. 522-531.

23. ___ (1946) The Chrysanthemum and the Sword. Boston: Houghton, Mifflin. --Japanese values in historical and psychological perspective.

24. Bennett, John W. (1946) The Interpretation of Pueblo Culture; A Question of Values. S.W. J. Anthrop. 2: 361-374. Also in: Douglas G. Haring, ed. Personal Character and Cultural Milieu. Syracuse: Syracuse Univ. Press, 1956. 203-216. --Influence of anthropologists' values on their research findings.

25. ___ (1949) Science and Human Rights; Reason and Action. Amer. Anthrop. 51: 329-336. --An argument for behavioral scientists to participate in social action.

26. +___ and McKnight, Robert K. (1956) Misunderstandings in Communication Between Japanese Students and Americans. Soc. Probl. 3: 243-256.

— Bidney, David. See Philosophy.

27. + Biebuyck, D. (1957) La société kumu face au Kitiwala. Zaïre (Brussels) 11: 7-40. --Detailed analysis of a nativistic movement in

-46-

relation to pre-contact conceptual and institutional characteristics.

28. Boas, Franz (1911) The Mind of Primitive Man. Rev. ed. New York: Macmillan. --See especially: Chs. 11-12, values and their change with the development of civilization; distinguishes biological from cultural development, in opposition to racist evolutionism.

29. ___ (1927) Primitive Art. Oslo: Instituttet for Sammenlignende Kulturforskning. --Republished: Irvington-on-Hudson, N.Y.: Capitol Publishing, 1951.

30. ___ (1930) Anthropology; Ethics. IN: Encyclopedia of the Social Sciences 2: 97-98. New York: Macmillan. --Moral universals listed.

31. ___ (1932) The Aims of Anthropological Research. Science 76: 605-613.

32. +Bohannan, Paul (1955) A Tiv Political and Religious Idea. S.W. J. Anthrop. 11: 137-149. --Linguistic factors in the views of society and of the universe held by the Tiv of central Nigeria.

33. Bruner, Edward M. (1956) Cultural Transmission and Cultural Change. S.W. J. Anthrop. 12: 191-199. --Persistence of the value system of the Mandan-Hidatsa Indians of North Dakota seen as support for the hypothesis that what is internalized in infancy and early childhood is most resistant to change in contact situations.

34. Bryson, Lyman, Finkelstein, Louis, MacIver, Robert M. and McKeon, Richard, eds. (1954) Symbols and Values; An Initial Study. Symp. Sci. Phil. Relig. 13. --An interdisciplinary symposium.

35. Bunzel, Ruth L. (1938) Art. IN: Franz Boas, ed. General Anthropology. New York: Heath. 535-588. --Survey of the plastic arts of primitive peoples; comments on relevant esthetic theories.

36. ___ (1938) The Economic Organization of Primitive Peoples. IN: Franz Boas, ed. General Anthropology. New York: Heath. 327-408. -- Surveys economic customs from the theoretical position that economics must be studied in the context of each culture's concept of the good life.

37. Burrows, Edwin G. (1952) From Value to Ethos on Ifaluk Atoll. S.W. J. Anthrop. 8: 13-35. -- The values of a Micronesian culture, with special attention to values related to ranked status.

38. Busia, K. A. (1954) The Ashanti of the Gold Coast. IN: C. D. Forde, ed. African Worlds; Studies in the Cosmological Ideas and Social Values of African Peoples. London: Oxford Univ. Press. 190-209.

―― Carstairs, G. Morris. See Psychology.

39. Caudill, William (1952) Japanese-American Personality and Acculturation. Provincetown, Mass.: Journal Press (Genetic Psychol. Monographs 45.) --Relation of modal personality traits to cultural value-orientations and conflicts in values.

40. ___ and De Vos, George (1956) Achievement, Culture and Personality; The Case of the Japanese Americans. Amer. Anthrop. 58: 1102-1126. --Examines achievement goals emphasized in the value system, processes by which they are implemented, and personality adjustment to them.

41. +Cazeneuve, Jean (1958) Les rites et la condition humaine. Paris: Presses Universitaires de France. --A study of primitive man as seeking a "human condition" sensed as a properly human way of life beyond what is actually experienced.

42. Chapple, Eliot D. (1950) Anthropology and Ethics. Symp. Sci. Phil. Relig. 10: 79-85. --The concept of equilibrium proposed to test the "ethically desirable"; scientific inquiry and experiment expected to produce a universally acceptable ethics.

43. Cloutier, George (1951) An Analysis of Cross-Cultural Marriage, Using Profiles of Cultural Orientation. Honors Thesis, Harvard College. -- Analysis of a sample of cross-cultural marriages in the American Southwest, with strain successfully predicted from differences in cultural value-orientation profiles.

44. Cohen, Yehudi A. (1955) Character Formation and Social Structure in a Jamaican Community. Psychiatry 18: 275-296.

45. +Colson, Elizabeth (1953) Social Control and Vengeance in Plateau Tonga Society. Africa 23: 199-212.

46. Committee on Ethics, Report (1949) Human Organization 8: 20-21. --A "Code of Ethics" for anthropologists, drawn up by the Society for Applied Anthropology.

47. +Coon, Carleton S. (1946) The Universality of Natural Groupings in Human Societies. J. Educ. Sociol. 20: 163-168.

48. Culwick, A. T. (1942) Good Out of Africa; A Study of the Relativity of Morals. London: Oxford

Univ. Press (Rhodes-Livingstone Papers, No. 8). --Survival value proposed as the test of social institutions; criticizes attempt to impose Christian values on Africans and describes disorganization resulting from the attempt.

49. Curtiss, William E. (1905) Education and Morals among the Navajos and Pueblos. Amer. Antiquarian 27: 259-265. --An early study; very general statements, based largely upon the opinions of an Indian agent.

50. Douglas, Mary (1954) The Lele of Kasai. IN: C. D. Forde, ed. African Worlds; Studies in the Cosmological Ideas and Social Values of African Peoples. London: Oxford Univ. Press. 1-26.

51. Driberg, J. H. (1928) Primitive Law in Eastern Africa. Africa 1: 63-72.

52. Dube, S. C. (1955) Indian Village. London: Routledge and Kegan Paul. --See especially: Chs. 4-7, values in relation to religion, family and caste; Ch. 8, change involving values.

53. DuBois, Cora (1936) The Wealth Concept as an Integrative Factor in Tolowa-Tututni Culture. IN: R. H. Lowie, ed. Essays in Anthropology in Honor of Alfred Louis Kroeber. Berkeley: Univ. of California Press. 49-65. --The extent and limits of the influence of wealth as a value.

54. ___ (1955) The Dominant Value Profile of American Culture. Amer. Anthrop. 57: 1232-1239.

55. ___ (1956) Foreign Students and Higher Education in the United States. Washington: Amer. Council on Education. --See especially: Ch. 6, selected American values related to adjustment problems of foreign students in the United States.

56. Edel, May and Edel, Abraham (1959) <u>Anthropology and Ethics.</u> Springfield, Ill.: Thomas (Marvin Farber, ed. American Lectures in Philosophy). --A combination of philosophical ethics with anthropology, to establish "coordinates" for mapping cultural ethics, to explore the relations of morality to culture patterns and social processes, and to examine refinements and reformulations of philosophical ethical issues in relation to cultural content.

57. Edmonson, Munro S. (1952) <u>Los Manitos; Patterns of Humor in Relation to Cultural Values.</u> Ph. D. Thesis, Harvard Univ. --Relates prohibitions and permissions of humor to values, with descriptive materials from Spanish-American villages.

58. Eggan, Dorothy (1956) Instruction and Affect in Hopi Cultural Continuity. <u>S. W. J. Anthrop.</u> 12: 347-370. --Strong emotional conditioning during the learning process as an instrument in cultural conditioning, especially in the persistence of values.

59. Eglar, Zekiye (1957) Panjabi Village Life. IN: Stanley Maron, ed. <u>Pakistan; Society and Culture.</u> New Haven: Human Relations Area Files. 62-80. --Summary of social organization, with relevant ideals and values described.

60. Ehrenfels, U. R. (1953) Social Ethics in the Anthropological Age. <u>Women's Welfare J.</u> (Madras, India) 9: 1-8. --Hindu values and anthropological theories of diffusion as they relate to values.

61. Elbert, Samuel H. (1951) Hawaiian Literary Style and Culture. <u>Amer. Anthrop.</u> 53: 345-354. --Analysis of folktales, their content related to cultural values and linguistic structure.

-51-

62. Elwin, Verrier (1955) The Religion of an Indian Tribe. New York: Oxford Univ. Press. --See especially: the last three chapters, The Saora Ethic, The Regard for Human Life, Values and Motives.

63. Embree, John F. (1943) Resistance to Freedom; An Administrative Problem. Appl. Anthrop. 2: 10. --Values in relation to applied anthropology.

64. ___ (1945) Applied Anthropology and Its Relation to Anthropology. Amer. Anthrop. 47: 635-637.

65. ___ (1949) The Indian Bureau and Self-Government. Human Organization 8: 211-214.

66. ___ (1950) Standardized Error and Japanese Character; A Note on Political Interpretation. World Pol. 2: 439-443.

67. Epstein, A. L. (1954) Juridical Techniques and the Judicial Process; A Study in African Customary Law. Manchester: Manchester Univ. Press. (Rhodes-Livingstone Papers, No. 23).

68. Erasmus, Charles J. (1952) Changing Folk Beliefs and the Relativity of Empirical Knowledge. S. W. J. Anthrop. 8: 411-428. --On the inter-relations of normative and existential statements.

69. Evans-Pritchard, E. E. (1937) Witchcraft, Oracles and Magic among the Azande. London: Oxford Univ. Press. --See especially: Ch. 7, description of moral notions.

70. ___ (1940) The Nuer; A Description of the Modes of Livelihood and Political Institutions of a Nilotic People. Oxford: Clarendon Press. --See especially: 25, 263, 265, references to values. One of the earliest ethnographies to take the

concept of values as central in the theoretical framework.

71. ___ (1949) Two Nuer Ritual Concepts. Man 49: 74-76. --Counterparts of "respect" and "sin" in Nuer belief.

72. ___ (1956) Nuer Religion. Oxford: Clarendon Press. -- See especially: Ch. 7, Sin; Ch. 13, Some Reflections on Nuer Religion, on Nuer moral judgments related to religious thought and practice.

73. Firth, Raymond (1929) Primitive Economics of the New Zealand Maori. New York: Dutton. -- See especially: Ch. 12, primitive economic values.

74. ___ (1939) Primitive Polynesian Economy. London: Routledge. --Tikopian economic system and values.

75. ___ (1949) Authority and Public Opinion in Tikopia. IN: Meyer Fortes, ed. Social Structure; Studies Presented to A. R. Radcliffe-Brown. London: Oxford Univ. Press. 168-188. --Description and analysis of social sanctions and relevant social structures in the enforcement of the society's moral code.

76. ___ (1951) Elements of Social Organization. New York: Philosophical Library. --See especially: Ch. 2, a comparative sociological treatment of the value concept; Ch. 3, values and social change; Ch. 4, economic values; Ch. 6, moral standards and sanctions; Ch. 7, religious values.

77. ___ (1953) The Study of Values by Social Anthropologists. Man 53: 146-153.

78. Fletcher, Alice C. and La Flesche, Francis (1911)
Rites Pertaining to the Individual; Introduction
of the Omaha Child to the Cosmos. IN: The
Omaha Tribe, Twenty-Seventh Annual Report
of the Bureau of American Ethnology, 1905-06.
Washington, D.C.: U.S.G.P.O. 115-133.
Also in: Douglas G. Haring, ed. Personal
Character and Cultural Milieu. Syracuse:
Syracuse Univ. Press, 1956. 289-301.

79. Forde, C. D., ed. (1954) African Worlds; Studies in
the Cosmological Ideas and Social Values of
African Peoples. Published for the International African Institute. London: Oxford Univ.
Press.

80. Fortes, Meyer (1949) The Web of Kinship Among the
Tallensi. London and New York: Oxford Univ.
Press. --"Kinship taken as a system of values...
is unique in that it is the master principle both
for particular activities and for the social
structure as a whole." (p. 340) (The "essence"
of such a kinship system lies) "in its function
as the primary mechanism through which the
basic moral axioms of a society of the type
represented by the Tallensi are translated into
the give and take of social life." (p. 346)

81. Foster, George M. (1952) Relationships Between Theoretical and Applied Anthropology; A Public
Health Program Analysis. Human Organization
11: 5-16.

___ Francis, E. K. See Sociology.

82. Fried, Jacob (1953) The Relation of Ideal Norms to
Actual Behavior in Tarahumara Society. S.W.
J. Anthrop. 9: 286-295. --An American Indian
culture.

83. Fürer-Haimendorf, Christophe von (1941) Religion and Ethics among the Konyak Nagas and Other Indian Tribes. IN: J. P. Mills et al., eds. Essays in Anthropology. Lucknow: Maxwell. 158-168. --India.

84. Garth, Thomas R., Jr. (1945) Emphasis on Industriousness among the Atsugewi. Amer. Anthrop. 47: 554-566. --A California Indian culture permeated by a dominant value of industriousness.

85. Geertz, Clifford (1951) Drought, Death and Alcohol in Five Southwestern Cultures. Harvard Values Study. Dittoed. --Comparative analysis of responses to crises in the light of different histories and value-orientations of five cultures.

86. ___ (1957-58) Ethos, World-View and the Analysis of Sacred Symbols. Antioch Rev. 17: 421-437. -- The relationship between evaluative-normative and cognitive-existential elements in culture; description of the integration of Javanese values and metaphysics.

87. Geertz, Hildred (1956) Javanese Values and Family Relationships. Ph. D. Thesis, Radcliffe College.

— Gehlen, Arnold. See Philosophy.

88. Gillin, John (1944) Cultural Adjustment. Amer. Anthrop. 46: 429-447. --A theory of cultural compatibility to external conditions and internal consistency, with a schema for locating compatibilities and consistencies of cultures.

89. ___ (1948) The Ways of Men. New York: Appleton-Century-Crofts. --See especially: Chs. 22-24, values as integrators in a conceptual scheme to analyze culture patterns and integration.

-55-

90. ___ (1955) National and Regional Cultural Values in the United States. Soc. Forces 34: 107-113.

91. Gluckman, Hermann Max (1955) The Judicial Process among the Barotse of Northern Rhodesia. Published for the Rhodes-Livingstone Institute. Manchester: Manchester Univ. Press. Also: Glencoe, Ill.: Free Press.

92. Goldenweiser, Alexander (1937) Anthropology. New York: Crofts. --See especially: Ch. 25, primitive values as part of "primitive life and thought."

93. Goldfrank, Esther (1945) Socialization, Personality, and the Structure of Pueblo Society (with Particular Reference to Hopi and Zuni). Amer. Anthrop. 47: 516-539. Also in: Douglas G. Haring, ed. Personal Character and Cultural Milieu. Syracuse: Syracuse Univ. Press, 1956. 303-327.

94. Goldschmidt, Walter (1951) Ethics and the Structure of Society; An Ethnological Contribution to the Sociology of Knowledge. Amer. Anthrop. 53: 506-524. --Social structure, rather than specific economic implementation of that structure, seems to have crucial involvement with the ethical system; Hupa-Yurok Indian and modern Western comparisons.

95. ___ (1951) Notes (on "Death of a Salesman"). Amer. Quart. 3: 259-269. --Observations on American values.

96. ___ (1953) Values and the Field of Comparative Sociology. Amer. Sociol. Rev. 18: 287-293. --The concept of values as universal imperatives and as functionally related to other parts of culture viewed as social anthropology's contribution to general sociological theory; thesis

illustrated by analysis of relation of subsistence
economy to the value of land.

97. Goodman, Mary Ellen (1957) Values, Attitudes, and
Social Concepts of Japanese and American
Children. Amer. Anthrop. 59: 979-999.

98. Gorer, Geoffrey (1942) Themes in Japanese Culture.
New York Acad. Sci. Series II, 5: 106-124.
Also in: Douglas G. Haring, ed. Personal
Character and Cultural Milieu. Syracuse:
Syracuse Univ. Press, 1948. 237-255. --
Japanese values as determined by child-rearing
practices.

99. ____ (1955) Modification of National Character; The
Role of the Police in England. J. Soc. Issues
11: 24-32. Also in: Douglas G. Haring, ed.
Personal Character and Cultural Milieu.
Syracuse: Syracuse Univ. Press, 1956. 329-
339.

100. Griaule, Marcel (1938) Masques Dogons. Paris:
Institut d'Ethnologie. --Description of complex
Sudanese philosophical system and symbolism.

101. ____ (1948) Dieu d'Eau, Entretiens avec Ogotemméli.
Paris: Editions du Chêne.

102. ____ and Dieterlen, Germain (1954) The Dogon of the
French Sudan. IN: C. D. Forde, ed. African
Worlds; Studies in the Cosmological Ideas and
Social Values of African Peoples. London:
Oxford Univ. Press. 83-110.

103. +Hall, Edward T., Jr. (1955) The Anthropology of
Manners. Sci. Amer. 192: 84-90.

104. +____ and Trager, G. L. (1953) The Analysis of Culture. Washington, D. C.: U.S.G.P.O.,
Foreign Service Institute, Department of State.

--An approach to culture through analogies with linguistics; discriminates different levels of analysis; uses a biological base to free the analytic categories from cultural preconceptions.

105. Hallowell, A. Irving (1950) Values, Acculturation and Mental Health. Amer. J. Orthopsychiat. 20: 732-743. --Values in relation to adjustment and personality function, exemplified in Ojibwa Indians under acculturative pressures.

106. Haring, Douglas G. (1946) Aspects of Personal Character in Japan. Far Eastern Quart. 6: 12-22. Also in: Douglas G. Haring, ed. Personal Character and Cultural Milieu. Syracuse: Syracuse Univ. Press, 1956. 412-423.

107. ___, ed. (1948) Personal Character and Cultural Milieu. Syracuse: Syracuse Univ. Press. --Reprinted in 1956.

108. ___ (1953) Japanese National Character; Cultural Anthropology, Psychoanalysis, and History. Yale Review 42: 373-392. Also in: Douglas G. Haring, ed. Personal Character and Cultural Milieu. Syracuse: Syracuse Univ. Press, 1956. 424-437.

109. Henry, Jules and Boggs, Joan W. (1952) Child Rearing, Culture, and the Natural World. Psychiatry 15: 261-272.

110. Herskovits, Melville J. (1942) On the Values in Culture. Sci. Monthly 54: 557-560. --Cultural relativism extended to include appreciation of the values of one's own culture.

111. ___ (1948) Man and His Works; The Science of Cultural Anthropology. New York: Knopf. --See

especially: Ch. 5, The Problem of Cultural
Relativism, differentiates universals from absolutes; views cultural relativism as essential
to inductive extraction of universals; Ch. 21,
Religion: The Problem of Man and the Universe, esp. 353; Ch. 22, Religion: The Control of the Universe, esp. 375, on the ethical
content of religions.

112. ___ (1951) Tender and Tough-Minded Anthropology
and the Study of Values in Culture. S. W. J.
Anthrop. 7: 22-31. --Cultural relativism defended and distinctions drawn between methodological, philosophical and practical relativism.

113. ___ (1955) Cultural Anthropology. New York:
Knopf. --See especially: Ch. 19, Cultural Relativism and Cultural Values.

114. ___ (1958) Some Further Comments on Cultural Relativism. Amer. Anthrop. 60: 266-273. --
Urges extension of documenting relativism in
ethics and values to documenting relativism of
cultural perception, concepts of time and space
and other elements in world-view.

115. Hitchcock, John T. (In Press) The Idea of the Mar-
tial Rajput. J. Amer. Folklore. --Summary of
the values of a major caste-group of India.

116. Hobson, Richard (1954) Navaho Acquisitive Values.
Peabody Museum, Harvard, 42. --Clusters of
values of wealth accumulation and associated
socio-economic values related to the dominant
value-motifs of the Navaho.

117. Hockett, Charles F. (1951) Review: Science and the
Goals of Man, A Study in Semantic Organization: by Anatol Rapoport. Etc. 8: 132-141. --
Criticizes Rapoport's argument but accepts his
major thesis that scientific practice generates
an ethic. (See 1965.)

118. Hoebel, E. Adamson (1954) The Law of Primitive Man; A Study in Comparative Legal Dynamics. Cambridge: Harvard Univ. Press. --Theoretical and descriptive study of law as an aspect of culture, with descriptions of legal norms of several primitive cultures.

119. +Hogbin, H. Ian (1947) Shame; A Study of Social Conformity in a New Guinea Village. Oceania 17: 273-288.

120. +Hoijer, Harry, ed. (1954) Language in Culture; Proceedings of a Conference on the Interrelations of Language and Other Aspects of Culture. Amer. Anthrop. Assn. Memoir No. 79. Also: Chicago: Univ. of Chicago Press. --Methodologically interesting for analogies between intercultural study of language and of values.

121. Holleman, J. F. (1950) An Anthropological Approach to Bantu Law (with special reference to Shona law). Human Probl. in Brit. Central Africa 10: 51-64. --Contrasts between the presuppositions of Western and African (especially Shona) law.

122. Honigmann, John J. (1949) Culture and Ethos of Kaska Society. New Haven: Yale Univ. Press (Yale Publications in Anthrop. 40). --The value system and personalities of a Canadian Indian group, with Rorschach results, autobiographical materials and discussion of the concepts of ethos and world-view.

123. ___ (1949) Incentives to Work in a Canadian Indian Community. Human Organization 8: 23-28.

124. +___ (1950) Culture Patterns and Human Stress. Psychiatry 13: 25-34. --Cultural determination of stress and provision for relief of stress, with much comparative data; the problem of relieving stress without disrupting culture.

125. Howell, P. P. (1954) A Manual of Nuer Law. Published for the International African Institute.
New York: Oxford Univ. Press. --Codes and
sanctions of a segmentary social system based
on the value premise of balanced opposition of
groups, the highest value being loyalty to one's
group.

126. +Hsu, Francis L. K. (1952) Religion, Science and
Human Crisis; A Study of China in Transition
and Its Implications for the West. London:
Routledge and Kegan Paul.

127. ___ (1953) Americans and Chinese; Two Ways of
Life. New York: Schuman. --Universal beliefs
and values, acculturation in China, with comparisons of the two cultures.

128. Hu Hsien-Chin (1944) The Chinese Concepts of 'Face.'
Amer. Anthrop. 46: 45-64. Also in: Douglas
G. Haring, ed. Personal Character and Cultural Milieu. Syracuse: Syracuse Univ. Press,
1956. 447-467.

129. Hulse, Frederick S. (1948) Convention and Reality in
Japanese Culture. S.W. J. Anthrop. 4: 345-
355. --Relationship between ideal formal values
and behavioral norms among the Japanese.

130. Human Organization (formerly Applied Anthropology)
1949 Editorial: Colonialism and the United
Nations. 8: 3-4.
1949 Editorial: "Understanding" is Not
Enough. 8: 2-3.
1950 Editorial: Other Lessons from Bikini.
9: 4.
1952 Editorial: Research - Business or Schol-
arship? 11: 3-4.
--Editorials on the ethics of applied anthropology, modern science and colonialism.

131. +Keesing, Felix M. (1949) Cultural Dynamics and Administration. Seventh Pacific Sci. Congress, Proc. 7: 102-117.

132. ___, ed. (1953) Anthropological Contributions to Value Theory. Department of Anthropology, Stanford University. Dittoed. --Excerpts from 49 authors, mainly anthropologists, with an introductory essay by the editor, The Historical Place of Value Concepts in Anthropological Theory.

133. ___, ed. (1955) Anthropological Contributions to Value Theory, rev. issue, to May 1955. Dittoed. Stanford University Department of Sociology and Anthropology, Committee for Anthropological Research. --A new introduction by the editor, Value Concepts in Anthropological Theory; additional excerpts.

134. +___ and Keesing, Marie M. (1956) Opinion Formation and Decision-Making. IN: Elite Communication in Samoa; A Study of Leadership. Stanford: Stanford Univ. Press (Stanford Anthrop. Series, no. 3). Ch. 5.

135. Kimball, Solon T. (1946) The Crisis in Colonial Administration. Appl. Anthrop. 5: 8-16. -- Values relating to caste and race relations in Asian colonial policy and United States Indian policy.

136. +Kluckhohn, Clyde (1941) Patterning as Exemplified in Navaho Culture. IN: Leslie Spier, A. I. Hallowell and S. S. Newman, eds. Language, Culture, and Personality; Essays in Memory of Edward Sapir. Menasha: Sapir Memorial Publication Fund. 109-130. --Concepts of culture patterns formulated, their analytic use illustrated with Navaho data. Distinguishes ideal from real patterns, idea from action patterns, configurations from behavioral patterns.

137. +___ (1943) Covert Culture and Administrative Problems. Amer. Anthrop. 45: 213-227. --Further
progress in U. S. Indian Service Administration depends upon advances in anthropological
theory; pattern theory sketched.

138. ___ (1949) The Philosophy of the Navaho Indians.
IN: F. S. C. Northrop, ed. Ideological Differences and World Order. New Haven: Yale
Univ. Press. 356-384. --Navaho system of
metaphysics, logic and ethics.

139. ___ (1950) The Special Character of Integration in an
Individual Culture. Proc. Stillwater Conference: The Nature of Concepts; Their Inter-
Relation and Role in Social Structure. New
York: Foundation for Integrated Education.
78-87. --The concept of culture proposed as of
suitable breadth to cut across traditional academic disciplines and as relevant to the study
of universal values.

140. ___ (1951) An Anthropological Approach to the Study
of Values. Bull. Amer. Acad. Arts and Sci. 4:
2-3. --Separation of science from values, especially as reinforced by relativism, challenged;
the possibility of discovering universal values,
based on the "givens" of human life explored.

141. ___ (1951) A Comparative Study of Values in Five
Cultures. Foreword to Evon Z. Vogt, Navaho
Veterans. Peabody Museum, Harvard, 41.

142. ___ (1951) Values and Value-Orientations in the
Theory of Action. IN: Talcott Parsons and
Edward Shils, eds. Toward a General Theory
of Action. Cambridge: Harvard Univ. Press.
388-433. --Definitions and classificatory principle for values and value-orientations, the
latter related to operational and observational
referents; "value" distinguished from related
concepts.

143. ___ (1952) Universal Values and Anthropological Relativism. IN: Modern Education and Human
Values. Pittsburgh: Univ. of Pittsburgh Press
(Pitcairn-Crabbe Foundation Lecture Series 4).
87-112. --Notes convergences and cultural variations of values.

144. +___ (1953) Universal Categories of Culture. IN:
Alfred L. Kroeber, ed. Anthropology Today,
Chicago: Univ. of Chicago Press. 507-523.

145. +___ (1954) Culture and Behavior. IN: Gardner
Lindzey, ed. Handbook of Social Psychology.
Vol. II. Cambridge: Addison-Wesley. 921-
976. --Relates concepts of culture to psychological concepts; discusses universal behaviors
and the relations of psychology and anthropology.

146. ___ (1955) Ethical Relativity; Sic et Non. J. Phil.
52: 663-677. --Reviews contributions of social
sciences to ethical theory, finds the evidence
makes "the position of radical cultural relativity
untenable."

147. ___ (1955) Implicit and Explicit Values in the Social
Sciences Related to Human Growth and Development. Merrill-Palmer Quart. 1: 131-140.

148. ___ (1955) Indian Americans in a White Man's
World; A Study of Indian American Values and
Culture Change. Advance (Congregational
Christian Journal) 147: 13-15.

149. ___ (1956) Navaho Morals. IN: Vergilius Ferm, ed.
Encyclopedia of Morals. New York: Philosophical Library. 383-390.

150. ___ (1956) Some Navaho Value Terms in Behavioral
Context. Language 32: 140-145.

151. ___ (1956) Toward a Comparison of Value-Emphases
in Different Cultures. IN: L. D. White, ed.
The State of the Social Sciences. Chicago:
Univ. of Chicago Press. 116-132. --Following
a model from linguistics, proposes binary opposition of cross-cultural core value-emphases.

152. ___ (1957) Cultures, Values, and Education. Bull.
Res. Inst. Comp. Educ. and Culture (English
ed. 1, Fukuoka, Japan: Kyushu University):
44-61.

153. ___ (1958) The Evolution of Contemporary American
Values. Daedalus, Spring: 78-109 (Issued as
vol. 87, No. 2, Proc. Amer. Acad. Arts and
Sci.). --Surveys recent studies of American
values, noting a shift from the Puritan Ethic
towards group values, stability and hetero-
geneity.

154. ___ and Kluckhohn, Florence R. (1947) American
Culture; Generalized Orientation and Class
Patterns. Symp. Sci. Phil. Relig. 7: 106-128.

——Kluckhohn, Florence, R. See Sociology.

155. +Koppers, Wilhelm (1952) Primitive Man and His
World Picture. Trans. by Edith Raybould.
London and New York: Sheed and Ward.

156. Krige, J. D. and Krige, E. J. (1954) The Lovedu of
the Transvaal. IN: C. D. Forde, ed. African
Worlds; Studies in the Cosmological Ideas and
Social Values of African Peoples. London:
Oxford Univ. Press. 55-82.

157. Kroeber, Alfred L. (1910) The Morals of Uncivilized
People. Amer. Anthrop. 12: 437-447. --One
of the earlier American anthropological papers
to discuss cultural ethics; deals with moral
universals, the cultural relativity of morals
and the non-rational nature of morality.

158. ___ (1948) Anthropology. New York: Harcourt. --
One of the first anthropology textbooks to deal
explicitly with values. See: 294, 840-849.

159. ___ (1949) Values as a Subject of Natural Science Inquiry. Natl. Acad. Sci. Proc. 35: 261-264.
--Values as "natural phenomena occurring in
nature."

160. ___ (1952) The Nature of Culture. Chicago: Univ.
of Chicago Press. --See especially: 104-106,
118-135, 136-138, and 152-166, discussion
and recommendation of objective study of
values.

161. + ___ (1957) Style and Civilizations. Ithaca: Cornell
Univ. Press. --The concept of "style" applied
to decorative and fine arts and to civilizations.

162. ___ and Kluckhohn, Clyde (1952) Culture. Peabody
Museum, Harvard, 47. --See especially: 174-
180, Values and Relativity. Other references
to values in the text, passim.

163. Kropotkin, Petr A. (1926) Ethics, Origin and Development. Trans. by Louis S. Friedland and
Joseph R. Piroshnikoff. New York: McVeigh,
Dial Press. --Mutual aid as a law of nature
and, together with progressive evolution, the
basis of a scientific ethics.

164. LaBarre, Weston (1954) The Human Animal.
Chicago: Univ. of Chicago Press. --Discusses
moral values (Why Man is Human) and primitive belief systems (Superstition and the Soul),
in a biological-psychoanalytic framework, with
a naturalistic attack on "metaphysical" values.

165. Lee, Dorothy D. (1940) A Primitive System of Values.
Phil. Sci. 7: 355-378. --Metalinguistic analysis
of the culture of Trobriand Islanders.

166. ___ (1948) Are Basic Needs Ultimate? J. Abnorm.
Soc. Psychol. 43: 391-395. Also in: Clyde
Kluckhohn, Henry Murray and David Schneider,
eds. Personality in Nature, Culture and
Society. New York: Knopf, 1953. 335-341. --
"Values" asserted to be more basic than "needs"
in explaining cultural variation; culture an expression of a society's basic values, not of its
adjustive needs.

167. ___ (1949) Being and Value in a Primitive Culture.
J. Phil. 46: 401-415. --Through linguistic
analysis primarily, "being" found to be the
dominant philosophical Wintu motif and value.

168. ___ (1953) Freedom and Authority as Integral to Culture and Structure. Symp. Sci. Phil. Relig.
12: 335-344.

169. ___ (1954) Freedom, Spontaneity and Limit in
American Linguistic Usage. Explorations 4:
6-14.

170. ___ (1954) Symbolization and Value. Symp. Sci.
Phil. Relig. 13: 73-85. Also in: Explorations
7: 56-66 (1957).

— Leighton, Alexander H. See Psychology.

— Leighton, Dorothea. See Psychology.

171. +Lévi-Strauss, Claude (1945) French Sociology. IN:
Georges Gurvitch and Wilbert Moore, eds.
Twentieth Century Sociology. New York:
Philosophical Library. 503-537. --Discussion
of cultural universals; controversy with A. L.
Kroeber on this point.

— Lévy-Bruhl, Lucien. See Sociology.

172. Lewis, Oscar (1951) Life in a Mexican Village; Tepoztlán Restudied. Urbana: Univ. of Illinois Press. --A descriptive study, with some mention of values. See especially: 296 ff., 418 ff., 422.

173. Li An-Che (1937) Zuni; Some Observations and Queries. Amer. Anthrop. 39: 62-76. --Interprets disagreements about Zuni as reflecting the different values of anthropological observers.

174. Lienhardt, Godfrey (1954) The Shilluk of the Upper Nile. IN: C. D. Forde, ed. African Worlds; Studies in the Cosmological Ideas and Social Values of African Peoples. London: Oxford Univ. Press. 138-163.

175. Linton, Ralph (1949) Discussion. IN: S. Stansfield and Marian W. Smith, eds. Culture and Personality, Proc. Interdisciplinary Conference. New York: Viking Fund. 123-124. --Examples of abrupt changes in the value systems of primitive societies.

176. ___ (1952) Universal Ethical Principles; An Anthropological View. IN: R. N. Anshen, ed. Moral Principles of Action. New York: Harper. 645-660.

177. ___ (1954) The Problem of Universal Values. IN: Robert F. Spencer, ed. Method and Perspective in Anthropology; Papers in Honor of Wilson D. Wallis. Minneapolis: Univ. of Minnesota Press. 145-168. --Distinguishes instrumental from conceptual values; lists and discusses values found in all cultures.

178. Little, Kenneth (1954) The Mende in Sierra Leone. IN: C. D. Forde, ed. African Worlds; Studies in the Cosmological Ideas and Social Values of

African Peoples. London: Oxford Univ. Press.
111-137.

179. Llewellyn, Karl and Hoebel, E. Adamson (1941) The
Cheyenne Way; Conflict and Case Law in Primitive Jurisprudence. Norman: Univ. of Oklahoma Press.

180. Lowie, Robert H. (1920) Primitive Society. New
York: Liveright. --See especially: Chapters
on property, rank and justice for cross-cultural
differences in these values.

181. ___ (1921) A Note on Esthetics. Amer. Anthrop. 23:
170-174. --Quantitative comparison of esthetic
predilections of Crow and Shoshoni Indians.

182. McAllester, David P. (1954) Enemy Way Music; A
Study of Social and Esthetic Values as Seen in
Navaho Music. Peabody Museum, Harvard,
41. --Detailed musicological analysis of the
secular music of the Enemy Way and discussion of relationships of esthetic to other values.

183. McArthur, C. C. (1952) Cultural Values as Factors
in Imaginal Productions. Ph. D. Thesis,
Harvard Univ.

184. McFeat, Thomas F. S. (1957) Value Patterns in a
Design for Learning; A Study in Contextual
Shift. Ph. D Thesis, Harvard Univ. --Based
on Zuni data.

185. McNair, Robert (1948) The Ideas of the Good in the
Mythology of The Navaho Indians. Ph. D.
Thesis, Harvard Univ.

186. Malinowski, Bronislaw (1926) Crime and Custom in
Savage Society. London: Kegan Paul, Trench,
Trubner. --Moral and legal code and social
sanctions of the Trobrianders.

187. ___ (1944) Freedom and Civilization. Chapel Hill:
       Univ. of North Carolina Press. --Value con-
       ceived as a culturally determined driving force;
       a call to anthropologists to reaffirm values
       needed to maintain and advance culture.

188. Mandelbaum, David G. (1953) On the Study of Na-
       tional Character. Amer. Anthrop. 55: 174-
       187. --Critique of Mead's paper, National
       Character (see 200).

189. ___ (1955) The World and the World View of the
       Kota. IN: McKim Marriott, ed. Village
       India. Chicago: Univ. of Chicago Press.
       223-254.

190. Maquet, Jacques J. (1954) The Kingdom of Ruanda.
       IN: C. D. Forde, ed. African Worlds; Studies
       in the Cosmological Ideas and Social Values of
       African Peoples. London: Oxford Univ. Press.
       164-189.

191. Marett, R. R. (1931) The Beginnings of Morals and
       Culture; An Introduction to Social Anthropology.
       IN: W. Rose, ed. An Outline of Modern Knowl-
       edge. London: Gollancz. 395-430.

192. ___ (1935) Head, Heart and Hands in Human Evolu-
       tion. London: Hutchinson's Scientific Books.
       --See especially: 43-61, Fact and Value. Fact
       reportable by science, but "the core of reality
       is constituted not by fact but by inspiration"
       and is thus in the domain of the "framers of
       ideals."

193. Matthews, Washington (1899) The Study of Ethics
       among the Lower Races. J. Amer. Folklore
       12: 1-9. --One of the first papers in descrip-
       tive ethics by an American ethnographer.

194. Mead, Margaret (1935) Sex and Temperament in
        Three Primitive Societies. New York:
        Morrow. --Includes discussion of sex-role
        values, their internalization and the origins
        of deviance in three New Guinea tribes.

195. ___, ed. (1937) Co-operation and Competition among
        Primitive Peoples. New York: McGraw-Hill.
        --Internalization of values in 13 societies, with
        a theory of personality development and a form-
        ulation of the shame-guilt distinction.

196. +___ (1939) On the Concept of Plot in Culture. Trans.
        New York Acad. Sci., Series 2, 2: 24-31.

197. ___ (1942) And Keep Your Powder Dry. New York:
        Morrow. --Includes treatment of American
        values.

198. ___ (1942) The Comparative Study of Cultures and
        the Purposive Cultivation of Democratic Values.
        Symp. Sci. Phil. Relig. 2: 55-69. --Also,
        comments by Ruth Benedict, Clyde Kluckhohn,
        Dorothy D. Lee, Geoffrey Gorer, Gregory
        Bateson, 69-98.

199. ___ (1950) The Comparative Study of Cultures and the
        Purposive Cultivation of Democratic Values,
        1941 - 1949. Symp. Sci. Phil. Relig. 10: 87-
        108. --Also comments by Karl W. Deutsch,
        Geoffrey Gorer, Rhoda Métraux.

200. ___ (1953) National Character. IN: Alfred L.
        Kroeber, ed. Anthropology Today. Chicago:
        Univ. of Chicago Press. 642-667. --Methods
        of national character research and their place
        in the field of culture and personality. (For
        criticism, see 188.)

201. ___, Chapple, Eliot D. and Brown, G. Gordon (1949)
        Report of the Committee on Ethics (Society for

Applied Anthropology). <u>Human Organization 8:</u> 20-21. --Reprinted in <u>Human Organization 10:</u> 32. A code of ethics for applied anthropologists.

202. ___ and Métraux, Rhoda, eds. (1953) <u>The Study of Culture at a Distance.</u> Chicago: Univ. of Chicago Press. --Methods of national character research and results of studies of European and Asian cultures.

203. Mercier, Paul (1954) The Fon of Dahomey. <u>IN:</u> C. D. Forde, ed. <u>African Worlds; Studies in the Cosmological Ideas and Social Values of African Peoples.</u> London: Oxford Univ. Press. 210-234.

204. Métraux, Rhoda and Mead, Margaret (1954) <u>Themes in French Culture; A Preface to a Study of French Community.</u> Hoover Institute Studies, Communities, No. 1, Series <u>D</u>, Stanford: Stanford Univ. Press. --Analysis of selected aspects of French life, revealing values; techniques and concepts from cultural anthropology, clinical psychology and psychiatry.

205. Mills, George (1953) <u>Navaho Art and Culture; A Study of the Relations Among Art Styles, Art Values, and Cultural Premises.</u> Ph. D. Thesis, Harvard Univ.

— Montagu, Ashley. See Ashley Montagu, M. F.

— Munch, Peter A. See <u>Sociology.</u>

206. Murdock, George P. (1945) Common Denominator of Cultures. <u>IN:</u> Ralph Linton, ed. <u>The Science of Man and the World Crisis.</u> New York: Columbia Univ. Press. 123-142. --Universal culture pattern, in terms of learning theory and biological adaptation.

207. Nadel, S. F. (1951) <u>Foundations of Social Anthro-</u>
<u>pology</u>. London: Cohen and West. --See es-
pecially: 48-55, values of anthropologists;
264-265, definition and discussion of "value";
final chapter, holistic conceptions of culture.

208. Norbeck, Edward and Norbeck, Margaret (1956)
Child Training in a Japanese Fishing Community. <u>IN</u>: Douglas G. Haring, ed. <u>Per-</u>
<u>sonal Character and Cultural Milieu</u>. Syra-
cuse: Syracuse Univ. Press. 651-673.

209. Olson, Ronald L. (1956) Channelling of Character in
Tlingit Society. <u>IN</u>: Douglas G. Haring, ed.
<u>Personal Character and Cultural Milieu</u>.
Syracuse: Syracuse Univ. Press. 675-687. --
An American Indian culture.

210. Opler, Marvin K. (1955) Cultural Values and Attitudes on Child Care. <u>Children 2</u>: 45-50. --
Effects of cultural milieu on child-care practices and associated behavior, as exemplified
in various American Indian tribes, Japanese-
Americans, and other cultures in transition.

211. ___ (1956) <u>Culture, Psychiatry and Human Values;</u>
<u>The Methods and Values of a Social Psychiatry</u>.
Springfield, Ill.: Thomas. --Survey of mental
illnesses among the peoples of the world;
theoretical analysis linking cultural, psychiatric and value-theory components.

212. Opler, Morris E. (1941) <u>An Apache Life-Way</u>.
Chicago: Univ. of Chicago Press. --Detailed
ethnography, presented in the order in which
an Apache Indian learns his culture; largely in
the words of Apache informants, with data on
socialization, sex values and belief systems.

213. ___ (1945) Social Science and Democratic Policy.
<u>Appl. Anthrop. 4</u>: 11-15.

214. +___ (1945) Themes as Dynamic Forces in Culture.
Amer. J. Sociol. 51: 198-206. --Proposal to
analyze cultures in terms of "themes"; factors
limiting expression of themes in behavior.
(For criticism, see 682.)

215. +___ (1946) An Application of the Theory of Themes
in Culture. J. Washington Acad. Sci. 36: 137-
166. --Twenty themes in the culture of the Lipan
Apache Indians.

216. +___ (1946) Rejoinder. Amer. J. Sociol. 52: 43-44.
--Defends concept of "themes" against critique
of A. K. Cohen (see 682).

217. +___ (1948) Some Recently Developed Concepts Relating to Culture. S. W. J. Anthrop. 4: 107-
122. --Review of work by Benedict, Linton,
Kluckhohn, Kroeber, Murdock, C. S. Ford,
Gillin et al., with the emphasis on patterns,
themes and premises in cultural content.

218. Palau Marti, Montserrat (1956) Métaphysique noire et
psychologie. Rev. de Psychologie des Peuples
(Paris) 11: 174-180. --In Bantu thinking, supreme values expressed in terms of "life" or
"vital force." Dualisms of "self" and "other,"
now being rejected by psychological theory in
the European tradition, have never had a place
in Bantu thinking.

219. Parsons, Elsie C. (1915) Links Between Religion and
Morality in Early Culture. Amer. Anthrop. 17:
41-57. --Supernatural sanctions in non-literate
societies.

220. Pelzel, John C. and Kluckhohn, Florence R. (1957)
A Theory of Variation in Values Applied to
Aspects of Japanese Social Structure. Bull.
Res. Inst. Comp. Educ. and Culture (English
ed. 1, Fukuoka, Japan: Kyushu University):
62-76.

221. Pitt-Rivers, Julian A. (1954) The People of the Sierra. New York: Criterion. --Study of a Spanish village, including values.

222. +Portilla, Miguel (1956) La Filosofia Nahuatl, Estudiada en Sus Fuentes. Mexico, D. F.: Ed. Instituto Indigenista Interamericano. -- Cosmological, metaphysical and theological ideas; Nahuatl texts appended.

223. Powdermaker, Hortense (1939) After Freedom. New York: Viking. --See especially: Part VI, American Negro values.

224. ___ (1950) Hollywood, the Dream Factory; An Anthropologist Looks at the Movie-Makers. Boston: Little, Brown.-- "Movie values" and American values.

225. ___ (1956) Social Change Through Imagery and Values of Teen-Age Africans in Northern Rhodesia. Amer. Anthrop. 58: 783-814.

226. Radcliffe-Brown, A. R. (1939) Taboo. Cambridge: Cambridge Univ. Press. --The relation of rituals and ritual values to the constitution of human society, with the theoretical view: "A social system can be conceived and studied as a system of values." (p. 20)

227. +Radin, Paul (1927) Primitive Man as a Philosopher. New York: Appleton. --Denies a separate primitive mentality, maintaining that there are philosophical and intellectual individuals in primitive groups.

228. ___ (1931) Concept of Right and Wrong. IN: V. F. Calverton, ed. The Making of Man. New York: Modern Library. 818-827.

229. Rangeley, W. H. J. (1948) Notes on Cewa Tribal Law. Nyasaland J. 1: 5-68. --An African legal system.

230. Rapoport, Robert N. (1954) Changing Navaho Religious Values; A Study of Christian Missions to the Rimrock Navahos. Peabody Museum, Harvard, 41. --Statistical, historical and psychological analyses of Navaho converts to Christianity.

231. Read, K. E. (1955) Morality and the Concept of the Person among the Gahuku-Gama (New Guinea). Oceania 25: 233-282.

232. Read, Margaret (1938) The Moral Code of the Ngoni and Their Former Military State. Africa 11: 1-24.

233. Redfield, Robert (1948) The Art of Social Science. Amer. J. Sociol. 54: 181-190. --The value problem in the humanities and social sciences.

234. +___ (1952) The Primitive World View. Proc. Amer. Phil. Soc. 96: 31-36. --Human universals assumed in the study of world view.

235. ___ (1953) The Primitive World and Its Transformations. Ithaca: Cornell Univ. Press. --World view as an approach to value-belief systems; change of moral order that accompanies development of urban civilization; impossibility of ethical neutrality for the anthropologist seen to follow from recognition of moral progress in human history.

236. ___ (1955) The Little Community; Viewpoints for the Study of a Human Whole. Chicago: Univ. of Chicago Press. --Using the concepts of values, world-view and ethos, urges and explores the possibilities of a more holistic viewpoint in the understanding of humanity.

237. +Reichard, Gladys A. (1955) Anthropologic View of a Primitive Religion. Internatl. Record of Med. and General Practice Clinics 168: 768-773.

238. Richards, Audrey (1940) Bemba Marriage and Present Economic Conditions. Livingstone, Northern Rhodesia: Rhodes-Livingstone Institute (Rhodes-Livingstone Papers, No. 4). -- Sex and marital values and changing family structure in industrialization in Central Africa.

239. Roberts, John M. (1957) Four Southwestern Men; A Study in Culture, Cultural Control, and Values. Lincoln: Univ. of Nebraska Press.

240. ___ and Vogt, Evon Z., eds. (In progress) A Social Scientific Study of Values; Theory and Interpretations (Tentative Title). Evanston, Ill.: Row, Peterson. --Theoretical implications of the Harvard Comparative Study of Values in Five Cultures project. (See also, 287.)

241. Sapir, Edward (1924) Culture, Genuine and Spurious. Amer. J. Sociol. 29: 401-429. Also in: David G. Mandelbaum, ed. Selected Writings of Edward Sapir in Language, Culture, and Personality. Berkeley: Univ. of California Press, 1949. 308-331. --An evaluation of societies on the basis of their degree of cultural integration and their creative expression of a "national genius."

242. Sayres, William C. (1956) Disorientation and Status Change. S.W. J. Anthrop. 12: 79-86. --Conflicting status-value orientations related to status shifts in a group of Colombian Indians.

243. Schapera, Isaac (1937) Law and Justice. IN: Isaac
     Schapera, ed. The Bantu-Speaking Tribes of
     South Africa. London: Routledge and Kegan
     Paul. 197-219.

244. ___ (1949) The Tswana Conception of Incest. IN:
     Meyer Fortes, ed. Social Structure; Studies
     Presented to A. R. Radcliffe-Brown, London:
     Oxford Univ. Press. 104-120. --Enforcement
     of a sexual taboo in a South African tribe, with
     case histories.

245. Schapiro, Meyer (1953) Style. IN: Alfred L.
     Kroeber, ed. Anthropology Today. Chicago:
     Univ. of Chicago Press. 287-312. --Reviews
     psychological, sociological and economic
     theories of style in relation to art history, cul-
     tural integration and esthetic value judgments.

246. Schneider, David M. (1957) Political Organization,
     Supernatural Sanctions and the Punishment for
     Incest on Yap. Amer. Anthrop. 59: 791-800.
     --Distinguishes prescribed sanctions from
     behavior in analysis of taboo violations in a
     Pacific Island culture.

247. Shah, A. M. and Shroff, R. G. (In Press) Barots of
     Gujarat (Foreword by M. N. Srinivas). J.
     Amer. Folklore. --Summary of the values of "A
     Caste of Genealogists and Mythographers - The
     Vahivancha" of India.

248. Shimkin, Demitri B. and Sanjuan, Pedro (1953) Cul-
     ture and World View; A Method of Analysis
     Applied to Rural Russia. Amer. Anthrop. 55:
     329-348. --Content analysis and adapted
     Rorschach scoring of proverbs from three
     Russian districts, with a study of the relations
     between the social-value contents of the
     proverbs and other cultural differences among
     the districts.

249. Siegel, Bernard J. (1948) Currents of Anthropological Theory and Value Concepts. S. W. J. Anthrop. 4: 199-210. --Value concepts and value judgments in anthropological writings.

250. Singer, Milton (1949) How the American Got His Character. Ethics 60: 62-66.

251. ___ (1956) Cultural Values in India's Economic Development. Philadelphia: Annals Amer. Acad. Pol. Soc. Sci.: 81-91. --"...The traditional Indian philosophy of renunciation is ... functionally linked to the material side of Indian life."

252. ___, ed. (In Press) Cultural Values and India's Economic Development; A Discussion. J. Econ. Development and Cultural Change. --Discussion of Singer (see 251), by John Goheen, M. N. Srinivas, D. G. Karve and Milton Singer on the question whether traditional Indian values will promote or frustrate the modernization program of India.

253. ___ (In Press) The Great Tradition in a Metropolitan Center; Madras. J. Amer. Folklore.

254. +___, ed. (In Press) Traditional India; Structure and Change. A Symposium. J. Amer. Folklore. --Discussions of social organization, cultural performances and media, problems and processes of culture change.

255. Slotkin, James S. (1950) Social Anthropology; The Science of Human Society and Culture. New York: Macmillan. --See especially Ch. 3, definitions of "values" and "value systems"; Chs. 5-10, examination of naturalistic, supernaturalistic, esthetic and mystical world-views.

256. Smith, Watson and Roberts, John (1954) Zuni Law; A Field of Values. Peabody Museum, Harvard, 43. --Cases heard before the Zuni Council, categorized according to U. S. legal system terminology, related values described and discussed.

257. Speck, Frank (1933) Ethical Attributes of the Labrador Indians. Amer. Anthrop. 35: 559-594. -- Reports Naskapi usages as utilitarian, arising from deliberate, rationalized thought about social conduct.

258. Spencer, Katherine (1957) Mythology and Values; An Analysis of Navaho Chantway Myths. Philadelphia: Amer. Folklore Soc. (Amer. Folklore Soc. Memoirs 48).

259. +Spier, Leslie (1927) The Association Test as a Method of Defining Religious Concepts. Amer. Anthrop. 29: 267-270. --Proposes a word association test to discover individual variation in religious beliefs, with some Havasupai Indian data.

260. Spindler, George D. (1948) American Character as Revealed by the Military. Psychiatry 11: 274-281.

261. ___ (1955) Education and Anthropology. Stanford: Stanford Univ. Press. --Value judgments in anthropological and educational research and in applied anthropology; cultural values; universals; other aspects of values.

262. ___ (1955) Education in a Transforming American Culture. Harvard Educ. Rev. 25: 145-156. -- "Traditional" and "emergent" American values.

263. +Spiro, Melford E. (1954) Human Nature in Its
     Psychological Dimensions. Amer. Anthrop.
     56: 19-30. --Universals of human behavior and
     personality structure.

264. Steed, Gitel P. (1955) Notes on an Approach to a
     Study of Personality Formation in a Hindu
     Village in Gujarat. IN: McKim Marriott, ed.
     Village India. Chicago: Univ. of Chicago
     Press.

265. Steiner, Franz (1956) Taboo. Laura Bohannan, ed.
     London: Cohen and West. Also: New York:
     Philosophical Library. --The social function of
     taboo, especially as an element "in which atti-
     tudes to values are expressed in terms of danger
     behavior."

266. Steward, Julian (1948) Comments on the Statement on
     Human Rights. Amer. Anthrop. 50: 351-352.
     --Criticizes A. A. A. 1947 statement (see 6),
     arguing for ethical neutrality of anthropologists.

267. Stoetzel, Jean (1955) Without the Chrysanthemum
     and the Sword; A Study of the Attitudes of
     Youth in Post-War Japan. New York: Colum-
     bia Univ. Press. --Results of questionnaires,
     interviews, projective tests and autobiographies,
     showing chief life aims and other attitudes of
     post-war Japanese youth. 80 tables, 12-page
     bibliography.

268. +Tax, Sol (1941) World View and Social Relations in
     Guatemala. Amer. Anthrop. 43: 27-42.

269. ___, Eiseley, Loren C., Rouse, Irving and Voegelin,
     Carl F., eds. (1953) An Appraisal of Anthro-
     pology Today. Chicago: Univ. of Chicago
     Press. --See especially: 181-188; 322-326,
     335-336; 372-376; discussions of the study of
     values and of the values of anthropologists by
     Robert Redfield, Clyde Kluckhohn, Claude
     Lévi-Strauss, David Bidney, Margaret Mead,
     Ralph Linton et al.

270. ter Haar, Barend (1948) Adat Law in Indonesia. Trans. and ed. by E. Adamson Hoebel and A. A. Schiller. New York: International Secretariat, Institute of Pacific Relations.

271. Thompson, Laura (1945) Logico-Aesthetic Integration in Hopi Culture. Amer. Anthrop. 47: 540-553. Also in: Douglas G. Haring, ed. Personal Character and Cultural Milieu. Syracuse: Syracuse Univ. Press, 1956. 729-743. --A highly integrated American Indian value system.

272. ___ (1946) In Quest of an Heuristic Approach to the Study of Mankind. Phil. Sci. 13: 53-66. --Values for the social scientist, their use in research illustrated by reference to work with Hopi Indians.

273. ___ (1947) In Quest of an Heuristic Approach to the Study of Mankind. Symp. Sci. Phil. Relig. 6: 503-526. --Additions, including pictorial illustrations, to the 1946 paper of the same title (see 272).

274. ___ (1948) Attitudes and Acculturation. Amer. Anthrop. 50: 200-215. --Belief in the immanent justice of nature in five Indian cultures, the effects of acculturation on these world views.

275. ___ (1950) Culture in Crisis; A Study of the Hopi Indians. New York: Harper. --The values of Hopi Indians and of Indian Service administrators.

276. ___ (1950) Science and the Study of Mankind. Symp. Sci. Phil. Relig. 10: 65-77. --Values in relation to applied social science.

277. ___ (1951) Operational Anthropology as an Emergent Discipline. Etc. 8: 117-128. --Argument for

the involvement of anthropologists in social action; values in applied anthropology; the holistic approach to culture advocated.

— Tumin, Melvin. See Sociology.

278. Untereiner, Wayne (1952) Self and Society; Orientations in Two Cultural Value Systems. Ph. D. Thesis, Harvard Univ. --Cognitive, cathectic and value orientations of Texan and Zuni communities.

279. Van der Kroef, Justus M. (1953) The Origin of Trade in Indonesia. Sci. Monthly 76: 284-289. -- Economic practices of non-Westernized Indonesians with a kinship-based, dualistic value pattern.

280. Vansina, Jan (1954) Les valeurs culturelles des Bushong. Zaïre (Brussels) 8: 889-910. --A Belgian Congo society.

281. Van Valkenburg, R. F. (1936-1938) Navaho Common Law. Museum Notes, Museum of Northern Arizona 9: 17-22, 51-54; 10: 39-45.

282. Voget, Fred W. (1954) The Folk Society--An Anthropological Application. Soc. Forces 33: 105-113. --Extending Redfield's "folk society" concept, constructs four types of sociocultural systems in terms of antithetical collective and individualistic value sentiments and attitudes.

283. Vogt, Evon Z. (1951) Navaho Veterans; A Study of Changing Values. Peabody Museum, Harvard, 41. --Differential value-acculturation of a sample of Navaho veterans and non-veterans in terms of personality, social and cultural variables.

284. ___ (1955) Modern Homesteaders; The Life of a
Twentieth-Century Frontier Community.
Cambridge: Harvard Univ. Press, Belknap. --
Community study centering on analysis of
values.

285. ___ and O'Dea, Thomas F. (1953) A Comparative
Study of the Role of Values in Social Action in
Two Southwestern Communities. Amer. Sociol.
Rev. 18: 645-654. --Comparison of effects of
differences in Texan and Mormon values on responses to similar problems, the influence of
situational factors having been taken into account.

286. ___ and Roberts, John M. (1956) A Study of Values.
Sci. Amer. 195: 25-31. --Brief account of the
Harvard Comparative Study of Values in Five
Cultures project.

287. ___ , eds. (In Progress) The Peoples of Ramah; A
Comparative Study of Value Systems (Tentative
Title). Evanston, Ill.: Row, Peterson. --
Results of the Harvard Comparative Study of
Values in Five Cultures project. (See also,
240.)

288. Von Mering, Otto (1956) The Patterning of Individual
and Cultural Valuations. Ph. D. Thesis,
Harvard Univ. --A comparative analysis of
American Indian and American communities.

289. Wagner, Gunter (1954) The Abaluyia of Kavirondo
(Kenya). IN: C. D. Forde, ed. African
Worlds; Studies in the Cosmological Ideas and
Social Values of African Peoples. London:
Oxford Univ. Press. 27-54.

290. Wallis, Wilson D. (1952) Values in a World of Cultures. Amer. Anthrop. 54: 143-146. --
Criticism of the ethical relativism of anthro-

pologists and a plea for the "evaluation of values."

291. Warner, W. Lloyd (1953) American Life; Dream and Reality. Chicago: Univ. of Chicago Press. -- Modern American values and social structure. Annotated bibliography.

292. ___, Meeker, Marchia and Eells, Kenneth (1949) Social Class in America. Chicago: Chicago Sci. Res. Assn. --The techniques of "evaluated participation" and "index of status characteristics" explained for researchers. Annotated bibliography.

293. Westermarck, Edward (1906) Origin and Development of Moral Ideas. London and New York: Macmillan. 2 vols.

294. ___ (1936) Christianity and Morals. New York: Macmillan. --Variation in morality attributed to environmental differences and unresolvable moral differences; moral standards relative to the moral emotions of a place and era, evolving towards a disinterested utilitarian ethic; disapproval socially more useful than approval; "this is good" defined as "this is impartially approved."

295. +White, Leslie (1943) Energy and the Evolution of Culture. Amer. Anthrop. 45: 335-356. -- "Energy" as a universal scale of cultural development.

296. ___ (1949) The Science of Culture. New York: Farrar, Straus. --Ameliorative hopes of behavioral scientists criticized as assuming free will; cultural determinism upheld and an evolutionist theory of human history presented, with technology the standard for evaluating cultural development.

-85-

297. Whiting, John W. M. and Child, Irvin L. (1953) Child
     Training and Personality; A Cross-Cultural
     Study. New Haven: Yale Univ. Press. --In-
     cludes exploration and test of psychoanalytic
     theory of internalization of moral values.

298. Whorf, Benjamin L. (1956) Language, Thought, and
     Reality; Selected Writings. J. B. Carroll, ed.
     Cambridge: Technology Press of Mass. Inst.
     Technology. Also: New York: John Wiley;
     London: Chapman and Hall. --See especially:
     57-87, 246-270, the influence of linguistic
     morphology upon values and their conceptuali-
     zation.

299. Wilson, Godfrey (1936) An African Morality.
     Africa 9: 75-98.

300. Wilson, Monica (1951) Good Company; A Study of
     Nyakyusa Age-Villages. London: Oxford Univ.
     Press. --See especially: Ch. 4, values under-
     lying a Central African social structure.

301. +Wissler, Clark (1923) Man and Culture. New York:
     Crowell. --One of the first American anthro-
     pologists to discuss the "universal ground plan"
     of all cultures.

302. Zborowski, Mark (1949) The Place of Book Learning
     in Traditional Jewish Culture. Harvard Educ.
     Rev. 19: 87-109. --A valued role among East
     European Jews.

303. Zingg, Robert M. (1942) The Genuine and Spurious
     Values in Tarahumara Culture. Amer.
     Anthrop. 44: 78-92. --Application of Sapir's
     categories of genuine and spurious culture to
     description of spiritual and emotional values
     of an Indian tribe of Chihuahua, Mexico.

II. PSYCHOLOGY, SOCIAL AND EDUCATIONAL PSYCHOLOGY, PSYCHIATRY AND PSYCHOANALYSIS

304. Abel, Theodora M. (1941) Moral Judgments among Subnormals. J. Abnorm. Soc. Psychol. 36: 378-392. --Comparison of moral realism in institutionalized and non-institutionalized adolescent subnormal girls, using Piaget technique.

305. Adams, Joe K. (1955) Expressive Aspects of Scientific Language. IN: Heinz Werner, ed. On Expressive Language; Papers Presented at the Clark University Conference on Expressive Language Behavior. Worcester: Clark Univ. Press. 47-52. --"Scientific language ... expresses many values, attitudes, ways of perceiving and dealing with the world. "

306. Adler, Alfred (1927) Understanding Human Nature. Trans. by Walter Béran Wolfe. Garden City, N. Y.: Greenberg. --See especially: 161-286, The Science of Character.

307. +Adorno, T. W., Frenkel-Brunswik, Else, Levinson, D. J., Sanford, R. N. et al. (1950) The Authoritarian Personality. New York: Harper. -- Ethnocentric, anti-Semitic and anti-democratic attitudes; data from attitude scales and clinical interviews.

308. Alexander, Franz (1950) Values and Science. J. Soc. Issues 6: 28-32.

309. Allport, Floyd H. (1934) The J-Curve Hypothesis of Conforming Behavior. J. Soc. Psychol. 5: 141-183. Also in: Theodore M. Newcomb and Eugene Hartley, eds. Readings in Social Psychology. New York: Holt, 1947. 55-67. --

-87-

A graphic means of expressing the conformity of individuals to group norms.

310.   ___ (1939) Rule and Custom as Individual Variations of Behavior Distributed upon a Continuum of Conformity. Amer. J. Sociol. 44: 897-921.

311.   ___ (1955) Theories of Perception and the Concept of Structure. New York: Wiley. --See especially: 345-361, "the directive-state theory of perception" in relation to values.

312. Allport, Gordon W. (1947) Scientific Models and Human Morals. Psychol. Rev. 54: 182-192. Also in: The Nature of Personality; Selected Papers. Cambridge: Addison-Wesley Press, 1954. --Suggests a "moral science" to take up the slack between morality and modern technology.

313.   ___ (1950) The Individual and His Religion; A Psychological Interpretation. New York: Macmillan. --The place of religious sentiments in the mature personality; the relation of rationality and mental health to religious values.

314.   ___ and Vernon, Philip E. (1931) A Study of Values. Boston: Houghton, Mifflin. --A scale for measuring theoretical, economic, esthetic, social, political and religious value-emphases and a statistical analysis of American value profiles.

315.   ___ Vernon and Lindzey, Gardner (1951) Manual; A Study of Values. New York: Houghton, Mifflin.--Revision of Allport and Vernon, 1931.

316. Anderson, Rose G. (1948) Subjective Ranking versus Score Ranking of Interest Values. Personnel Psychol. 1: 349-355.

317. Arnheim, Rudolf (1952) Agenda for the Psychology of Art. J. Aesthetics and Art Criticism 10: 310-314.

318. Arsenian, Seth (1943) Change in Evaluative Attitude during Four Years of College. J. Appl. Psychol. 27: 338-349. --Uses Allport-Vernon scale.

319. ___ (1943) The Relation of Evaluative Attitudes to Vocational Interest and Social Adjustment. J. Soc. Psychol. 17: 17-24. --Correlation of responses from Allport-Vernon Test and Cleeton Vocational Interest Inventory.

320. Asch, Solomon E. (1952) Social Psychology. New York: Prentice-Hall. --See especially: Chs. 12, 13, "rules and values" and "the fact of culture and the problem of relativism."

321. Auerbach, J. G. (1950) Value Changes in Therapy. Personality 1: 63-67. --"Real values" substituted for "pseudo-values" in therapy as the neurotic learns to see himself objectively.

322. Balint, M. (1951) On Punishing Offenders. IN: G. B. Wilbur and Warner Muensterberger, eds. Psychoanalysis and Culture. New York: International Universities Press. 254-279. -- Possible psychoanalytic contributions to resolving the moral problems in penology; a social analysis of deviations from moral codes in society.

323. Barker, Roger G., Kounin, Jacob S. and Wright, Herbert F., eds. (1943) Child Behavior and Development; A Course of Representative Studies. New York: McGraw-Hill.

324. Barkley, Key L. (1942) Development of the Moral Judgment of College Students. Character and

Pers. 10: 199-212. --Descriptive study and review of literature on moral judgment.

325. +Bauer, Raymond A. (1952) The New Man in Soviet Psychology. Cambridge: Harvard Univ. Press.

326. ___ (1953) The Psychology of the Soviet Middle Elite; Two Case Histories. IN: Clyde Kluckhohn, Henry Murray and David Schneider, eds. Personality in Nature, Culture, and Society. New York: Knopf, 1953. 633-650. --Two valued personality types engendered by the Soviet social system.

327. Bavelas, Alex (1942) A Method for Investigating Individual and Group Ideology. Sociometry 5: 371-377. --The moral ideology of children.

328. Beaglehole, Ernest (1931) Property; A Study in Social Psychology. London: Allen and Unwin. -- Methods of comparative psychology, anthropology and individual psychology in a study of ascription of value to objects. See especially: Ch. 5, Magic, Animism and Property Values; Ch. 6, Sentiments of Ownership in Savage Society; Ch. 7, The Social Patterning of Property Values.

329. ___ (1944) Character Structure. Psychiatry 7: 145-162. --Internalization of group character and values and its relation to social change, illustrative material from primitive and Western societies.

330. Bennis, Warren G. (1956) Values and Organization in a University Social Research Group. Amer. Sociol. Rev. 21: 555-563.

331. Bills, Robert E. (1952) The Effect of a Value on Learning. J. Pers. 21: 217-222. --Agreement or disagreement between students' and instruc-

tor's values influences even marks based on objective examinations.

332. Blanchard, William H. (1956) Medieval Morality and Juvenile Delinquency. Amer. Imago 13: 383-398.

333. Blondel, Charles (1928) The Troubled Conscience and the Insane Mind. London: Kegan Paul, Trench, Trubner.

334. Boder, David P. (1954) The Impact of Catastrophe; I. Assessment and Evaluation. J. Psychol. 38: 3-50. --Traumatic Inventory and Scale of Traumatic Values to analyze interviews with European displaced persons.

335. Boisen, A. T. (1932) The Problem of Values in the Light of Psychopathology. Amer. J. Sociol. 38: 51-63. --Moral self-judgment concluded to be among causative factors in 176 cases of dementia praecox; an individual case analyzed.

336. Bolton, Euri B. (1955) Brief Evaluation of Two Tests of Aesthetic Judgment. Peabody J. Educ. 32: 211-222. --Psychological questions relating to problems of measuring esthetic judgment; results of experiment involving the Meier and the Graves tests.

337. +Borgatta, Edgar F. (1954) Sidesteps Toward a Non-special Theory. Psychol. Rev. 61: 343-352. --Criticism of Freudianism, with implications for values and norms in theory construction.

338. Bovard, Everett W., Jr. (1953) Conformity to Social Norms in Stable and Temporary Groups. Science 117: 361-363.

—— Brentano, Franz. See Philosophy.

339. Bruner, Jerome S. and Goodman, Cecile C. (1947) Value and Need as Organizing Factors in Perception. J. Abnorm. Soc. Psychol. 42: 33-44. --Experiment on the perception of coin size by rich and poor children, motivational determinants stressed. (Cf. 348 and 467.)

340. ___ and Postman, Leo (1948) Symbolic Value as an Organizing Factor in Perception. J. Soc. Psychol. 27: 203-208. --Experimental study of effects of symbols - negative (swastika), neutral (square) and positive (dollar sign) - on the estimation of size.

341. Cantril, Hadley (1947) Understanding Man's Social Behavior; Preliminary Notes. Princeton: Office of Public Opinion Research. --See especially: Ethics and Morality.

342. ___ (1949) Toward a Scientific Morality. J. Psychol. 27: 363-376. --Perception psychology yields a concept of "effectiveness" which can be used for making scientific value judgments.

343. ___ (1950) The "Why" of Man's Experience. New York: Macmillan. --A multidisciplinary conceptual scheme, emphasizing man's ability to sense and seek enhancement of value in his experience.

344. ___ (1955) Ethical Relativity from the Transactional Point of View. J. Phil. 52: 677-687. --Emphasizes psychological bases of similarities among people of all cultures; views diverse ethical systems as equally satisfying the need for constancy and predictability "essential for the sharing of significances."

345. ___ and Allport, Gordon W. (1933) Recent Applications of the Study of Values. J. Abnorm. Soc. Psychol. 28: 259-273. --Evaluation of Allport-Vernon scale in light of empirical results.

346. ___, Ames, Adelbert, Jr., Hastorf, Albert H. and
Ittelson, William H. (1949) Psychology and
Scientific Research. Science 110: 461-464;
491-497; 517-522. --The transactional viewpoint and its relation to values.

347. Carstairs, G. Morris (1957) The Twice-Born; A
Study of a Community of High-Caste Hindus.
London: Hogarth.

348. Carter, Launor F. and Schooler, Kermit (1949)
Value, Need, and Other Factors in Perception.
Psychol. Rev. 56: 200-207. --Coin size estimation by rich and poor children; doubt raised
as to importance of value systems in perception of clear, physically present objects. (Cf.
339 and 467.)

349. Carter, T. M. (1932) Ethical Attitudes of 623 Men
and Women. Internatl. J. Ethics 43: 279-293.

350. Cattell, Raymond B. (1948) Ethics and the Social
Sciences. Amer. Psychol. 3: 193-198. --
Argues for the ethical neutrality of the social
sciences.

351. ___ (1950) The Scientific Ethics of "Beyond." J. Soc.
Issues 6: 21-27.

352. ___ (1951) The Integration of Psychology with Moral
Values. Brit. J. Psychol. 41: 25-34. --Social
scientists should state their own values and
examine the use being made of their results.

353. Centers, Richard (1948) Attitude and Belief in Relation to Occupational Stratification. J. Soc.
Psychol. 27: 159-185. --Quantitative data on
a wide variety of subcultural value differences
in the United States.

354. Chasdi, E. Hollenberg (1952) Child Training in a Pueblo; With Special Emphasis on the Internalization of Values. Ph. D. Thesis, Radcliffe College.

355. Child, Irvin L. (1954) Socialization. IN: Gardner Lindzey, ed. Handbook of Social Psychology. Vol. II. Cambridge: Addison-Wesley. 655-692.

356. Clark, W. H. (1950) The Psychology of Religious Values. Personality 1: 45-62.

357. Clippinger, John A. (1954) Recent Value Research and Its Significance for Religious Psychology. Relig. Educ. 49: 204-210. --Traces interest in science of values to Hegel; summarizes implications of recent findings for the psychology of personality and religion.

358. Cofer, Charles N. (1951) Verbal Behavior in Relation to Reasoning and Values. IN: Harold Guetzkow, ed. Groups, Leadership and Men. Pittsburgh: Carnegie Press. 206-217.

359. Cohen, Jozef B. (1941) A Scale for the Masurement of Attitude Toward the Aesthetic Value. J. Psychol. 12: 75-79. --An esthetic value scale constructed by Thurstone attitude scaling method and investigated in relation to the Allport-Vernon Test.

360. Coombs, Clyde H. (1954) Social Choice and Strength of Preference. IN: Robert M. Thrall, Clyde H. Coombs and Robert L. Davis, eds. Decision Processes. New York: Wiley. 69-86. --Relates group mechanisms to formal mechanisms to codify value judgments of operations used to determine a social utility.

361.   ___ and Beardslee, David C. (1954) On Decision-
       Making under Uncertainty. IN: Robert M.
       Thrall, Clyde H. Coombs and Robert L. Davis,
       eds. Decision Processes. New York: Wiley.

—— Creegan, Robert F. See Philosophy.

362. De Liz Ferreira, A. J. (1955) Some Notes on the
     Thonga Culture. Zaïre (Brussels) 9: 3-23. --
     Relations between implicit culture, values and
     the introduction of Western medicine in an
     African tribe.

363. Dembo, Tamara (1953) Investigation of Concrete
     Psychological Value Systems. U. S. Public
     Health Service, Institute Mental Health, Final
     Report. Dittoed. --Towards a theory and
     method for studying values as part of psycho-
     logical theory.

364. Deutsch, Morton and Gerard, Harold B. (1955) A
     Study of Normative and Informational Social
     Influences upon Individual Judgment. J. Ab-
     norm. Soc. Psychol. 51: 629-636.

365. Dicks, Henry V. (1950) In Search of Our Proper
     Ethic. Brit. J. Med. Psychol. 23: 1-14. --
     Mental health as a new value, understood as
     psychological integration of the personality.

366. Di Vesta, Francis J. (1949) Process, Concepts and
     Values in the Social and Personal Adjustment
     of Adolescents. Ithaca: Cornell Univ. (Ex-
     periment Station, Memoir 287).

367. Dollard, John (1945) The Acquisition of New Social
     Habits. IN: Ralph Linton, ed. The Science of
     Man in the World Crisis. New York: Columbia
     Univ. Press. 442-464. --Exploration of the
     possibilities of changing personal and group
     values of ethnic prejudice by psychotherapy.

368. Doob, Leonard W. (1940) The Values of Planning.
IN: The Plans of Men. New Haven: Yale Univ.
Press. 146-168.

369. ___ (1957) An Introduction to the Psychology of Acculturation. J. Soc. Psychol. 45: 143-160. --
Exploratory study of "traits" in three African
societies.

370. Dorr, Mildred and Havighurst, Robert J. (1949) The
Relation of Values to Character; Methods of
Studying Values. IN: Robert J. Havighurst and
Hilda Taba, eds. Adolescent Character and
Personality. New York: Wiley. 97-102; 284-
291.

371. Duffy, Elizabeth (1940) A Critical Review of Inves-
tigations Employing the Allport-Vernon Study
of Values and Other Tests of Evaluative Attitude. Psychol. Bull. 37: 597-612. --See 314.

372. ___ and Crissy, William J. E. (1940) Evaluative At-
titudes as Related to Vocational Interests and
Academic Achievement. J. Abnorm. Soc.
Psychol. 35: 226-245. --Correlation of Allport-
Vernon results with Strong Vocational Interest
scores and college grades.

373. Dukes, William F. (1955) Psychological Studies of
Values. Psychol. Bull. 52: 24-50. --Reviews
psychological literature on measurement of
group values, origin and development of values
in individuals and influence of values on cognitive life. Extensive bibliography.

374. Eagleson, Oran W. and Bell, Eleanor S. (1945) The
Values of Negro Women College Students. J.
Soc. Psychol. 22: 149-154. --Uses Allport-
Vernon Test.

375. Edwards, Ward (1954) The Theory of Decision Making. Psychol. Bull. 51: 380-417. --Reviews contributions from psychology, economics and mathematics on the theory of riskless choices and its application to welfare economics, theory of risky choices, transitivity of choices and theory of games, and statistical decision functions.

376. Ehrenfels, Christian von (1897-1898) System der Werttheorie. Volume I: Allgemeine Werttheorie, Psychologie des Begehrens; Volume II: Grundzüge einer Ethik. Leipsig: O. R. Reisland. --Early influence on general value theory. Value as a property of objects in relation to subjects and dependent on a broadly affective conception of desire.

377. Eissler, K. R. (1944) Balinese Character. Psychiatry 7: 139-144.

378. Erikson, Erik H. (1945) Childhood and Tradition in Two American Indian Tribes. IN: R. S. Eissler et al., eds. The Psychoanalytic Study of the Child. Vol. I. New York: International Universities Press. 319-350. Also in: Douglas G. Haring, ed. Personal Character and Cultural Milieu. Syracuse: Syracuse Univ. Press, 1956. 255-286.

379. ___ (1950) Growth and Crises of the "Healthy Personality." IN: M. J. E. Senn, ed. Supplement II, Trans. Fourth Conference on Infancy and Childhood, Josiah Macy, Jr. Foundation. Also in: Clyde Kluckhohn, Henry Murray and David Schneider, eds. Personality in Nature, Culture, and Society. New York: Knopf, 1953. 185-225. --The moral development of the individual in terms of psychoanalytic ego psychology.

380. Evans, Richard I. (1952) Personal Values as Factors in Anti-Semitism. J. Abnorm. Soc. Psychol. 47: 749-756.--Correlations between scores on Allport-Vernon Test and Levinson-Sanford Anti-Semitism Scale.

381. Eysenck, Hans J. (1954) The Psychology of Politics. London: Routledge and Kegan Paul. --Includes treatment of values in relation to decision-making.

382. Faigin, Helen (1952) Child Training in a Mormon Village with Special Emphasis on the Internalization of Values. Ph. D. Thesis, Radcliffe College.

383. Fenichel, Otto (1945) The Psychoanalytic Theory of Neurosis. New York: Norton. --See especially: Ch. 6, psychoanalytic approach to the development of moral values.

384. Fensterheim, Herbert and Tresselt, Margaret E. (1953) The Influence of Value Systems on the Perception of People. J. Abnorm. Soc. Psychol. 48: 93-98.

385. Ferguson, Leonard W., Humphreys, Lloyd G. and Strong, Frances W. (1941) A Factorial Analysis of Interests and Values. J. Educ. Psychol. 32: 197-204. --Uses the Strong Vocational Interest Blank and Allport-Vernon Test.

386. Festinger, Leon, Torrey, Jane and Willerman, Ben (1954) Self-Evaluation as a Function of Attraction to the Group. Human Relations 7: 161-174.

387. Fischer, Robert P. and Andrews, Avonne L. (1947) A Study of the Effect of Conformity to Social Expectancy on Evaluative Attitudes. Educ. and Psychol. Measurement 7: 331-335.

388. Fisher, Sarah C. (1948) Relationships in Attitudes, Opinions, and Values among Family Members. Berkeley: Univ. of California Press (University of California Publications in Culture and Society 2: 29-100). --Attitudes and values of two generations of the same families compared, intra-family correlations investigated.

389. Fletcher, John M. (1942) Science and the Problem of Human Values. Sci. Monthly 54: 259-265. -- Values, understood as interests, desires and cravings, are within the range of psychological inquiry and should be studied by psychologists.

390. Flügel, J. C. (1945) Man, Morals, and Society; A Psychoanalytic Study. New York: International Universities Press. Also: London: Duckworth. --Psychoanalytic social psychology approach to a theory of values and social attitudes, concluding with an assessment of moral progress.

391. Frank, Lawrence K. (1951) Nature and Human Nature; Man's New Image of Himself. New Brunswick: Rutgers Univ. Press. --In the light of new understanding, fulfillment of our values requires changes in beliefs and institutions.

392. +___ et al. (1948) Teleological Mechanisms. Annals, New York Acad. Sci. 50: 187-277. --New concepts and methods for the study of self-regulating processes make mechanistic formulations inadequate.

393. French, Thomas M. (1941) Goal, Mechanism and Integrative Field. Psychosomatic Med. 3: 226-252. --Psychoanalytic-field analysis of the mechanisms of goal-directed activity.

394. ___ (1952) Psychodynamic Analysis of Ethical and Political Orientations. Amer. J. Econ. Sociol. 12: 3-9.

395. French, Vera V. (1947-1948) The Structure of Sentiments. I. A Restatement of the Theory of
Sentiments. II. A Preliminary Study of Sentiments. III. A Study of Philosophicoreligious
Sentiments. J. Pers. 15, 16: 247-282; 78-108;
209-244.

396. Frenkel-Brunswik, Else (1948) Dynamic and Cognitive
Categorization of Qualitative Material. I. General Problems and the Thematic Apperception
Test. II. Application to Interviews with the
Ethnically Prejudiced. J. Psychol. 25: 253-
260; 261-277. --A method of interpreting data
based on "evaluation principles" applicable to
both interview and projective data; statistics
and case history method employed.

397. ___ (1948) A Study of Prejudice in Children. Human
Relations 1: 295-306. --Comparison of the
values and personality traits of prejudiced and
unprejudiced children.

398. ___ (1951) Patterns of Social and Cognitive Outlook
in Children and Parents. Amer. J. Orthopsychiat. 21: 543-558. --The values of ethnically
prejudiced children and parents, using questionnaires, interviews and T. A. T.

399. ___ (1954) Psychoanalysis and the Unity of Science.
Proc. Amer. Acad. Arts and Sci. 80: 271-350
(In cooperation with the Institute for the Unity
of Science). --See especially: 331-337, Psychoanalysis, Ethics and Rationality, on the ethical
factors in psychoanalytic theory.

400. ___ (1954) Social Research and the Problems of
Values; A Reply. J. Abnorm. Soc. Psychol.
49: 466-471. --Reply to a charge that the
values of the authors of The Authoritarian
Personality influenced research results (see
307).

401. Freud, Sigmund (1908) "Civilized" Sexual Morality
and Modern Nervousness. IN: Collected Papers.
Vol. II. London: Hogarth. 76-99. --Points out
the injurious effects of modern sexual prohibitions, outlines three stages in the cultural development of sexual morality.

402. ___ (1912) Totem and Taboo. IN: A. A. Brill, ed.
and trans. Basic Writings of Sigmund Freud.
New York: Modern Library, 1938. --The influence of childhood experience and family dynamics on taboos, rituals and symbol systems;
a theory of cultural evolution.

403. ___ (1922) Beyond the Pleasure Principle. Trans.
by C. J. M. Hubback. New York: Boni and
Liveright. --See especially: Ch. 4, hedonism
modified by the death wish as the source of
moral ideas.

404. ___ (1939) Civilization and Its Discontents. Trans.
by Joan Riviere. London: Hogarth. --The
superego as the psychological basis of civilized
values and morality the tool of society against
aggression, conscience the death wish turned
inward, values the "propping up of illusions
with arguments."

405. ___ (1949) The Future of an Illusion. Trans. by
W. D. Robson-Scott. London: Hogarth. --A
personal, idealistic view of ethics in a discussion of the functions of religion for the
individual and society.

406. Friedenburg, Edgar Z. and Havighurst, Robert J.
(1948) An Attempt To Measure Strength of
Conscience. J. Pers. 17: 232-243. --Subjects
asked to indicate how bad certain acts would be
and how they would feel if they committed them;
method reported as unsuccessful for measuring
but possibly useful as a projective device.

407. Friedman, Lawrence (1956) Psychoanalysis and the Foundation of Ethics. J. Phil. 53: 15-20. -- The psychoanalytic basis for development of the conscience; ethical theory must be based on the findings of psychology.

408. +Fromm, Erich (1941) Escape from Freedom. New York: Farrar and Rinehart. --Psychological analysis of Western man's capacity for freedom; Nazism viewed in neo-Freudian terms as an escape from freedom.

409. ___ (1947) Man for Himself; An Inquiry into the Psychology of Ethics. New York: Rinehart. --A humanistic ethic based on neo-Freudian analysis of character types in modern cultures and on ethical ideas of Aristotle, Nietzsche and Gide.

410. ___ (1950) Psychoanalysis and Religion. New Haven: Yale Univ. Press. --Psychoanalysts can examine the human reality and ethical problems of religious as well as non-religious symbol systems.

411. ___ (1955) The Sane Society. New York: Rinehart. -- A proposal for achieving personal and moral betterment.

412. Gillespie, James M. and Allport, Gordon W. (1955) Youth's Outlook on the Future. New York: Random House.

413. Ginsburg, Sol W. (1950) Values and the Psychiatrist. Amer. J. Orthopsychiat. 20: 466-478. --Primary needs of psychiatrists are a sound estimate of social dangers and a concept for normality in social structure as well as in the individual; value problems lie at the core of mores and beliefs.

414. Glasser, Edward M. and Maller, Julius B. (1940)
The Measurement of Interest Values. Charac-
ter and Pers. 9: 67-81. --The Interest-Values
Inventory proposed as an improvement on the
Allport-Vernon Study of Values.

415. Gloye, Eugene E. (1955) Learning as a Function of
Contexts Differentiated Through Antecedent
Value Experience. J. Experimental Psychol.
50: 261-264. --Evidence supporting the principle of value interference as more important in
learning than need reduction or emphasis.

416. Goldberg, Solomon C. (1954) Three Situational Determinants of Conformity to Social Norms.
J. Abnorm. Soc. Psychol. 49: 325-329. --
Distance, exposures and size of group as variables determining conformity to group norms.

417. +Goldstein, Kurt (1939) The Organism. New York:
American Book. --Includes a psychoanalytically-
oriented treatment of value-relevant concepts.

418. ___ (1947) Human Nature in the Light of Psycho-
Pathology. Cambridge: Harvard Univ. Press.

419. Grace, Gloria L. and Grace, Harry A. (1952) The
Relationship Between Verbal and Behavioral
Measures of Value. J. Educ. Res. 46: 123-
131. --Values categorized as: personal-
centered, interpersonal-centered and target-
centered; low correlations found between verbal
and sociometric-behavioral values.

420. Grace, Harry A. (1953) Charlie Chaplin's Films and
American Culture Patterns. J. Aesthetics and
Art Criticism 10: 353-363. --Seventy-six
films analyzed for American values.

421. Graham, James L. (1940) Some Attitudes Towards
Values. J. Soc. Psychol. 12: 405-414. --

College students' attitudes towards ethical, religious, political, economic and social values found to be distributed in J-curve.

422. Grasso, P. G. (1954) Gioventu' di Meta' Secolo; Risultati di Un' Inchiesta sugli Orientamenti Morali e Civili di 2000 Studenti Italiani. Roma: A. V. E. --Questionnaire results on ethical and political attitudes of 2,000 Italian students, chiefly from professional and white-collar families.

423. Green, Arnold W. (1946) Social Values and Psychotherapy. J. Pers. 14: 199-228. --Criticizes the value premises of several schools of psychotherapy; suggests canons for therapeutic policy with regard to social values.

424. Greenacre, Phyllis (1945) Conscience in the Psychopath. Amer. J. Orthopsychiat. 15: 495-509. --For criticism, see 459.

425. Guetzkow, Harold, ed. (1951) Groups, Leadership and Men. Pittsburgh: Carnegie Press. --Contains material on decision-making and other value-relevant phenomena.

426. Haigh, Gerard V. and Fiske, Donald W. (1952) Corroboration of Personal Values as Selective Factors in Perception. J. Abnorm. Soc. Psychol. 47: 394-398. --A relation found between value preference and speed of word recognition.

427. Hall, Roy M. (1950) Religious Beliefs and Social Values of College Students. Ph. D. Thesis, Syracuse Univ.

428. Harding, D. W. (1953) Social Psychology and Individual Values. London: Hutchinson's. --Analysis of "the psychological processes

associated with choices and evaluations," and "the conditions and processes affecting a social group's use of its human resources."

429. Harding, Lawry W. (1944) A Value-Type Generalizations Test; A Value-Type Problemmaire. J. Soc. Psychol. 19: 53-79; 115-144. --An attempt to develop a statistically sound test of values as manifested in general attitudes.

430. ___ (1948) Experimental Comparisons Between Generalizations and Problems as Indices of Values. J. Genl. Psychol. 38: 31-50. -- Problem or action tests better than personality-value tests as indices of values.

431. Harris, Daniel (1934) Group Differences in Values within a University. J. Abnorm. Soc. Psychol. 29: 95-102. --Allport-Vernon Test applied to college students and faculty.

432. Hartmann, George W. (1934) Sex Differences in Valuational Attitudes. J. Soc. Psychol. 5: 106-112. --An Allport-Vernon study.

433. ___ (1939) Value as the Unifying Concept of the Social Sciences. J. Soc. Psychol. 10: 563-575. --Program for the psychological study of values in order to bring about a better world.

434. Havighurst, Robert J. (1954) A Comparison of New Zealand and American Children on Emotional Response and Moral Ideology. IN: Robert J. Havighurst, Studies of Children and Society in New Zealand. Christchurch, N. Z.: Canterbury Univ. College, Dept. of Educ. (Limited publication; available by inter-library loan from Univ. of Chicago Library). --Finds American children more overtly concerned with personal and individualistic conduct, New Zealand children with their obligations to others; detailed tables of test results.

435. ___ and Neugarten, Bernice L. (1955) American Indian and White Children; A Sociopsychological Interpretation. Chicago: Univ. of Chicago Press. --See especially: Ch. 4, The Moral Ideology of Indian and White Children, describing the Bavelas test method, vith data from tests administered to several Indian and White groups; also, Ch. 5, Moral Judgment: Attitudes Toward Rules of Games.

436. ___, Robinson, Myra Z. and Dorr, Mildred (1946) The Development of the Ideal Self in Childhood and Adolescence. J. Educ. Res. 40: 241-257. --Interpretation of essays on "The Person I Would Like to Be Like," written by children from 8 to 18. (See 499.)

437. ___ and Ruddle, Susan M. (1954) The Moral Ideology of New Zealand Children. IN: Robert J. Havighurst. Studies of Children and Society in New Zealand, Christchurch, N. Z.: Canterbury Univ. College, Dept. of Educ. (Limited publication; available by inter-library loan from Univ. of Chicago Library). --Categories and results of the Moral Ideology Test, reflecting children's knowledge of cultural values rather than their overt behavior.

438. Heinicke, Christoph and Whiting, Beatrice (1953) Bibliographies on Personality and Social Development of the Child. New York: Social Science Research Council (Pamphlet 10).

439. Held, Doris (1955) Values and Attitudes; An Exploratory Study into Their Differing Functions for Personality. Dittoed (Can be obtained at Center for International Studies, Massachusetts Institute of Technology, Cambridge, Massachusetts).

440. Helper, Malcolm M. (1958) Parental Evaluations of
     Children and Children's Self-Evaluations.
     J. Abnorm. Soc. Psychol. 56: 190-194.

441. Hobbs, Nicholas (1950) Some Reflections on
     Empirical Investigation of Ethics. J. Soc.
     Issues 6: 56-60.

442. Hollingworth, Harry L. (1949) Psychology and
     Ethics; A Study of the Sense of Obligation.
     New York: Ronald. --An analysis of "ought"
     categories; a theory of value and system of
     ethical valuation; experimental methods for
     the measurement of individual differences in
     moral insight.

443. Holt, Edwin B. (1915) The Freudian Wish and Its
     Place in Ethics. New York: Holt. --Freudian,
     behavioristic and evolutionary elements com-
     bined in a moral theory; designed to replace
     acceptance of suppression by discriminating
     among positive alternatives.

444. Horney, Karen (1937) The Neurotic Personality of
     Our Time. New York: Norton. --See
     especially: Final chapter, for analysis of
     neurosis in terms of conflicting values and
     norms.

445. +Hovland, Carl I., Janis, Irving L. and Kelley,
     Harold H. (1953) Communication and Per-
     suasion; Psychological Studies of Opinion
     Change. New Haven: Yale Univ. Press.

446. Hughes, Julius H. and Thompson, George G. (1954)
     A Comparison of the Value Systems of Southern
     Negro and Northern White Youth. J. Educ.
     Psychol. 45: 300-309.

447. Hull, Clark L. (1944) Value, Valuation, and Natural
     Science Methodology. Phil. Sci. 11: 125-141.

--A "natural science theory of value," based on a primary need theory of value and developed in terms of reinforcement behavior theory.

448. ___ (1945) Moral Values, Behaviorism, and the World Crisis. Trans. New York Acad. Sci., Section of Psychol., Series II, 7: 90-94. -- There cannot be a normative science, but there can be a science which predicts moral behavior.

449. Hunt, Alice McCullough (1935) A Study of the Relative Value of Certain Ideals. J. Abnorm. Soc. Psychol. 30: 222-228. --Values scale based on opinions of 500 members of a community.

450. Hutt, Max L. and Miller, Daniel R. (1949) Social Values and Personality Development. J. Soc. Issues 5. --No. 4, Entire Number.

—— Inkeles, Alex. See Sociology.

451. Jacob, Philip E. (1957) Changing Values in College; An Exploratory Study of the Impact of College Teaching. New York: Harper.

—— Janowitz, Morris. See Sociology.

452. Jessor, Richard and Readio, Joel (1957) The Influence of the Value of an Event upon the Expectancy of Its Occurrence. J. Genl. Psychol. 56: 219-228. --Compares and interprets results of two tests of the hypothesis that the value of an event influences the expectancy of its occurrence.

453. Jones, Lyle V. and Morris, Charles (1956) Relations of Temperament to the Choice of Values. J. Abnorm. Soc. Psychol. 53: 345-349.

454. Josey, Charles C. and Snygg, Donald (1950) The
        Place of Psychology in the Development of
        Values. Personality 1: 1-6. --Psychologists
        can make ethical judgments by using the con-
        cept of adjustment; psychology must trans-
        form belief in individual dignity into an effec-
        tive moral code.

455. Jung, Carl G. (1939) The Integration of the Per-
        sonality. New York: Farrar and Rinehart. --
        "Collective unconscious" as the basis of per-
        sonality development; the "inner voice . . .
        places a man face to face with final moral
        decisions." See especially: 13, 52, 77, 289-
        296, 302-303.

456. +___ (1958) The Undiscovered Self. Trans. by R. F.
        C. Hull, Boston: Atlantic-Little, Brown. --
        Crises and destructive forces in modern
        society reflect the gulf between conscious and
        unconscious aspects of the individual psyche;
        Western scientific and rationalist philosophy
        of life judged to be as materialistic as Marxism.

457. Kalhorn, Joan (1944) Values and Sources of Authority
        among Rural Children. Univ. of Iowa Studies
        in Children's Welfare 20, 409: 99-151. --Com-
        pares Mennonite and non-Mennonite children,
        using the Bavelas moral ideology test.

458. Kardiner, Abram (1954) Sex and Morality. New
        York: Bobbs-Merrill. --Primarily for laymen,
        relates problems of sex and morality to
        socially conditioned emotional deprivation and
        the decline of values in modern society.

459. Karpman, Ben (1948) Conscience in the Psychopath;
        Another Version. Amer. J. Orthopsychiat. 18:
        455-491. --See 424.

460. Kates, Solis L. (1952) Conflicting Value-Orientations and Intra-Personality Conflicts. Proc. Oklahoma Acad. Sci. 33: 282-285. --Analyzes conflict of three value-orientations - external conformity, individual personality and secular rationality - all crucial for development of a healthy personality.

461. +Katona, George (1951) Psychological Analysis of Economic Behavior. New York: McGraw-Hill.

462. Kay, Lillian W. (1943) The Relation of Personal Frames of Reference to Social Judgments. New York: Archives of Psychology, 283. -- Experimental results indicate that when individuals judge the moral qualities of occupations, social norms are more important than subjective preferences and personal experiences.

463. Kelley, Harold H. (1952) Two Functions of Reference Groups. IN: Guy E. Swanson, Theodore M. Newcomb and Eugene L. Hartley, eds. Readings in Social Psychology. Rev. ed. New York: Holt. 410-414. --Distinguishes between normative and comparison (evaluation) functions of reference groups.

464. Kelley, E. Lowell (1949) Interest-Values Inventory. IN: Oskar Krisen Buros, ed. The Third Mental Measurements Yearbook. New Brunswick: Rutgers Univ. Press. 53-54.

465. Ketchum, J. D. (1951) Time, Values, and Social Organization. Canadian J. Psychol. 5: 97-109. --A cognitive approach to social perception and values.

466. Kilpatrick, Franklin P., ed. (1953) Human Behavior from the Transactional Point of View. Hanover, N. H.: Institute for Associated Research.

--Report on values and perception of the work
done by the Adelbert Ames and Hadley Cantril
group.

467. Klein, George S. , Schlesinger, Herbert J. and
Meister, David E. (1951) The Effect of Personal Values on Perception; An Experimental
Critique. Psychol. Rev. 58: 96-112. --Size
estimation experiment, finding no consistent
influence due to intensity of value and degree
of value significance. (Cf. 339 and 348.)

468. Klein, Melanie (1933) The Early Development of
Conscience in the Child. IN: Contributions to
Psychoanalysis 1921-1945 - Melanie Klein.
London: Hogarth Press and The Institute of
Psychoanalysis, 1948. 267-277.

469. Klineberg, Otto (1940) Social Psychology. New
York: Holt. --See especially: Chs. 5 and 6,
on "dependable motives" and variations in
values. See also: 2nd ed. , 1954, studies in
national characteristics.

470. Koffka, Kurt (1954) The Place of a Psychologist
among Scientists. Texas Reports Biology and
Med. 12: 98-109. --In studying both the observational and the reasoning levels of behavior, the psychologist is uniquely placed to
overcome seeming differences between fact
and value.

471. Köhler, Wolfgang (1938) The Place of Value in a
World of Facts. New York: Liveright. --A
philosophical theory of values as "required-
ness" in the phenomenological-objective world;
directed against the physicalist-reductionist
dehumanization of man.

472. ___ (1944) Value and Fact. J. Phil. 41: 197-212. --
Psychology cannot avoid the study of values in

motivation; value in a vector which issues from an object to the self, not the reverse.

473. Kris, Ernst (1952) Psychoanalytic Explorations in Art. New York: International Universities Press. --Psychoanalytic theory as an approach to art and its application to the analysis of the artist, in studies of the art of the insane, the comic, literary criticism and the creative processes. Extensive bibliography.

474. Lalande, André (1948) La Raison et les Normes. Paris: Hachette. --Attempts to establish the objectivity of ethical and esthetic norms, in opposition to scepticism and relativism; judgments about values held to underlie all rational thought.

475. ___ (1951) Le Comité International des Standards. Rev. Philosophique 141: 389-396. --Questionnaires and conferences on the normative principles of democracy.

476. Langner, Thomas S. (1953) A Test of Intergroup Prejudice Which Takes Account of Individual and Group Differences in Values. J. Abnorm. Soc. Psychol. 48: 548-554.

477. Lecky, Prescott (1945) Self-Consistency, a Theory of Personality. New York: Island Press. -- Values discussed in terms of personality integration; the effects of inconsistent elements on integration noted.

478. Lee, Alfred McClung (1945) The Analysis of Propaganda; A Clinical Summary. Amer. J. Sociol. 51: 126-135. --Classifies theoretical approaches to propaganda analysis and discusses means to discover to what extent propagandists are committed to the values of the group to which they belong.

479. ___ (1945) Levels of Culture as Levels of Social
      Generalization. Amer. Sociol. Rev. 10: 485-
      495. --Conceptual scheme for the study of
      moral behavior on the individual, group and
      societal levels.

480. ___ (1954) Social Pressures and the Values of Psy-
      chologists. Amer. Psychol. 9: 516-522. --
      Social roles of psychologists and social pres-
      sures relevant to such roles, in context of
      the APA Code of Ethics.

481. Leighton, Alexander H. (1945) The Governing of
      Men; General Principles and Recommendations
      Based on Experience at a Japanese Relocation
      Camp. Princeton: Princeton Univ. Press. --
      See especially: Appendix, theory and practice
      in intercultural problem-solving, related to
      the concept of systems of belief, including
      values.

482. ___ (1949) Human Relations in a Changing World.
      New York: Dutton. --See especially: Ch. 12,
      Social Sciences and Values.

483. Leighton, Dorothea and Kluckhohn, Clyde (1947)
      Children of the People. Cambridge: Harvard
      Univ. Press. --Internalization of values and
      acculturation among the Navaho; comparison of
      test results on shame, guilt and other moral-
      emotional responses in Navaho and white
      children.

484. Lerner, Daniel and Lasswell, Harold D. (1951) The
      Policy Sciences. Stanford: Stanford Univ.
      Press. --The sciences of society jointly "es-
      sential to the formulation and application of
      policy at every stage." Policy as a "body of
      principle to guide action," its application "a
      calculated choice."

485. Lerner, Eugene (1937) Constraint Areas and the Moral Judgment of Children. Menasha, Wis. : George Banta Publ. --Results of study support the Durkheim-Piaget hypotheses concerning adult-child relationships and moral realism in children.

486. +Lewin, Kurt (1948) Resolving Social Conflicts; Selected Papers on Group Dynamics, 1935-1946. Gertrude W. Lewin, ed. New York: Harper.

487. ___ and Grable, Paul (1945) Conduct, Knowledge and Acceptance of New Values. J. Soc. Issues 1: 53-64. --Re-education in connection with individual's change of cultural group.

488. +Likert, Rensis and Lippitt, Ronald (1953) The Utilization of Social Science. IN: Leon Festinger and Daniel Katz, eds. Research Methods in the Behavioral Sciences. New York: Dryden. 581-643. --Techniques for applying social science research to operating problems of organizations, professional workers, community leaders, government officials, business executives, etc.

489. Lippitt, Ronald (1950) Action-Research and the Values of the Social Scientist. J. Soc. Issues 6: 50-55.

490. Lo, C. F. (1942) Moral Judgments of Chinese Students. J. Abnorm. Soc. Psychol. 37: 264-269. --Rankings of "vices" and "ideals," comparison with American students.

491. London, Ivan D. (1948) Free-Will as a Function of Divergence. Psychol. Rev. 55: 41-47. --Concepts of divergence and natural selection used to reintroduce into psychology "free-will" as a scientific concept.

492. Lowe, Warner L. (1955) Value Systems in the
     Psychotherapeutic Process. Internatl. Record
     Med. and Gen. Practice Clinics 168: 786-789.
     --Values a significant therapeutic tool; the
     ultimate goal of therapy "the emergence of
     moral values, social activity, and universal
     concern in the egocentric personality."

493. Lurie, Walter A. (1937) A Study of Spranger's
     Value-Types by the Method of Factor Analysis.
     J. Soc. Psychol. 8: 17-37.

494. McClelland, David C., ed. (1955) Studies in Motiva-
     tion. New York: Appleton-Century-Crofts. --
     See especially: Sections on the social origins
     of motives and values and on the effects of
     motivation on behavior.

495. +___, Atkinson, John W., Clark, Russell A. and
     Lowell, Edgar L. (1953) The Achievement
     Motive. New York: Appleton-Century-Crofts.
     --Experimental studies in "need Achievement";
     includes discussion of animal and human mo-
     tives.

496. ___, Sturr, J. and Wendt, H. W. (1956) A Compari-
     son of Values and Motives in German and
     American Adolescent Boys. Dittoed (Can be
     obtained from D. C. McClelland, Department
     of Social Relations, Harvard University).

497. McCurdy, Harold G. (1954) Aesthetic Choice as a
     Personality Function. J. Aesthetics and Art
     Criticism 12: 373-377.

498. MacCurdy, J. T. (1950) Psychopathology and Social
     Psychology. Part III. Hierarchies of Interests.
     Brit. J. Psychol. 41: 1-13. --Criteria for an
     interest-values scale.

499. MacDonald, Donald V. (1954) The Development of
the Ideal Self in New Zealand Children. IN:
Robert J. Havighurst, Studies of Children and
Society in New Zealand. Christchurch, N. Z.:
Canterbury Univ. College, Dept. of Educ.
(Limited publication; available by inter-library
loan from Univ. of Chicago Library). --Analysis
of over 1700 children's essays on, "The Person
I Would Like to Be Like"; compares results with
similar data on American children.

500. McDougall, William (1920) The Group Mind. New
York: Putnam. --Social-psychological approach
to national character.

501. ___ (1927) Character and the Conduct of Life. New
York and London: Putnam. --Instincts lead to
sentiments, especially through maternity, that
produce genuine benevolence; custom provides
the content of morality; the sentiment of self-
respect needed to stabilize morality.

502. McGinnies, Elliott M. (1950) Personal Values as
Determinants of Word Association. J. Abnorm.
Soc. Psychol. 45: 28-36. --Correlation between
Allport-Vernon responses and latency of re-
sponse to value-loaded words.

503. ___ and Bowles, Warren (1949) Personal Values as
Determinants of Perceptual Fixation. J. Pers.
18: 224-235. --Other things equal, fixation oc-
curs more readily for percepts associated with
values.

504. McKeachie, Wilbert J. and Guetzkow, Harold (1952)
A Rating-Ranking Scale for Goals of Life.
Religious Educ. 47: 25-27.

505. MacRae, Duncan, Jr. (1950) The Development of
Moral Judgment in Children. Ph. D. Thesis,
Harvard Univ. Partially published as: A test

-116-

of Piaget's theories of moral development.
J. Abnorm. Soc. Psych. 49: 14-18.

506. Mannoni, O. (1950) Psychologie de la Colonisation.
Paris: Éditions du Seuil. --See especially:
Ch. 8, universal values arising out of "a
symmetric image of the unity of the person. "

507. Martin, R. T. (1953) Science and Social Engineering.
Australian J. Psychol. 5: 79-85. --Urges
psychologists not to give precedence to social
utility over the demands of scientific inquiry.

508. Martin, William E. (1954) Learning Theory and
Identification: III. The Development of Values
in Children. J. Genet. Psychol. 84: 211-217.

509. Maslow, Abraham H. (1948) Some Theoretical Consequences of Basic Need-Gratification. J. Pers.
16: 402-416. --Motivation in relation to personality, social attitudes and values.

510. ___ (1950) Self-Actualizing People; A Study of
Psychological Health. Personality 1: 11-34. --
A study of individuals developing towards self-
actualization.

511. ___ (1954) Normality, Health and Values; Psychological Progress in Understanding Human Nature and
a Scientific Ethics. Main Currents in Modern
Thought 10: 75-81. --Interdependence of
psychological and ethical inquiry.

512. Mason, Evelyn P. (1954) Some Factors in Self-
Judgments. J. Clinical Psychol. 10: 336-340.
--Uses Self-Concept Questionnaire and W. A. Y.
technique on three age-class status groups to
evaluate relationship of living conditions,
economic status and age to self-judgments.

513. Mausner, Bernard and Siegel, A. (1950) The Effect
     of Variation in "Value" on Perceptual Thresh-
     olds. J. Abnorm. Soc. Psychol. 45: 760-763.
     --An experiment on recognizing stamps of
     varying worth; negative evidence for the hypoth-
     esis that ease of perception is a function of the
     value of the perceived object.

514. Mayer, Charles L. (1954) In Quest of a New Ethics.
     Trans. by Harold A. Larrabee. Boston:
     Beacon Press. --An anti-collectivist materi-
     alism, self-interest as the foundation of ethics
     but with room for individual independence and
     idiosyncrasy.

515. Maynard, Adams E. (1957) Empirical Verifiability
     Theory of Factual Meaning and Axiological
     Truth. IN: Ray Lepley, ed. The Language of
     Value. New York: Columbia Univ. Press.
     94-105.

—— Mead, George H. See Philosophy.

—— Meinong, Alexius von. See Philosophy.

516. Melikian, Levon H. and Prothro, E. Terry (1957)
     Goals Chosen by Arab Students in Response to
     Hypothetical Situations. J. Soc. Psychol. 46:
     3-9. --Cross-cultural comparison of data on
     Arab and American student subjects.

517. Meng, Heinrich (1956) Psychoanalysis, Ethics and
     Worldly Care of the Soul. Amer. Imago 13:
     335-345.

518. Menninger, Karl A. (1938) Man Against Himself.
     New York: Harcourt. --Psychoanalytic view of
     man as a creature of intense inner conflicts,
     seeking escape from these conflicts through his
     own destruction by actual suicide or by "death by
     inches," e.g., alcoholism, functional disorders,
     etc.

519. Miller, Daniel R. and Hutt, Max L. (1949) Value
     Interiorization and Personality Development.
     J. Soc. Issues 5: 2-30.

520. ___ and Swanson, Guy E. (1956) The Study of Con-
     flict. IN: Marshall R. Jones, ed. Nebraska
     Symposium on Motivation, 1956. Lincoln:
     Univ. of Nebraska Press. --Needs, morals,
     defenses and expressive styles as elements in
     a classification of variables for analyzing inner
     conflicts and their resolution.

521. Mills, C. Wright (1951) White Collar; The American
     Middle Classes. New York: Oxford Univ.
     Press. --See especially: Part Three, Styles
     of Life, white collar values of work, leisure,
     status and success. See also: 332-342,
     relation of mass media and social structure to
     political values.

522. ___ (1956) The Power Elite. New York: Oxford
     Univ. Press. --American status and prestige
     system and its relation to power. See espe-
     cially: Ch. 4, The Celebrities; Ch. 13, The
     Mass Society; Ch. 15, The Higher Immorality,
     on values, moral uneasiness and "structural
     immorality. "

523. Money-Kyrle, Roger E. (1944) Towards a Common
     Aim - A Psychoanalytical Contribution to Ethics.
     Brit. J. Med. Psychol. 20: 105-117. --Psycho-
     logical bases of a universal morality, from a
     psychoanalytic point of view. Recommends
     study of moral attitudes of both normal and
     abnormal individuals as potentially useful in
     understanding political behavior.

524. ___ (1951) Psychoanalysis and Politics; A Contribution
     to the Psychology of Politics and Morals. New
     York: Norton. --In the good society, political

thinking is realistic and undistorted by unconscious fantasies; psychoanalytic insight fosters
the humanistic character needed for international peace.

525. ___ (1952) Psychoanalysis and Ethics. Internatl. J.
Psycho-Analysis 33: 225-234. --Psychoanalysis
works towards the elimination of morality
based on irrational anxiety; increased insight
would bring about convergences in political
ideology.

526. ___ (1955) The Anthropological and Psychoanalytic
Concept of the Norm. IN: Warner Muensterberger and Sidney Axelrad, eds. Psychoanalysis
and the Social Sciences. Vol. IV. New York:
International Universities Press. 51-60. --
Criticism of ethical theory from the psychoanalytic standpoint.

527. Mullahy, Patrick (1943) Values, Scientific Method
and Psychoanalysis. Psychiatry 6: 139-146. --
Psychoanalysis, interpreted in terms of interpersonal relations, has possibilities for a
scientific theory of values and value judgment.

528. ___ (1947) Psychiatric and Psychological Contributions to Ethics. J. Phil. 44: 380-391.

529. Murphy, Gardner (1947) Personality; A Biosocial
Approach to Origins and Structure. New York:
Harper. --See especially: Ch. 12, The World
of Values. Psychology and anthropology used
for a theory of values, further elaborated in
discussion of "ethos."

530. ___ (1954) The Internalization of Social Controls.
IN: Morroe Berger, Theodore Abel and Charles
H. Page, eds. Freedom and Control in Modern
Society. New York: Van Nostrand. 3-17. --

Socialization as what the young should "do, perceive, and value."

531. Murray, Henry A. (1947) Time for a Positive Morality. Survey Graphic 36: 195-196, 214-216. --Attributes high crime rate and weakening of Western culture to lack of creative, exhilarating, attainable, widely shared moral goals; discusses historical influences on moral values of "negative orientation" and indifference or cynicism.

532. ___ (1951) Toward a Classification of Interaction. IN: Talcott Parsons and Edward A. Shils, eds. Toward a General Theory of Action. Cambridge: Harvard Univ. Press. 434-464. --Concludes that "action tendencies must be linked with values."

533. ___ (1958) Individuality; The Meaning and Content of Individuality in Contemporary America. Daedalus, Spring: 25-47 (Issued as vol. 87, no. 2, Proc. Amer. Acad. Arts and Sci.). -- Using fictional dialogue, examines individuality as myth and as value.

534. ___ and Morgan, Christian D. (1945) A Clinical Study of Sentiments. Provincetown, Mass.: Journal Press. Genet Psychol. Monographs 32. --The place of sentiments in the total structure of personality, with a case study.

535. Nassar, Carlos (1951) Cultural Patterns and Their Influence on Child Education. Proc. 4th Internatl. Congr. Mental Health: 293-298.

536. Naumburg, Margaret (1955) Art as Symbolic Speech. J. Aesthetics and Art Criticism 13: 435-450. -- A theory of universal symbols, supported by

comparison of sexual symbols in Maori art, in the art of ancient and medieval cultures, and in drawings by patients in therapy.

537. Neumann, Erich (1949) Tiefenpsychologie und Neue Ethik. Zürich: Rascher Verlag.

538. Nichols, Claude A. (1930) Moral Education among the North American Indians. New York: Columbia Univ. , Teachers College Bureau of Publications.

539. Osgood, Charles E. and Suci, George J. (1955) Factor Analysis of Meaning. J. Experimental Psychol. 50: 325-338. --Evaluation, potency and activity found to be the connotative factors of meaningful judgments.

540. Peters, Henry N. (1942) The Experimental Study of Aesthetic Judgments. Psychol. Bull. 39: 273-305. --Review of the literature and a theory of esthetic experience as involving pleasant-ness-unpleasantness (response), perception (stimulus) and experience (the genetic aspect of affection).

541. ___ (1955) Toward a Behavioral Theory of Value. Etc. 12: 172-177.

542. Piaget, Jean (1929) The Moral Judgment of the Child. New York: Harcourt. --A theory of stages in the moral development of children, based on interviewing and observation of children's games and attitudes toward the rules.

543. Pickford, R. W. (1955) Factorial Studies of Aesthetic Judgments. IN: A. A. Roback, ed. Present-Day Psychology. New York: Philosophical Library. 913-929.

544. Piers, Gerhart and Singer, Milton B. (1953) Shame and Guilt; A Psychoanalytic and Cultural Study.

Springfield, Ill. : Thomas. --Development of
moral sanctions discussed in psychoanalytic
terms, with a critique and review of anthro-
logical literature on the subject.

545. Postman, Leo, Bruner, Jerome S. and McGinnies,
Elliott (1948) Personal Values as Selective
Factors in Perception. J. Abnorm. Soc.
Psychol. 43: 142-154. --Correlation found be-
tween Allport-Vernon responses and time taken
to recognize value-loaded words.

546. ___ and Schneider, Bertram H. (1951) Personal
Values, Visual Recognition, and Recall.
Psychol. Rev. 58: 271-284. --Personal values
have significant effects on perceptual thresholds
and recall of verbal stimuli, but frequency of
word usage is more important as a determinant
of recognition than of recall.

547. Precker, Joseph A. (1952) Similarity of Valuings as
a Factor in Selection of Peers and Near-Author-
ity Figures. J. Abnorm. Soc. Psychol. 47:
406-414.

548. ___ (1953) The Automorphic Process in the Attribution
of Values. J. Pers. 21: 356-363. --An individual tends to prefer those who have the same
values he has.

549. Prothro, E. Terry (1958) Arab Students' Choices of
Ways To Live. J. Soc. Psychol. 47: 3-7. --
Factor analysis of Christian and Moslem Arab
students' ratings of Charles W. Morris's "Ways
To Live," comparisons with ratings of students
of six other countries (Canada, China, India,
Japan, Norway, United States). (See 1625 and
1626.)

550. Pugh, Thomas J. (1951) A Comparative Study of the Values of a Group of Ministers and Two Groups of Laymen. J. Soc. Psychol. 33: 225-235. -- An Allport-Vernon study, with Negro subjects.

551. Ramírez-López, Ramón (1955) Valores e Ideales. Pedagogía, Río Piedras 3: 61-75. --Follows Spranger's typology, emphasizes the evaluation of values and ideals.

552. Raths, Louis (1940) Approaches to the Measurement of Values. Educ. Res. Bull. 19: 275-282; 304. --Criticism of objective techniques of value measurement as too restrictive and limited; suggestions for techniques to stimulate students to reconstruct and rethink their values.

553. ___ (1942) Appraising Changes in Values of College Students. J. Educ. Res. 35: 557-564.

554. Raup, R. Bruce (1950) Choice and Decision in Social Intelligence. J. Soc. Issues 6: 45-49.

555. Reid, John R. (1955) The Problem of Values in Psychoanalysis. Amer. J. Psychoanal. 15: 115-122. --Psychoanalytic contributions to understanding unconscious factors in value interpretations and moral judgments.

556. Ritchie, Benbow F. and Kaplan, Abraham (1940) A Framework for an Empirical Ethics. Phil. Sci. 7: 476-491. --Analysis of the relations between frequently used value terms (e. g. , activity, interest) and "a constitution of terms which will make these relations explicit. "

557. Rogers, Carl R. (1951) Client-Centered Therapy. Boston: Houghton, Mifflin. --See especially: Final chapter, a theory of personality and behavior in which the concept of values plays an important part.

558.   ___ and Skinner, B. F. (1956) Some Issues Concerning
        the Control of Human Behavior. Science 124:
        1057-1065. --Ends and values in relation to
        science. (Comments by Joseph Turner, editor-
        ial, same issue.)

559. +Roheim, Geza (1950) Psychoanalysis and Anthro-
        pology. New York: International Universities
        Press. --An approach to universals through the
        notion of the psychic unity of mankind.

560. Rommetveit, Ragnar (1955) Social Norms and Roles;
        Explorations in the Psychology of Enduring
        Social Pressures (with Empirical Contributions
        from Inquiries into Religious Attitudes and Sex
        Roles of Adolescents from Some Districts in
        Western Norway). Minneapolis: Univ. of
        Minnesota Press.

561. +Rose, Arnold M. (1946) Popular Logic; A
        Methodological Suggestion. Amer. Sociol.
        Rev. 11: 590-592. --Suggestions for the study
        of the logical consistency of group belief
        systems.

562.   ___ (1948) The Selection of Problems for Research.
        Amer. J. Sociol. 54: 219-227. --On the
        theoretical importance of practical,
        sociological research and the inevitability of
        value judgments in social research.

563.   ___ (1954) Theory and Method in the Social Sciences.
        Minneapolis: Univ. of Minnesota Press. --See
        especially: Values in Social Research.

564.   ___ (1956) Sociology and the Study of Values. Brit. J.
        Sociol. 7: 1-17. --Values predominantly social
        in origin, hence sociologists should play a major
        role in their analysis.

565. +Rosen, Bernard C. (1956) The Achievement Syndrome;
      A Psychocultural Dimension of Social Stratifica-
      tion. Amer. Sociol. Rev. 21: 203-211.

566. Rosenberg, Benjamin G. and Zimet, Carl N. (1957)
      Authoritarianism and Aesthetic Choice. J. Soc.
      Psychol. 46: 293-297. --California E- and F-
      scales and Barron-Welsh figure preference test
      indicate significant correlation between authori-
      tarianism and esthetic choice.

567. Rosenthal, David (1955) The Selection of Stimulus
      Words for Value; Duration Threshold Experi-
      ments. J. Abnorm. Soc. Psychol. 50: 403-
      404. --On the appropriateness of selected words
      for representing given values; psychological
      distinction between value as "interest" and value
      as "preference."

568. Rosenzweig, Saul (1950) Norms and the Individual in
      the Psychologist's Perspective. IN: M. L.
      Reymert, ed. Feelings and Emotions: The
      Mooseheart Symposium. New York: McGraw-
      Hill. 327-335. --Distinction between universal,
      group and individual norms, each accessible in
      the study of individual personality.

569. Ruesch, Jurgen and Bateson, Gregory (1951) Com-
      munications: The Social Matrix of Psychiatry.
      New York: Norton. --Definition and discussion
      of values by means of communication and
      information theory; analysis of American values
      and results of research on the values of American
      psychiatrists.

570. Sarbin, Theodore R. and Berdie, Ralph F. (1940)
      Relation of Measured Interests to the Allport-
      Vernon Study of Values. J. Appl. Psychol. 24:
      287-296.

571. Schaefer, Benjamin R. (1936) The Validity and
      Utility of the Allport-Vernon Study of Values
      Test. J. Abnorm. Soc. Psychol. 30: 419-422.
      --Confirmation of Allport-Vernon results.

572. Schmeidler, Gertrude R. (1952) Personal Values and
      ESP Scores. J. Abnorm. Soc. Psychol. 47:
      757-761.

573. Schrickel, Harry G. (1952) A Psycho-Anthropological
      Approach to Problems in Aesthetics. J.
      Aesthetics and Art Criticism 10: 315-322.

574. Seashore, Harold G. (1947) Validation of the Study of
      Values for Two Vocational Groups at the College
      Level. Educ. and Psychol. Measurement 7:
      757-763. --An Allport-Vernon study, showing
      usefulness of the test in educational-vocational
      guidance.

575. +Seward, Georgene H. (1954) Learning Theory and
      Identification. V. Some Cultural Aspects of
      Identification. J. Genet. Psychol. 84: 229-236.

576. Shand, Alexander F. (1920) The Foundations of Char-
      acter. London: Macmillan. --A science of
      character to guide moral education, combining
      purposive instinct psychology with a theory of
      conscience as the product of sentiments but
      relative to historical, national and sex difference.

577. Sherif, Muzafer (1936) The Psychology of Social Norms.
      New York: Harper.

578. Sherman, Murray H. (1957) Values, Religion, and the
      Psychoanalyst. J. Soc. Psychol. 45: 261-269.
      --Differences between Freudian and anti-
      Freudian "culturalist" psychoanalytic theorists
      in their attitudes towards values and treatment
      goals.

579. Siegel, Sidney (1957) Level of Aspiration and Decision Making. Psychol. Rev. 64: 253-262.

580. Sisson, E. Donald and Sisson, Bette (1940) Introversion and the Aesthetic Attitude. J. Genl. Psychol. 22: 203-208. --Correlates Allport-Vernon scale results with Bernreuter Personality Inventory scores and esthetic attitude questionnaires.

581. Skinner, B. F. (1955) Freedom and the Control of Men. Amer. Scholar 25: 47-65. --Scientific study of man does not threaten the tradition of Western democracy but is consistent with and probably inevitably derived from it.

582. Smith, Anthony J. (1957) Similarity of Values and Its Relation to Acceptance and the Projection of Similarity. J. Psychol. 43: 251-260. --Test results show causal relationship between perception of similarity in value systems of others and acceptance, correlation between acceptance and projection of similarity.

583. Smith, George Horsley (1946) Attitudes Toward Soviet Russia; II. Beliefs, Values, and Other Characteristics of Pro-Russian and Anti-Russian Groups. J. Soc. Psychol. 23: 17-33.

584. Smith, M. Brewster (1949) Personal Values as Determinants of a Political Attitude. J. Psychol. 28: 477-486. --Interviews of 250 men indicate the conditions under which general personal values become determinants of political attitudes.

585. ___ (1950) Optima of Mental Health. Psychiatry 13: 503-510. --Criteria of mental health applicable interculturally and intraculturally; multiple criteria of adjustment, integration and cognitive

adequacy as standards to evaluate conduciveness
to optimal mental health of sociocultural
conditions.

586. Snygg, Donald (1949) The Place of Psychology in the
Development of Values. Amer. Psychol. 4: 212.

587. ___ (1953) The Psychological Basis of Human Values.
IN: A. Dudley Ward, ed. Goals of Economic
Life. New York: Harper. 335-364.

588. Solomon, Richard L. and Howes, Davis H. (1951)
Word Frequency, Personal Values and Visual
Duration Thresholds. Psychol. Rev. 58:
256-270. --Visual duration thresholds indicate
frequency of word use rather than evaluative
perceptual processes.

589. Sommer, Robert and Killian, Lewis M. (1954)
Areas of Value Difference: I. A Method for
Investigation; II. Negro-White Relations. J.
Soc. Psychol. 39: 227-235; 237-244. --With
prejudiced and unprejudiced whites and Negroes
as subjects, a method for investigating valued
role behavior and intergroup relations, with
emphasis on "value differences, value conflicts,
and double standards. "

590. Speroff, Boris J. (1955) Job Satisfaction and Interpersonal Desirability Values. Sociometry 18:
69-72.

591. Spoerl, Dorothy Tilden (1952) The Values of the Post-
War College Student. J. Soc. Psychol. 35:
217-225. --Allport-Vernon Test results, com-
paring groups by college, religion and sex.

592. Spranger, Edward (1928) Types of Men; The Psychology and Ethics of Personality. Halle:
Niemeyer. --An early and influential classifica-

tion and theory of the value-aspects of
personality.

593. Stagner, Ross (1948) Psychology of Personality.
2nd ed. New York: McGraw-Hill. --See
especially: Part II, attitudes and values in the
description of personality; Part IV, social values
as determinants of personality.

594. Stanley, Julian C. (1951) Insight into One's Own
Values. J. Educ. Psychol. 42: 399-408. --
Correlation of Allport-Vernon responses and
self-ratings on values as a measure of insight.

595. ___ (1953) Study of Values Profiles Adjusted for Sex
and Variability Differences. J. Appl. Psychol.
37: 472-473. --Based on the Allport-Vernon
Study of Values.

596. Sutherland, Alexander (1898) The Origin and Growth
of the Moral Instinct. London: Longmans, Green.
--Psychological theory of moral sentiments as
biological, therefore universal, and associated
with prolonged parental care.

597. Tajfel, H. (1957) Value and the Perceptual Judgment
of Magnitude. Psychol. Rev. 64: 192-204. --
Critique of theory and methodology of tests of
perceptual overestimation due to value.
Bibliography of 28 items.

—— Taylor, William Stephens. See Philosophy.

598. Thorndike, Edward L. (1936) Science and Values.
Science 83: 1-8. --Reprinted in Etc. 1, 1943:
1-11. Judgments of value as judgments of fact
concerning consequences; values amenable to
scientific inquiry and discoverable, with difficulty, by scientific means.

599. ___ (1936) The Value of Reported Likes and Dislikes for Various Experiences and Activities as Indications of Personal Traits. J. Appl. Psychol. 20: 285-313. --A study of personal values, using a like-dislike scale.

600. ___ (1937) Valuations of Certain Pains, Deprivations, and Frustrations. J. Genet. Psychol. 51: 227-239. --"Cash value" as a measure of preferences.

601. ___ (1938) Individual Differences in Valuation. J. Abnorm. Soc. Psychol. 33: 71-85. --Questionnaire study of the amount of time unemployed college graduates would spend at hard labor for certain commodities.

602. ___ (1940) Human Nature and the Social Order. New York: Macmillan. --See especially: Part I, on conscience and value judgments and the possibility and desirability of a natural science of values; Part II, recommendations for improving the state of mankind.

603. Thurstone, L. L. (1927) The Method of Paired Comparisons for Social Values. J. Abnorm. Soc. Psychol. 21: 384-400. --Extends psychophysical measurement to social values, using seriousness of different crimes as a basis for measurement.

604. ___ (1954) The Measurement of Values. Psychol. Rev. 61: 47-58.

605. Todd, J. Edward (1941) Social Norms and the Behavior of College Students. New York: Columbia Univ., Teachers College, Contributions to Education 833.

606. Tolman, Edward C. (1951) Value Standards, Pattern
Variables, Social Roles, Personality. IN:
Talcott Parsons and Edward A. Shils, eds.
Toward a General Theory of Action. Cambridge:
Harvard Univ. Press. 343-354.

607. ___ and Brunswik, Egon (1935) The Organism and
the Causal Texture of the Environment.
Psychol. Rev. 42: 43-77. --Analysis of behavioral response of the organism to signs,
cues and means-objects in the means-end system.

608. Trow, William C. (1953) The Value Concept in Educational Psychology. J. Educ. Psychol. 44:
449-462.

609. Trueblood, Charles K. (1939) Beliefs and Personality.
J. Abnorm. Soc. Psychol. 34: 200-224. --
Belief, interest and value as interpenetrating
attitudes with which the individual responds to
situations.

610. Turner, William D. (1948) Altruism and Its Measurement in Children. J. Abnorm. Soc. Psychol.
43: 502-516.

611. Ugurel-Semin, Refia (1952) Moral Behavior and
Moral Judgment of Children. J. Abnorm. Soc.
Psychol. 47: 463-474. --An experiment in
generosity behavior, analyzed according to age,
sex and socio-economic group.

612. Vanderplas, James M. and Blake, Robert R. (1949)
Selective Sensitization in Auditory Perception.
IN: Jerome S. Bruner and David Krech, eds.
Perception and Personality; A Symposium.
Durham: Duke Univ. Press. --Using Allport-
Vernon value areas and Postman-Bruner-
McGinnies stimulus list, value orientation found
to be associated with aural recognition efficiency.

613. Van Dusen, Albert C. , Wimberly, Stan and Mosier,
     Charles I. (1939) Standardization of a Values
     Inventory. J. Educ. Psychol. 30: 53-62. --
     Scales for five evaluative attitudes (philistine,
     theoretical, religious, social, and esthetic),
     with data on college students.

614. Vernon, Philip E. and Allport, Gordon W. (1931) A
     Test for Personal Values. J. Abnorm. Soc.
     Psychol. 26: 231-248. --Description and ration-
     ale of the authors' value scale (see 314).

615. +Wegrocki, Henry J. (1939) A Critique of Cultural
     and Statistical Concepts of Abnormality.
     J. Abnorm. Soc. Psychol. 34: 166-178. Also
     in: Clyde Kluckhohn, Henry Murray and David
     Schneider, eds. Personality in Nature, Culture,
     and Society. New York: Knopf, 1953. 691-
     701. --The case for a pan-human standard of
     psychic normality, based on a concept of real-
     istic adjustment.

616. Weiss, Albert P. (1932) Value as an Objective Prob-
     lem for Psychology. J. Abnorm. Soc. Psychol.
     27: 111-129. --Definition of value in terms of
     biological survival and habit formation; the
     "problem of values" said to be introduced by
     planners.

617. White, Ralph K. (1944) Value Analysis; A Quantitative
     Method for Describing Qualitative Data. J. Soc.
     Psychol. 19: 351-358. --A method of classifica-
     tion and counting of recurrent value-judgments.

618. ___ (1947) Black Boy; A Value-Analysis. J. Abnorm.
     Soc. Psychol. 42: 440-461. --Illustration of the
     author's method of value-analysis.

619. ___ (1951) Value-Analysis, the Nature and Use of the
Method. Glen Gardner, N. J.: Libertarian
Press. Also: New York: Columbia Univ.
Press.

620. Whitely, Paul L. (1938) The Constancy of Personal
Values. J. Abnorm. Soc. Psychol. 33: 405-
408. --The Allport-Vernon Test used in a
three-year study of college students.

621. Wickert, Frederic L. (1940) A Test for Personal
Goal-Values. J. Soc. Psychol. 11: 259-274. --
Nine items representing a continuum of human
desires prepared in a form similar to the Allport-
Vernon Test.

622. Wolfenstein, Martha (1950) Some Variants in Moral
Training of Children. IN: R. S. Eissler et
al., eds. The Psychoanalytic Study of the
Child. Vol. V. New York: International
Universities Press. 310-328.

623. ___ (1951) The Emergence of Fun Morality. J. Soc.
Issues 7: 15-25. --". . . Fun, from having
been suspect if not taboo, has tended to become
obligatory. " This change examined through a
study of changes in child training over a thirty-
five year period.

624. Wolff, Werner (1950) One Plus One = ? An Inquiry
into Methodology, Perception and Values.
Personality Symposium 1: 68-74. --The role
of the individual's value system in the cognitive
process of adding.

625. ___ (1950) Values and Personality; An Existential
Psychology of Crisis. New York: Grune-Stratton.
--Existential psychology as "an interpretation
of data in terms of an individual's value system"
and as important for psychotherapy.

626. Woodruff, Asahel D. (1942) Personal Values and the Direction of Behavior. School Rev. 50: 32-42. --A technique for measuring distinctive patterning of personal values, administered to 350 subjects; results indicate close relationship between value patterns and individual behavior.

627. ___ (1943) Students' Verbalized Values. Religious Educ. (Sept.-Oct.): 321-324. --Ranking of twelve values of students grouped by church membership; results indicate that attitudes depend on individual value concepts.

628. ___ (1944) The Relationship Between Functional and Verbalized Motives. J. Educ. Psychol. 35: 101-107. --Basic and functional motives do not change rapidly, but degree of awareness of basic values may be greatly influenced by immediate experiences when such values are seriously involved.

629. ___ (1945) Personal Values and Religious Background. J. Soc. Psychol. 22: 141-147. --The effect of religious experience on the value patterns of young people of different backgrounds.

630. ___ and Di Vesta, Francis J. (1948) The Relationship Between Values, Concepts, and Attitudes. Educ. Psychol. Measurement 8: 645-659. -- "A Study of Choices," Thurstone Attitude Scales and a fraternity attitude scale administered to college students and intercorrelations of results investigated.

631. Wundt, Wilhelm (1897-1901) Ethics. Trans. by Edward B. Titchner, Julia H. Gulliver and Margaret F. Washburn. London: Sonnenschein. Also: New York: Macmillan.

632. Young, Paul Thomas (1955) The Role of Hedonic
     Processes in Motivation. IN: Marshall R.
     Jones, ed. Nebraska Symposium on Motiva-
     tion: 1955. Lincoln: Univ. of Nebraska Press.
     193-238. --Reviews experimental evidence
     showing importance of affective processes in
     motivation; presents four experimental pro-
     cedures for changing the value systems of rats.

633. Zilboorg, Gregory (1950) Clinical Variants of Moral
     Values. Amer. J. Psychiat. 106: 744-747. --
     Distinguishes a pathological sense of guilt from
     normal guilt feelings.

III. SOCIOLOGY

634. Adler, Franz (1956) The Value Concept in Sociology. Amer. J. Sociol. 62: 272-279. --A survey; bibliographical footnotes.

635. Albrecht, Milton C. (1956) Does Literature Reflect Common Values? Amer. Sociol. Rev. 21: 722-729. --Analysis of methodology and statistical results of studies of stories in wide-circulation magazines; finds support for the hypothesis that such stories reflect norms and values regarding the American family.

636. Angell, Robert C. (1949) Moral Integration and Interpersonal Integration in American Cities. Amer. Sociol. Rev. 14: 245-251. --Statistical comparison of survey data from four cities, concluding that level of moral integration is a function of city-wide interpersonal integration.

637. ___ (1958) Free Society and Moral Crisis. Ann Arbor: Univ. of Michigan Press. --Analysis of contemporary crisis in relation to rapid change and personal anonymity; proposes extensive use of social science to bring about "moral and social integration in a free society."

638. +Arensberg, Conrad M., Barkin, Solomon, Chalmers, W. Ellison, Wilensky, Harold L., Worthy, James C. and Dennis, Barbara D. (1957) Research in Industrial Human Relations--A Critical Appraisal. New York: Harper. --Contributions from sociologists, personnel directors, and union officials, on the practice and philosophy of labor relations viewed as human relations.

639. Aubert, Vilhelm (1958) Legal Justice and Mental
     Health. Psychiatry 21: 101-113. --Value con-
     flicts and the "collision of norms" between the
     psychiatric-psychological approach and the
     legal approach to handling human problems.

640. Bain, Read (1949) Natural Science and Value-Policy.
     Phil. Sci. 16: 182-192. --Social scientific
     knowledge useful in the formulation of method-
     policy and value-policy.

641. ___ (1952) The Scientist and His Values. Soc. Forces
     31: 106-109. --The scientist as such makes no
     value judgments but must promote scientific
     knowledge as a value and not avoid action-
     problems.

642. Bales, Robert F. and Couch, Arthur S. (1956)
     Factor Analysis of the Domain of Values.
     Cambridge: Harvard University, Laboratory
     of Social Relations. Dittoed.

643. Barber, Bernard (1952) Science and the Social Order.
     Glencoe, Ill.: Free Press. --See especially:
     62-66, 85-94 and 246-247, moral values and the
     scientist.

644. Barnes, Harry E. and Becker, Howard (1952)
     Social Thought from Lore to Science.
     Washington: Harren Press. --Includes discus-
     sion of value system terminology and the in-
     fluence of values upon the work of social
     scientists.

645. Barrabee, Paul (1954) How Cultural Factors Affect
     Family Life. IN: National Conference of
     Social Work; The Social Welfare Forum, 1954.
     New York: Columbia Univ. Press. 17-30. --
     Analyzes family life with special reference to
     ethnic membership and its concomitant values;

urges social workers to be sensitive to their clients' cultural values and world views.

646. Becker, Howard (1941) Supreme Values and the Sociologist. Amer. Sociol. Rev. 6: 155-172. --Ethical neutrality in social research supported, but social scientists should accept the value of "control," the supreme value of science.

647. ___ (1950) Through Values to Social Interpretation; Essays on Social Contexts, Actions, Types and Prospects. Durham: Duke Univ. Press. -- Six essays on the role of values and value systems in the current study of social affairs, with a typology of value systems.

648. ___ (In progress) Value. IN: UNESCO Dictionary of Social Science. --Definition, with historical review of origins and usage.

649. Bellah, Robert N. (1957) Tokugawa Religion; the Values of Pre-Industrial Japan. Glencoe, Ill.: Free Press. --Preindustrial Japanese values permitted more rapid industrialization than in any other non-Western country, without a major internal crisis.

650. ___ (1958) Religious Aspects of Modernization in Turkey and Japan. Amer. J. Sociol. 64: 1-5. --Accommodation to changes in political and economic institutions involves a shift from "prescriptive" to "principal" value system, differentiating religion and ideology.

651. +Bendix, Reinhard (1951) Social Science and the Distrust of Reason. Berkeley: Univ. of California Press (Univ. of California Publications in Sociology and Social Institutions, 1). -- Anti-rationalism and "method" as a substitute for reason in recent social science.

652. ___ (1956) Work and Authority in Industry. New York:
      Wiley. Also: London: Chapman and Hall. --
      Comparative analysis of ideologies associated
      with management justification of employers'
      discipline and authority.

653. +___ and Lipset, Seymour M., eds. (1953) Class,
      Status and Power. Glencoe, Ill.: Free Press.

654. Benne, Kenneth D. and Swanson, G. E. (1950) The
      Problem of Values and the Social Scientist.
      J. Soc. Issues 6: 2-7.

655. ___, eds. (1950) Values and the Social Scientist.
      J. Soc. Issues 6. --A symposium on the desira-
      bility of the scientific study of values.

656. +Berelson, Bernard R. and Janowitz, Morris (1950)
      Readings in Public Opinion and Communication.
      Rev. ed. Glencoe, Ill.: Free Press.

657. +___, Lazarsfeld, Paul F. and McPhee, William N.
      (1954) Voting; A Study of Opinion Formation in
      a Presidential Campaign. --Further development
      of the approach used in Lazarsfeld et al.
      (see 783).

658. Berger, Morroe, Abel, Theodore and Page, Charles
      H. (1954) Freedom and Control in Modern
      Society; In Honor of Robert Morrison MacIver.
      New York: Nostrand. --Essays by sociologists,
      political scientists, and others on individual and
      social interests in social control.

659. Bernard, Jessie S. (1949) American Community
      Behavior. New York: Dryden. --A theory of
      conflict between overt ideals and actually sought
      goals in the American scene; sociology as
      competent to provide relevant facts but not
      solutions for value problems.

660. ___ (1950) The Validation of Normative Social Theory. J. Phil. 47: 481-493. --Standards of validation of normative social theory "are the perfectly natural facts of human cultural values," not natural science postulates, as claimed by Northrop (see 1646, 1647, 1650).

661. ___ (1954) The Theory of Games of Strategy as a Modern Sociology of Conflict. Amer. J. Sociol. 59: 411-424. --Concepts from game theory as basis for a sociology of conflict; conceptual, technical, practical and ethical problems of various strategies exposed.

662. Bernard, L. L. (1936) The Conflict Between Primary Group Attitudes and Derivative Group Ideals in Modern Society. Amer. J. Sociol. 41: 611-623. --Analysis of the lack of social control in modern life; recommendations for achieving a "new social idealism" by expanding group sympathies.

663. Bierstedt, Robert (1948) Social Science and Social Policy. Bull. Amer. Assn. Univ. Professors 34: 310-319. --Behavioral science must be ethically neutral but can be used to determine means and to throw light on morally important problems.

664. Blackwell, Gordon W. (1958) Community Analysis. IN: Roland Young, ed. Approaches to the Study of Politics. Evanston: Northwestern Univ. Press. 305-317. --Value system as one of the dimensions of community.

665. Bouglé, C. C. (1926) The Evolution of Values. Trans. by Helen S. Sellars. New York: Holt. --An influential sociological study.

666. Bowman, Claude C. (1943) Evaluations and Values Consistent with the Scientific Study of Society. Amer. Sociol. Rev. 8: 306-312.

667. ___ (1945) Must the Social Sciences Foster Moral Scepticism? Amer. Sociol. Rev. 10: 709-715. --Attack on ethical neutrality in the social sciences, adapting Deweyean arguments.

668. ___ (1946) Hidden Valuations in the Interpretation of Sexual and Family Relationships. Amer. Sociol. Rev. 11: 536-544. --Examines bias in some sociological studies, recommends value judgments of future investigators be made explicit.

669. ___ (1954) Social Change as Reflected in the Kinsey Studies. Soc. Probl. 2: 1-6. --The Kinsey reports reflect a trend ". . . away from the traditional morality toward an ideology of sexual humanism. "

670. ___ (1956) Is Sociology Too Detached? Amer. Sociol. Rev. 21: 563-568. --Objectivity does not require non-evaluative detachment; greater social science interest in policy-related research anticipated.

671. Brown, J. S. (1952) A Comparative Study of Deviations from Sexual Mores. Amer. Sociol. Rev. 17: 135-146. --Statistical study of data on punishment for sex activity in 110 societies.

672. Burgess, Ernest W. (1935) Social Planning and the Mores. IN: Ernest W. Burgess and Herbert Blumer, eds. The Human Problems of Social Planning; Selected Papers from The Proceedings of the American Sociological Society. Chicago: Amer. Sociol. Soc. 1-18.

673. ___ (1954) Economic, Cultural, and Social Factors
          in Family Breakdown. Amer. J. Orthopsychiat.
          24: 462-470. --American values of individualism,
          competition and democracy, in emphasizing
          individual development, may weaken the in-
          stitutional bonds of the family.

674. ___ (1954) Values and Sociological Research. Soc.
          Problems 2: 16-20. --". . . The essential
          data for sociological research are values";
          examines the role of the sociologist in changing
          values and proposes that sociologists defend
          the value of academic freedom by doing research
          on the ways it is threatened or curtailed.

675. Caiger, George, ed. (1953) The Australian Way of
          Life. London: Heinemann (Way of Life Series).
          Also: New York: Columbia Univ. Press,
          1954. --Survey of Australian values, ideals,
          institutions and aspirations.

676. Calpin, G. H., ed. (1953) The South African Way of
          Life; Values and Ideals of a Multi-Racial Society.
          London: Heinemann (Way of Life Series).
          Also: New York: Columbia Univ. Press,
          1954. --Education, politics and economics of
          six major ethnic groups.

677. Case, Clarence Marsh (1939) The Value Concept in
          Sociology and Related Fields. Sociol. Soc.
          Res. 23: 403-430. --Uses of the term "value"
          by economists and philosophers, historical
          development of the sociological concept of
          values as "the selected objects of the evaluators
          themselves. "

678. ___ (1944) Essays in Social Values. Los Angeles:
          Univ. of Southern California Press. --Relates
          the objective investigation of values with their
          philosophic standardization; discusses the
          relationship between specifically social values

and other complexes of values in modern civilization.

679. Catton, William R. , Jr. (1954) Exploring Techniques for Measuring Human Values. Amer. Sociol. Rev. 19: 49-55. --Report of three experiments that demonstrate the quantitative commensurability of qualitatively unlike values; standard scaling techniques used.

680. ___ (1954) Propaganda Effectiveness as a Function of Human Values. Ph. D. Thesis, Univ. of Washington.

681. ___ (1956) A Retest of the Measurability of Certain Human Values. Amer. Sociol. Rev. 21: 357-359.

682. +Cohen, Albert K. (1946) An Evaluation of "Themes" and Kindred Concepts. Amer. J. Sociol. 52: 41-42. --Critique of Opler's concept of themes (see 214), attempt to make thematic analysis of culture more systematic.

683. ___ (1948) On the Place of "Themes" and Kindred Concepts in Social Theory. Amer. Anthrop. 50: 436-443. --Relationships between the integration of value systems and the functional necessities of social systems.

684. Coleman, Lee (1941) What Is American? A Study of Alleged American Traits. Soc. Forces 19: 492-499. --Summarizes data and conclusions on "alleged American characteristics, ideals, and principles, " with a list of traits upon which there is relative agreement among various authors.

685. Collins, Jerome (1957) Changing Values in the Best Sellers of the 1930-1935 and 1950-1955 Periods. Honors Thesis, Harvard Univ.

686. Comte, Auguste (1875-1877) System of Positive Polity. London: Longmans, Green. Vol. I: General View, trans. by J. H. Bridges; Vol. II: Social Statics, trans. by F. Harrison; Vol. III: Social Dynamics, trans. by E. S. Beesly et al.; Vol. IV: Theory of the Future of Man, trans. by R. Congreve. --Classical positivist treatise, consummated by the proposal of science as a religion and value system for the modern world.

687. Coser, Lewis A. (1957) Social Conflict and the Theory of Social Change. Brit. J. Sociol. 8: 197-207. --Social conflict involving purposive action generates "a group-forming and value-forming response" and the formation of new value systems; tension-release mechanisms preserve the system at the risk of destructive, unrealistic conflict.

688. Cottrell, William F. (1955) Energy and Society; The Relation Between Energy, Social Change, and Economic Development. New York: McGraw-Hill. --See especially: 177-178 and 236. Values - "the factors that within physical and physiological limits affect choice" - intermediate between environment and actual production of energy.

689. ___ (1955) Research to Establish the Conditions for Peace. J. Soc. Issues 11: 13-20. --Program for the study of the values of the elite; social values; the socio-psychological attributes of values and of correlate social and power structures; methods to create or alter values; goal-attainment in relation to available resources and means.

690. Cuber, John F. and Harper, Robert A. (1948) Problems of American Society; Values in Conflict. New York: Holt. --New edition, with

William F. Kenkel, 1956. Social problems as
value conflicts; judgments of what are social
problems presuppose value-premises.

691.   ___ and Pell, Betty (1941) A Method for Studying
Moral Judgments Relating to the Family. Amer.
J. Sociol. 47: 12-23. --Describes a question-
naire based on hypothetical situations.

692. Davis, Allison (1948) Social Class Influences upon
Learning. Cambridge: Harvard Univ. Press.
--Compares values and child-rearing practices
of middle and lower classes in the United States;
discusses effects of these on school situations;
cultural determinants of mental abilities.

693. Davis, Arthur K. (1951) Conflict Between Major
Social Systems; The Soviet-American Case.
Soc. Forces 30: 29-36. --Values described and
contrasted.

694. DeGre, Gerard (1955) Science as a Social Institution.
New York: Random House. --On social change
and the norms of science and the cultural values
of modern science.

695. Dodd, Stuart C. (1950) How to Measure Values. Res.
Stud. Washington 18: 163-168.

696.   ___ (1951) On Classifying Human Values; A Step in
the Prediction of Human Valuing. Amer. Sociol.
Rev. 16: 645-653. --Proposed variables:
desiderata, intensity of desiring, persons, time,
space and residual condition.

697.   ___ (1951) Historic Ideals Operationally Defined.
Publ. Opin. Quart. 15: 547-556. --Proposes
moment formulas be used in defining and
measuring ideals and values.

698. ___ (1953) A Statement of Human Wants. Educ. Theory 3: 179-181. --Universal needs as basic to universal values.

699. ___ and Catton, William R., Jr. (1954) Symbolizing the Values of Others. Symp. Sci. Phil. Relig. 13: 485-496.

700. Dubin, Robert (1956) Industrial Workers' Worlds; A Study of the 'Central Life Interests' of Industrial Workers. Soc. Probl. 3: 131-142. --In three middle-western plants, workers' value orientations towards job interest, primary human relations, valued social experience.

701. Duncan, Hugh D. (1953) Language and Literature in Society. Chicago: Univ. of Chicago Press. --Sociological esthetic theory.

702. ___ (1957) Sociology of Art, Literature and Music; Social Contexts of Symbolic Experience. IN: Howard Becker and Alvin Boskoff, eds. Modern Sociological Theory in Continuity and Change. New York: Dryden. 482-497. --Surveys recent theory.

703. Durkheim, Emile (1920) Introduction à la Morale. Rev. Philosophique (Paris) 90: 79-97.

704. ___ (1933) On the Division of Labor in Society. Trans. by G. Simpson. New York: Macmillan. --Criticism of past moral theories for starting with moral formula instead of facts; ethics should become a science of moral facts of social disapprovals; moral authority resides in society as a whole, but there is room for individualism in differentiation of society.

705. ___ (1953) Sociology and Philosophy. Trans. by D. F. Pocock. Glencoe, Ill.: Free Press. --See

especially: 35-62, on "The Determination of
Moral Facts" and sections on value judgments
and judgments of reality.

706. ___ (1957) Professional Ethics and Civic Morals.
Trans. by Cornelia Brookfield. London:
Routledge and Kegan Paul. Also: Glencoe,
Ill.: Free Press. --Lectures first delivered
1890-1900, revised and published as Leçons
de Sociologie; Physique des moeurs et du droit.

707. Du Wors, Richard E. (1952) Persistence and Change
in Local Values of Two New England Communities. Rural Sociol. 17: 207-217. --Holistic,
historical study of values in the social systems
of adjacent communities in Maine.

708. +Eisenstadt, S. N. (1949) The Perception of Time
and Space in a Situation of Culture-Contact.
J. Royal Anthrop. Inst. 79: 63-68. --Anomie
and discontinuities in time and space orientation
in a Jewish section of Jerusalem.

709. ___ (1954) Studies in Reference Group Behaviour;
1. Reference Norms and the Social Structure.
Human Relations 7: 191-216. --Reference-group
orientation as a normative process through
which "the various concrete roles which an
individual performs are related to the wider
values of society, and to its basic identifications. "

710. +___ (1957) Sociological Aspects of Political Development in Underdeveloped Countries. Econ. Development and Cultural Change 5: 289-307.
--Internal dynamics of social and political
systems changing from traditional to Western
type.

711. Fairchild, Henry Pratt (1950) Versus; Reflections of
a Sociologist. New York: Philosophical
Library. --Essays on the general theme that

human choice is between two goods or evils, not between good and evil. (Cf. 1472.)

712. Fichter, Rev. Joseph H. (1939) Roots of Change. New York: Appleton-Century. --Effects of economic changes on values and related phenomena.

713. ___ (1956) Religious Values and the Social Personality. Amer. Catholic Sociol. Rev. 17: 109-116. --Religious role and value-norms in the conduct of the modal Roman Catholic, in relation to his other major social roles and to the secular values of urban culture.

714. ___ and Kolb, William L. (1953) Ethical Limitations on Sociological Reporting. Amer. Sociol. Rev. 18: 544-550. --On the sociologist's responsibility to the people he studies; recommendations to decide issues of publishing possibly harmful information.

715. Folsom, Joseph K. (1937) Changing Values in Sex and Family Relations. Amer. Sociol. Rev. 2: 717-726. --Definition and theory of values, analysis of changes in modern society.

716. ___ and Strelsky, Nikander (1944) Russian Values and Character. Amer. Sociol. Rev. 9: 296-307. --Cognitive orientations and ethos, using configurational concepts of O. Spengler, R. Benedict and C. W. Morris.

717. Foote, Nelson N. (1954) Sex as Play. Soc. Probl. 1: 159-163. --Compares Swedish and American attitudes on sex as play; proposes research to explore "the morals and values which might emerge from a forthright public acceptance of sex as play. "

718. Francastel, P. (1949) Art et Sociologie. L'Année
    Sociologique (1940-1948), 3me Série (Paris)
    2: 491-527. --Esthetic values in relation to
    social organization.

719. Francis, E. K. (1955) In Search of Utopia -- The
    Mennonites in Manitoba. Glencoe, Ill.: Free
    Press. --Changes in value orientation and social
    structure of Russian emigrants of the 1870's
    and their descendants, showing that economic
    adaptation does not necessarily mean failure to
    maintain a central core of values.

720. Frazier, E. Franklin (1957) Black Bourgeoisie; The
    Rise of a New Middle-Class in the United States.
    Glencoe, Ill.: Free Press. --French edition:
    Bourgeoisie Noire. Paris: Librairie Plon,
    1955. Values and behavior of the American
    Negro middle class; socio-psychological
    analysis of the compensatory "world of make
    believe" created by the Negro elite.

721. Geiger, Theodor (1955) Evaluational Nihilism. Acta
    Sociol. 1: 18-25. --Value judgments neither
    objectively valid nor theoretically meaningless;
    the problem of value judgments has urgent
    social implications in a society where moral
    autonomy has become a social institution.

722. Gerth, Hans and Mills, C. Wright (1953) Character
    and Social Structure; The Psychology of Social
    Institutions. New York: Harcourt. --See
    especially: Ch. 10, Symbol Spheres, inter-
    nalized common values as justifying and sanc-
    tioning institutionalized authority and motivating
    personal conduct; Ch. 11, Stratification and
    Institutional Orders, stratification as "classi-
    fication in terms of valued things and experi-
    ences ... [and] the ranking of people with
    respect to such values ...."

723. Ginsberg, Morris (1938-1939) The Function of
        Reason in Morals. Proc. Aristotelian Soc. 39:
        249-270.

724. ___ (1942) National Character. Brit. J. Psychol.
        32: 183-295.

725. ___ (1944) Moral Progress. Glasgow: Glasgow
        Jackson. --Evolutionary ethical theory.

726. ___ (1952) Psycho-Analysis and Ethics. Brit. J.
        Sociol. 3: 287-304. --Review of Freud, Flügel
        and Fromm, concluding that psychoanalytic
        theory is compatible with different concepts of
        moral judgment and contributes to ethics
        through the study of comparative moral pathol-
        ogies and by revealing the irrational elements
        in moral judgments.

727. ___ (1953) On the Diversity of Morals. J. Royal
        Anthrop. Inst. 83: 117-135.

728. ___ (1953) The Idea of Progress; A Revaluation.
        Boston: Beacon Press.

729. ___ (1955) Moral Bewilderment. Soc. Forces 34:
        5-10. --Social philosophy, not science,
        competent to analyze and resolve basic moral
        problems.

730. ___ (1957) Essays in Sociology and Social Philosophy.
        Vol. I, On the Diversity of Morals. New York:
        Macmillan. --See especially: Part One, on
        moral bewilderment, morality and political
        conflict, ethical relativity, psychoanalysis
        and ethics, basic needs in relation to moral
        ideals, and responsibility.

731. Goffman, Erving (1956) The Nature of Deference and
        Demeanor. Amer. Anthrop. 58: 473-502. --

Personal interactions in a mental hospital as
the basis of exploring relations of individuals
to social rules of conduct.

732. Grafton, Thomas H. (1947) The Sociology of Right
and Wrong. Amer. Sociol. Rev. 12: 86-95. --
The concepts of right and wrong as acts and
action-systems.

733. Graham, Saxon (1957) American Culture; An Analysis
of Its Development and Present Characteristics.
New York: Harper.--Conceptual and emotional elements of values basic to motivation
of behavior in American society; "values" the
theoretical basis for explaining the uniqueness
of institutional forms.

734. Gross, Edward (1956) Social Science Techniques; A
Problem of Power and Responsibility. Sci.
Monthly 83: 242-247. --See especially: Concluding section on moral obligations, arguing
that the scientific behavior of social scientists
must rest ultimately on moral considerations.

735. Gross, Feliks, ed. (1948) European Ideologies; A
Survey of 20th Century Political Ideas. New
York: Philosophical Library. --Twenty-four
papers, defending or attacking a wide variety
of political philosophies, chiefly varieties of
socialism.

736. ___ (1950) The Planner and "The Planned"; The
Peasants of East Europe - A Case Study.
Modern Rev. 3: 3-13. --Conflict between the
values of East European peasants and those of
Soviet planners.

737. ___ (1951) Language and Value Changes among the
Arapaho. Internatl. J. Amer. Linguistics 17:
10-17. --Linguistic indicators of value changes
of a Plains Indian group.

738. Gurvitch, Georges (1937) Morale Théorique et Science des Moeurs; Leurs Possibilités, Leur Conditions. Paris: Presses Universitaires de France.

739. ___ (1938) La Science des Faits Moraux et la Morale Théorique chez E. Durkheim. Essais de Sociologie. Paris: Librairie du Recueil 279-306.

740. ___ (1943) Is Moral Philosophy a Normative Theory? J. Phil. 40: 141-148. --Rejects the view that ethics is normative, i.e., that it enjoins what it is "right to do."

741. Hart, Hornell (1945) A Reliable Scale of Value Judgments. Amer. Sociol. Rev. 10: 473-481. --Experiments in value-scaling.

742. ___ (1947) Factuality and the Discussion of Values. Soc. Forces 25: 290-294. --Statistical analysis of relationships between factuality and discussion of values in a sample of sociological writings.

743. ___ (1948) Atomic Cultural Lag; The Value Frame. Sociol. Soc. Res. 32: 768-775. --Concludes that most Americans choose the same world goals.

744. ___ (1949) Social Science and the Atomic Crisis. J. Soc. Issues, Supplement Series 2: 1-30. --A "Manhattan Project of Social Sciences" proposed to correct problems in moral lag; scientific analysis of social values to be part of the project.

745. Hartung, Frank E. (1954) Cultural Relativity and Moral Judgments. Phil. Sci. 21: 118-126. -- Cultural relativity is "surreptitiously moral, and . . . deprives man of rational grounds for decision in certain crucial areas." (For criticism, see 1146.)

746. Hauser, Philip M. (1949) Social Science and Social
     Engineering. Phil. Sci. 16: 209-218. --It is
     not the province of the social scientist as such
     to give advice or to participate in policy deci-
     sions and action programs.

747. Hayes, Edward Cary (1921) Sociology and Ethics.
     New York, London: Appleton. --Outline of a
     science of ethics, with illustrations.

748. Herman, Abbott P. (1949) Values of Individualism.
     Sociol. Soc. Res. 33: 196-203. --Description
     and classification, based on American com-
     munity studies.

749. Himes, Joseph S. (1952) Value Consensus in Mate
     Selection among Negroes. Marriage and
     Family Living 14: 317-321. --Personality
     traits found to be more important than sex
     standards or leisure interests.

750. ___ (1955) Value Analysis in the Theory of Social
     Problems. Soc. Forces 33: 259-262. --Typology
     of value conflicts in the United States for value
     analysis of social problems.

751. Hobhouse, L. T. (1906) Morals in Evolution. London:
     Chapman and Hall.

752. ___ (1921) The Rational Good; A Study in the Logic of
     Practice. London: Allen and Unwin.

753. +Homans, George (1950) The Human Group. New
     York: Harcourt. --Analysis of small groups;
     norms and values treated passim.

754. Horton, Paul B. and Leslie, Gerald R. (1955) The
     Sociology of Social Problems. New York:
     Appleton-Century-Crofts. --Social problems
     analyzed in terms of social change, social

disorganization, emergence of value conflicts and the influences of personal deviation. Annotated bibliographies.

755. Hyman, Herbert (1953) The Value Systems of Different Classes; A Social Psychological Contribution to the Analysis of Stratification. IN: Reinhard Bendix and Seymour M. Lipset, eds. Class, Status and Power. Glencoe, Ill.: Free Press. 426-442.

756. +Inkeles, Alex (1950) Public Opinion in Soviet Russia; A Study in Mass Persuasion. Cambridge: Harvard Univ. Press.

757. ___ and Levinson, Daniel (1954) National Character; The Study of Modal Personality and Sociocultural Systems. IN: Gardner Lindzey, ed. Handbook of Social Psychology. Vol. II. Cambridge: Addison-Wesley Press. 977-1020.

758. +International Sociological Association, in Collaboration with Jessie Bernard, T. H. Pear, Raymond Aron and Robert C. Angell (1957) The Nature of Conflict; Studies on the Sociological Aspects of International Tensions. Paris: UNESCO. -- Four chapters on sociological, historical and psychological approaches to conflict, with values treated in passing; bibliography of 1160 related titles.

759. Janowitz, Morris (1954) Some Observations on the Ideology of Professional Psychologists. Amer. Psychol. 9: 528-532.

760. + ___ and Marvick, Dwaine (1953) Authoritarianism and Political Behavior. --Publ. Opin. Quart. 17: 185-201. --With two nation-wide samples of the American public, explores the "feasibility of considering personality tendencies as dimensions

of American political behavior," using concepts
developed by Adorno et al. (see 307).

761. +___ (1956) Competitive Pressure and Democratic
      Consent; An Interpretation of the 1952 Presi-
      dential Election. Ann Arbor: Univ. of
      Michigan, Bureau of Government, Institute of
      Public Administration. --See especially: Ch. 1,
      The Criteria for Competitive Democracy; Ch.
      4, The Quality of the Electorate's Deliberation;
      Ch. 7, The Final Balance: Consent Versus
      Manipulation.

762. Johns-Heine, Patricke and Gerth, Hans H. (1949)
      Values in Mass Periodical Fiction: 1921-1940.
      Publ. Opin. Quart. 13: 105-113. --Shifts in
      treatment of heroes and themes reflect important
      social trends.

763. Jonassen, Christian T. (1947) The Protestant Ethic
      and the Spirit of Capitalism in Norway. Amer.
      Sociol. Rev. 12: 676-686. --Assesses the
      relative influence of religious values and
      economic factors in the development of Norwegian
      capitalism, with a discussion of Weber and Marx.

764. Jones, Arthur H. (1943) Sex, Educational and Religious
      Influences on Moral Judgments Relative to the
      Family. Amer. Sociol. Rev. 8: 405-411. --
      Results of a study of the family and sex values
      of 888 persons, using the Cuber-Pell situational
      questionnaire.

765. Kahl, Joseph A. (1957) The American Class Structure.
      New York: Rinehart. --See especially: Income,
      Wealth and Style of Life; Classes as Ideal Types:
      Emergent Values. Annotated bibliography.

766. Keeley, Benjamin J. (1954) Factors Associated with Value Convergence in a Social System; With Special Reference to the Marriage Group. Ph.D. thesis Univ. of Nebraska.

767. Kirby, John D. (1954) Moral Ideals and Institutions. Amer. J. Econ. Sociol. 13: 349-356. --On the conditions necessary for the "emergence of a new morality" opposite in tendency to prevailing ideologies.

768. ___ (1955) Are Morals Subversive? Amer. J. Econ. Sociol. 14: 335-346. --New moral ideals tend to be opposed to the values of an existing social order and to produce social change; historical examples given of the Compensatory Moral Ideal.

769. Klapp, Orrin E. (1954) Heroes, Villains and Fools, as Agents of Social Control. Amer. Sociol. Rev. 19: 56-62. --A typology of kinds of deviance from a normative behavioral center that serve a group as simplified norms of self-judgment and guarantors of socially shared sentiments.

770. Kluckhohn, Florence R. (1950) Dominant and Substitute Profiles of Cultural Orientations; Their Significance for the Analysis of Social Stratification. Soc. Forces 28: 376-393. --Conceptual scheme for cross-cultural study of value-orientations, with a re-evaluation of American class structure.

771. ___ (1953) American Women and American Values. IN: Lyman Bryson, ed. Facing the Future's Risks. New York: Harper. 175-199.

772. ___ (1953) Dominant and Variant Value-Orientations.
IN: Clyde Kluckhohn, Henry Murray and David
Schneider, eds. Personality in Nature, Culture
and Society. New York: Knopf. 342-357. --A
conceptual scheme for the cross-cultural study
of variations of basic value-orientations concerning human nature, man and nature, time,
personality and social relationships.

773. ___ (1956) Value Orientations. IN: Roy R. Grinker,
ed. Toward a Unified Theory of Human Behavior. New York: Basic Books. 83-93.

774. ___, Strodtbeck, Fred L. and Roberts, John M., with
the assistance of Kimball Romney and Clyde
Kluckhohn. (In progress) Variations in Value-
Orientations. Evanston, Ill.: Row, Peterson.
--Analysis of questionnaire results of a five-
culture study in New Mexico, showing dominant
and variant value-orientations.

775. Kobrin, Solomon (1951) The Conflict of Values in
Delinquency Areas. Amer. Sociol. Rev. 16:
653-662. --High delinquency rates in certain
urban areas attributed to "a duality of conduct
norms."

776. Kolb, William L. (1953) A Social-Psychological
Conception of Human Freedom. Ethics 63:
180-189. --Universal psychic needs as the basis
of the study of man.

777. ___ (1953) Values, Positivism, and the Functional
Theory of Religion; The Growth of a Moral
Dilemma. Soc. Forces 31: 305-311. --Dilemma
of sociologists of religion: the social risk in
spreading the idea that "belief in the ultimate
validity of values is necessary but illusory"
against the alternative of depriving people "of
the knowledge necessary for their freedom and
dignity."

778. ___ (1954) The Impingement of Moral Values on
     Sociology. Soc. Probl. 2: 66-70. --Moral
     norms governing the relationship between
     scientists and their subjects limit procedures
     and concepts without entering research as value
     biases.

779. ___ (1957) The Changing Prominence of Values in
     Modern Sociological Theory. IN: Howard
     Becker and Alvin Boskoff, eds. Modern Soci-
     ological Theory in Continuity and Change. New
     York: Dryden. 93-132. --The value concept in
     sociology linked to the normative and its devel-
     opment from the time of Thomas and Znaniecki's
     work in 1918 (see 888) reviewed.

780. Kosa, John (1957) The Rank Order of Peoples; A
     Study in National Stereotypes. J. Soc. Psychol.
     46: 311-320. --Value judgments of other ethnic
     groups from 112 Hungarians living in Canada.

781. Krishan, Daya (1954) Social Change; An Attempt at a
     Study in Conflicting Patterns of Social Action.
     Phil. Phen. Res. 14: 567-573. --Social action
     as perpetuating or changing existing values;
     the difference in means between totalitarian
     and democratic social control is the difference
     between regarding persons manipulatively or
     affectively.

782. Landis, Paul H. (1947) Social Policies in the Making.
     Boston: Heath.

783. +Lazarsfeld, Paul F., Berelson, Bernard and Gaudet,
     Hazel (1944) The People's Choice; How the
     Voter Makes Up His Mind in a Presidential
     Campaign. New York: Duell, Sloan and
     Pearce. --2nd ed. New York: Columbia Univ.
     Press, 1948. Method and theory to account for
     "all those conditions which determined the poli-

tical behavior of people," including ideology, interest, predispositions, pressures, etc.

—— Lee, Alfred McC. See Psychology.

784. Lévy-Bruhl, Lucien (1905) Ethics and Moral Science. Trans. by Elizabeth Lee. London: Constable. --Theoretical normative science logically impossible; recommends a sociology of morality that describes ethical data.

785. Lowenthal, Leo (1957) Literature and the Image of Man; Sociological Studies of the European Drama and Novel, 1600-1900. Boston: Beacon.

786. Lundberg, George A. (1939) Foundations of Sociology. New York: Macmillan. --See especially: Ch. 1, positivistic-pragmatic argument for the sociological study of values.

787. ___ (1947) Can Science Save Us? New York: Longmans, Green. --Prediction in ethics possible through scientific investigation.

788. ___ (1948) Semantics and the Value Problem. Soc. Forces 27: 114-117. --Positivist-linguistic analysis combined with pragmatist-cognitivist interpretation of ethical statements.

789. ___ (1949) Applying the Scientific Method to Social Phenomena. Sociol. Soc. Res. 34: 3-12. -- The potential benefit of the moral effects of applying social science in our society outweighs the possibility of use of science for immoral ends.

790. ___ (1950) Can Science Validate Ethics? Bull. Amer. Assn. Univ. Professors 36: 262-275. --Goals cannot be provided by science, but scientific prediction can help decide courses of action.

791. ___ (1952) Science, Scientists, and Values. Soc.
Forces 30: 373-379. --Argues for the separation
of science qua science from moral direction and
value judgments.

792. ___ (1955) Occupations and "Class" Alignments in the
United States, 1870-1950. Soc. Forces 34:
128-130.

793. Lyman, Elizabeth L. (1955) Occupational Differences
and the Values Attached to Work. Amer. J.
Sociol. 61: 138-144.

794. Lynd, Robert S. (1939) Knowledge for What? The
Place of Social Science in American Culture.
Princeton: Princeton Univ. Press. --See
especially: Ch. 5, Values and the Social
Sciences, a plea for the constructive use of
social science in social amelioration.

795. MacIver, Robert M. (1942) Social Causation. New
York: Ginn. --See especially: On values, 218-
219, 296-297, 308-313, 372-374, 388-389,
526-527.

796. ___ (1953) Government and the Goals of Economic
Activity. IN: A. Dudley Ward, ed. Goals
of Economic Life. New York: Harper.
181-203.

797. ___ (1955) Academic Freedom in Our Time. New
York: Columbia Univ. Press. --A report of the
American Academic Freedom Project of Columbia
University.

798. ___ (1955) The Social Significance of Professional
Ethics. Annals Amer. Acad. Pol. Soc. Sci.
297: 118-124. --Reprint from the May, 1922
issue.

799. Mannheim, Karl (1936) Ideology and Utopia; An
     Introduction to the Sociology of Knowledge.
     Trans. by Louis Wirth and Edward Shils. New
     York: Harcourt. --Moral norms and values,
     like all other ideas, vary with socio-economic
     patterns.

800. ___ (1943) Diagnosis of Our Time. London: Kegan
     Paul, Trench, Trubner. --See especially: 15-
     34, The Crisis in Valuation; 109-112 and 131-
     135, on religion and values. Recommends
     linking the study of values to knowledge of
     social process.

801. Mayer, Kurt B. (1955) Class and Society. New York:
     Doubleday. --See especially: Ch. 5, Prestige,
     Style of Life, and Status Groups in American
     Society, on value orientations and consumption
     patterns; Ch. 7, Class Awareness and Class
     Consciousness, on status awareness, prestige
     perspectives, class consciousness and the
     American Dream.

802. Mendenhall, Robert C. (1957) Differential Strains
     and Values in Two Mormon Ways of Life. Ph. D.
     Thesis, Harvard Univ.

803. Merrill, Francis E. (1955) Social Character and
     Social Problems. Soc. Probl. 3: 7-12. --
     Social problem defined as a threat to established
     social value; perception of social problems re-
     lated to Riesman's typology of social character.

804. Merton, Robert K. (1949) The Role of Applied Social
     Science in the Formation of Policy. Phil. Sci.
     16: 161-181. --Sociological analysis of applied
     social research in America, with attention to
     the value framework of the policy-maker and
     the research worker.

805. (1957) Social Theory and Social Structure. Rev. ed.
Glencoe, Ill.: Free Press. --See especially:
Ch. 4, Social Structure and Anomie; Ch. 5,
Continuities in the Theory of Social Structure
and Anomie; Ch. 6, Bureaucratic Structure and
Personality; Ch. 8, Contributions to the Theory
of Reference Group Behavior (with Alice S.
Rossi); Ch. 9, Continuities in the theory of
Reference Groups and Social Structure; Ch. 18,
Puritanism, Pietism, and Science.

—— Mills, C. Wright. See Psychology.

806. Moore, Wilbert E. (1945) Sociology of Economic
Organization. IN: Georges Gurvitch and
Wilbert E. Moore, eds. Twentieth Century
Sociology. New York: Philosophical Library.
438-465. --Economic behavior related to the
social order as a whole, including institutional
arrangements, social norms, value systems
and the "status of ends and motives. "

807. Morris, Richard T. (1956) A Typology of Norms.
Amer. Sociol. Rev. 21: 610-613.

808. Mosteller, Frederick and Nogee, P. (1951) An
Experimental Measurement of Utility. J. Pol.
Econ. 59: 371-404.

809. Mukerjee, Radhakamal (n. d.) The Institutional Theory
of Economics. London: Macmillan. --Norms of
social welfare and justice in the foundation of
institutional economics.

810. ___ (1946) The Conservation and Synthesis of Values
and Ideals by Institutions. Soc. Forces 25:
121-130.

811. ___ (1946) The Sociology of Values. Sociol. Soc.
Res. 31: 101-109.

812. ___ (1949) The Social Structure of Values. London: Macmillan. --Valuation as the fundamental factor in the sociological study of human relations, groups and institutions.

813. ___ (1950) Bridging Individual and Social Ethics. Soc. Forces 28: 262-270.

814. ___ (1952) The Dynamics of Morals. London: Macmillan.

815. ___ (1954) The Social Function of Art. New York: Philosophical Library. --Study in the comparative sociology of art, centered on the stable social values expressed and consolidated by art in different cultures and ages.

816. Munch, Peter A. (1954) The Peasant Movement in Norway; A Study in Class and Culture. Brit. J. Sociol. 5: 63-77. --Conflicts of norms, values and loyalties in the urbanization process.

817. Naegele, Kaspar D. (1949) From De Tocqueville to Myrdal; A Research Memorandum on Selected Studies of American Values. Harvard Values Study. Dittoed. --Summarizes conceptions of American values found in the literature and discusses problems of describing values and formulating value theory.

818. ___, O'Dea, Thomas F., Spencer, Katherine, Vidich, Arthur J. and Vogt, Evon Z. (1949) Memorandum; Some Problems in Value Research. Harvard Values Study. Dittoed. --Problems of definition and methodology in the study of values.

819. Narain, Dhirendra (1957) Hindu Character (A Few Glimpses). Bombay: Univ. of Bombay Press (Univ. of Bombay Publications in Sociology Series, No. 8). --A national character study

of Hindus, with Chinese data used for contrast;
analysis of proverbs; examination of the determination of Hindu ideals by the Bhagavadgītā.

820. Nisbet, Robert A. (1953) The Quest for Community;
A Study in the Ethics of Order and Freedom.
New York: Oxford Univ. Press. --Groups as
intermediate between individuals and society;
historical explanation of the contemporary
sense of difficulty in the realm of human relationships and values.

821. Nordskog, John E. (1954) Contemporary Social
Reform Movements. New York: Scribner's. --
A textbook, with an extensive bibliography.

822. Nottingham, Elizabeth K. (1954) Religion and
Society. New York: Doubleday. --Functional
analysis of the meaning of religious beliefs,
practices, symbols and moral values.

823. +O'Dea, Thomas F. (1954) The Sociology of Religion.
Amer. Cath. Sociol. Rev. 15: 73-103. --
Current analyses in the sociology of religion
criticized; proposal of a non-normative study
of religion. Extensive bibliography.

824. ___ (1957) The Mormons. Chicago: Univ. of Chicago
Press. --Historical and ethnographic study of
Mormon values and their influence on Mormon
life. See especially: Ch. 6, The Values of
Mormonism.

—— Pareto, Vilfredo. See Economics.

825. Parsons, Talcott (1935) The Place of Ultimate Values
in Sociological Theory. Ethics 45: 282-316.

826. ___ (1951) The Social System. Glencoe, Ill.: Free
     Press. --See especially: Chs. 8-9, theory of
     values and value-orientations, their influence
     on social structure and their use in analyzing
     social systems in the theory of social action.

827. ___ (1954) Essays in Sociological Theory. Rev.
     ed. Glencoe, Ill.: Free Press. --Conflicts,
     integration and systems of values; values
     related to kinship, political ideologies, sex,
     social class, the professions.

828. ___ (1954) The Incest Taboo in Relation to Social
     Structure and the Socialization of the Child.
     Brit. J. Sociol. 5: 101-117.

829. ___ (In Progress) On American Society. Glencoe,
     Ill.: Free Press. --See especially: Section
     on American Values.

830. ___ and Bales, Robert F. and Shils, Edward A.
     (1953) Working Papers in the Theory of Action.
     Glencoe, Ill.: Free Press. --Emendation of
     theory of action, including value-orientation
     pattern.

831. ___ and Shils, Edward A., eds. (1951) Toward a
     General Theory of Action. Cambridge: Harvard
     Univ. Press. --See especially: Part II, Values,
     Motives, and Systems of Action, patterns of
     value-orientations in the organization of person-
     ality, social systems and culture.

832. ___ and White, Winston (In Progress) Continuity and
     Change in American Values. IN: Seymour
     M. Lipset and Leo Lowenthal, eds. Continuities
     of Social Research (Tentative Title). Glencoe,
     Ill.: Free Press.

833. Polanyi, Michael (1946) Science, Faith and Society. London: Oxford Univ. Press.

834. ___ (1951) The Logic of Liberty. Chicago: Univ. of Chicago Press.

835. Ramsey, Charles E. and Nelson, Lowry (1956) Change in Values and Attitudes Toward the Family. Amer. Sociol. Rev. 21: 605-609.

836. Reid, Ira De A. (1955) Social Protest; Cue and Catharsis. Phylon 16: 141-147. --"Social protest" as a conceptual tool for more precise exploration of social change, social action and social conflict; analysis of social protest will reveal new value systems and the value systems that are in conflict.

837. Rieff, Philip (1957) Freudian Ethics and the Idea of Reason. Ethics 67: 169-183. --Compares Freudian and Platonic psychology, discusses Freud's concept of ego as leading to rational grasp of "reality" as the ultimate value.

838. Riemer, Svend (1949) Values and Standards in Research. Amer. J. Sociol. 55: 131-136. -- Ways in which the objectivity of social research may be affected by the level of abstraction on which it is conducted; the necessity for adequate standards to deal with concrete value specifications.

839. Riesman, David (1950) The Lonely Crowd; A Study of the Changing American Character. New Haven: Yale Univ. Press. --The effects of changes in population, economic structure and child-rearing on the social character and values of Americans, particularly urban upper-middle class.

840. ___ (1952) Some Observations on the Study of American Character. Psychiatry 15: 333-338.

841. ___ (1952) Values in Context. Amer. Scholar 22: 29-39. --The dangers of behavioral science manipulation of human beings noted, a restrained approach to scientific normativeness advocated.

842. ___ (1954) Individualism Reconsidered and Other Essays. Glencoe, Ill.: Free Press. --Values of minority groups, American popular culture, the aging process, public opinion reviewed. Attacks "groupism" in favor of a new individualism; attacks normative behavioral science programs in favor of "moral experimentalism."

843. Rioux, Marcel (1956) Remarques sur les Valeurs et les Attitudes des Adolescents d'une Communauté Agricole du Québec. Contributions à l'Etude des Sciences de l'Homme, Montréal 3: 133-143.

844. Roethlisberger, Fritz J. (1942) Management and Morale. Cambridge: Harvard Univ. Press. -- Social values, social structure and efficiency in industry.

845. ___ and Dickson, W. J. (1939) Management and the Worker. Cambridge: Harvard Univ. Press. -- Report on the Hawthorne experiments in the social organization, morale and efficiency of industrial workers.

___ Rose, Arnold M. See Psychology.

846. Rosenberg, Morris (1949) The Social Roots of Formalism. J. Soc. Issues 5: 14-23. --Relates middle-class values, functional in the status-prestige race, to emotional suppression and overemphasis on forms.

847.   ___ and Bellin, Seymour (1950) Value Patterns in the
       Trade Union Press. Internatl. J. Opinion and
       Attitude Research 3: 555-574.

848.   ___, with Suchman, Edward A. and Goldsen, Rose K.
       (1957) Occupations and Values. Glencoe, Ill. :
       Free Press. --The importance of personality
       differences and interpersonal factors in oc-
       cupational choices of college students, with
       special attention to changes of occupation.

849. Rossi, Peter H. (1958) Community Decision-Making.
      IN: Roland Young, ed. Approaches to the
      Study of Politics. Evanston: Northwestern
      Univ. Press. 363-382. --Critical review of
      approaches through decision-maker studies,
      decision process studies and studies of partisans.

850. Rubin, Morton (1958) Localism and Related Values
      among Negroes in a Southern Rural Community.
      Soc. Forces 36: 263-267. --Value orientations
      in relation to personal background data show
      that this sub-society "no longer fits the model
      of the folk society, if it ever did. "

851. Ryan, Bryce F. and Straus, Murray A. (1954) The
      Integration of Sinhalese Society. Res. Stud.
      Washington 22: 179-227. --Flexibility of norms,
      tolerance of non-normative behavior and un-
      developed values of group organization related
      to the concept of a "loosely structured" society.

852. Salisbury, W. Seward (1958) Religion and Seculariza-
      tion. Soc. Forces 36: 197-205. --Degrees of
      internalization of selected sacred values in
      relation to behavior consistent with the sacred
      value involved; United States undergraduate
      student sample.

853. Saunders, Lyle (1954) Cultural Difference and Medical Care; The Case of the Spanish-Speaking People of the Southwest. New York: Russell Sage Foundation. --The negative influence of beliefs and values of Spanish-speaking Americans on their reaction to modern medicine.

854. Schneider, Louis and Brodbeck, Arthur J. (1955) Some Notes on Moral Paradoxes in Race Relations. Phylon 16: 149-158. --Difficulties in a simple, moralistic interpretation of race relations between white and Negro; suggests a "morally relevant" social science approach through establishing specific links between situation and moral response.

855. Schücking, L. L. (1944) The Sociology of Literary Taste. London: Kegan Paul, Trench and Trubner.

856. Seeman, Melvin (1947) Moral Judgment; A Study in Racial Frames of Reference. Amer. Sociol. Rev. 12: 404-411. --An experiment on the attitudes of college students towards sex and family morality of Negroes and whites, with discussion of the relation of moral judgment to prejudice.

857. ___ (1956) Intellectual Perspective and Adjustment to Minority Status. Soc. Probl. 3: 142-153. -- Adjustment to value conflict in marginal status situation leads to learning the value of and techniques for questioning "givens" and seeking new solutions, hence to creativity; methodology and findings on Jewish sample.

858. Segerstedt, Torngy T. (1956) The Uppsala School of Sociology. Acta Sociol. 1: 85-119. --Swedish sociology, developed from social philosophy,

concerned with methodological problems and values; theoretical definitions and group model for empirical research on communication of norms.

859. Shepard, Herbert A. (1956) Basic Research and the Social System of Pure Science. Phil. Sci. 23: 48-57. --Discusses the central value system and the personal and social norms of pure science.

860. Shils, Edward A. (1949) Social Science and Social Policy. Phil. Sci. 16: 219-242. --Historical and analytic review of the role of social scientists in the formulation of the social policy of modern nations.

861. +___ (1956) The Torment of Secrecy; The Background and Consequences of American Security Policies. Glencoe, Ill.: Free Press. --"An essay in sociological analysis and political philosophy," analyzing McCarthyism.

862. ___ (1957) Primordial, Personal, Sacred and Civil Ties; Some Particular Observations on the Relationships of Sociological Research and Theory. Brit. J. Sociol. 8: 130-145. --On the role of primary groups in the integration of society and the varying intensities of attachment to the ultimate values of the society.

863. Simmel, Georg (1892-93) Einleitung in die Moral-wissenschaft; Eine Kritik der ethischen Grundbegriffe. Berlin. 2 vols.

864. +___ (1950) The Sociology of Georg Simmel. Trans. by Kurt H. Wolff. Glencoe, Ill.: Free Press. --Principally formal sociology, but with treatment of freedom and other ethico-philo-sophical ideas.

865. Simpson, George (1950) The Scientist -- Technician or Moralist? Phil. Sci. 17: 95-108. --Failure to understand the unity of reason and morality explains bifurcation of science and morality; contemporary science is not non-moral but uncritically accepts conventional social values.

866. ___ (1953) Science as Morality; An Essay Towards Unity. Yellow Springs, Ohio: Humanist Press. --Explores the possibility of unifying science and morality, arguing that unity already exists, warning social scientists against becoming mere technicians.

867. Sims, Newell L. (1940) Democracy under Three Different Cultures. Amer. Sociol. Rev. 5: 56-66. --The character structure of Englishmen, Frenchmen and Americans, with particular reference to political behavior and central cultural values.

868. +Sjoberg, Gideon (1955) The Comparative Method in the Social Sciences. Phil. Sci. 22: 106-117. --Methodological problems in deriving and applying "universal categories" and "invariant points of reference" in cross-cultural research and analysis.

869. Small, Albion W. (1905) General Sociology. Chicago: Univ. of Chicago Press. --See especially: Ch. 41. "Good" defined as the promotion of social process, with values to be adapted to specific situations.

870. Smith, Harvey L. (1954) The Value Context of Psychology. Amer. Psychol. 9: 532-535. --The psychologist's position in relation to other psychotherapists and the "institutional complex within which psychology is defining its place. "

871. Sorokin, Pitirim (1942) Man and Society in Calamity.
New York: Dutton. --Historical-sociological
analysis of moral behavior in war, famine, and
other crises.

872. ___ (1950) Altruistic Love; A Study of American
"Good Neighbors" and Christian Saints. Boston:
Beacon Press. --Proposals for "altruistic
individualism" and critique of various plans for
attaining world peace and cooperation.

873. Spencer, Herbert (1895) Principles of Ethics. New
York: Appleton. --Happiness as the goal of ethics;
the good identified with the more evolved, the
bad with the less evolved.

874. Srinivas, M. N. (1956) A Note on Sanskritization and
Westernization. Far Eastern Quart. 15: 481-
496. Reprinted in: Introduction to the Civilization of India. Chicago: Univ. of Chicago Press,
Syllabus Division, 1957. 365-380.

875. Stein, Herman D. and Cloward, Richard A., eds.
(1957) Social Perspectives on Behavior.
Glencoe, Ill.: Free Press. --See especially:
Part I, on values.

876. Stouffer, Samuel A. (1949) An Analysis of Conflicting
Social Norms. Amer. Sociol. Rev. 14: 707-
717. --A study, in terms of role theory, of
student values concerning cheating on examinations.

877. +___ (1955) Communism, Conformity and Civil
Liberties. Garden City, N.Y.: Doubleday.

878. ___ and Toby, Jackson (1951) Role Conflict and
Personality. Amer. J. Sociol. 56: 395-406. --
Explores procedures to link study of social

norms with study of personality predispositions; questionnaire data from students on hypothetical situations.

879. Straus, Jacqueline H. and Straus, Murray A. (1953) Suicide, Homicide and Social Structure in Ceylon. Amer. J. Sociol. 58: 461-469. -- Suicide and homicide related to values.

880. Strodtbeck, Fred L. (1958) Family Interaction, Values and Achievement. IN: D. McClelland, A. Baldwin, U. Bronfenbrenner and F. L. Strodtbeck, eds. Talent and Society. New York: Nostrand. --Value-orientations related to power positions in face-to-face groups; data from a 4-place value-attitude scale, used with American Jewish and Italian fathers and sons as subjects.

881. +__ and Hare, A. Paul (1954) Bibliography of Small Group Research (from 1900 through 1953). Sociometry 17: 107-178.

882. Suchman, Edward A., Williams, Robin M., Jr. and Goldsen, Rose K. (1953) Student Reaction to Impending Military Service. Amer. Sociol. Rev. 18: 293-304. --Personal, ideological and value factors as determinants of attitudes.

883. Sumner, William Graham (1906) Folkways. Boston: Ginn. --Reprinted 1934. Morality, both social and philosophical, as part of the folkways, therefore expressions of custom, not rational judgments.

884. Sutton, Francis X., Harris, S. E. and Kaysen, K. (1956) The American Business Creed. Cambridge: Harvard Univ. Press.

885. Tambiah, S. J. and Ryan, Bryce (1957) Secularization
    of Family Values in Ceylon. Amer. Sociol. Rev.
    22: 292-299. --Exposure to secularizing in-
    fluence of urban contact an inadequate measure
    of secularization of family values; changes occur
    first in "ideological systems not possessing
    such central moral significance."

886. Thomas, John L. (1954) Sex and Society. Soc. Order
    4: 242-248. --Three divergent attitudes in
    contemporary United States towards sex be-
    havior as a moral question.

887. Thomas, William I. (1936) The Comparative Study of
    Cultures. Amer. J. Sociol. 42: 177-185. --
    An examination of values as related to the
    comparative method.

888. ___ and Znaniecki, Florian (1918-1921) The Polish
    Peasant in Europe and America. Boston:
    Richard G. Badger. 5 vols. --Reissued in 1927,
    New York: Knopf, 2 vols. A pioneer use of the
    value concept in a detailed study of acculturation.

889. Tomasic, Dinko (1948) Personality and Culture in
    Eastern European Politics. New York: Stewart.
    --Comparison of institutions and ideologies,
    culture and personality, changes from rural
    to urban patterns, of Dinaric and Zadruga groups
    of Eastern Europe.

890. Tonnies, Ferdinand (1940) Fundamental Concepts of
    Sociology. Trans. and Supplemented by
    Charles P. Loomis. New York: American
    Book. --Classic discussion of economic,
    political and spiritual values and of morality
    and law in the historical shift from Gemeinschaft
    to Gesellschaft.

891. Tumin, Melvin (1945) Culture, Genuine and Spurious; A Re-Evaluation. Amer. Sociol Rev. 10: 199-207. --Comparison of Ladino and Indian values in Guatemala; relations of genuine to folk culture and spurious to secular culture.

892. ___ (1954) Obstacles to Creativity. Etc. 11: 261-271. --Creativity in relation to social milieu; modern social conditions as producing four anti-creative "pathologies"; suggests redirecting social rewards for creativity.

893. ___ and Feldman, Arnold S. (1956) Status, Perspective and Achievement; Education and Class Structure in Puerto Rico. Amer. Sociol. Rev. 21: 464-472. --Effect of socio-economic status on perspective and achievement; "relatively small increments of education and income make relatively large differences in the intelligence and ambition with which new values are pursued, once a minimum level has been reached."

894. Turner, Ralph H. (1951) The Experience of Vertical Mobility and Personal Values. Proc. Pacific Sociol. Soc., published as Res. Stud. Washington 19: 89-92.

895. ___ (1952) Moral Judgment; A Study in Roles. Amer. Sociol. Rev. 17: 70-77. --Reactions of individuals to hypothetical moral deviation in friends.

896. +___ (1953) The Quest for Universals in Sociological Research. Amer. Sociol. Rev. 18: 604-611.

897. ___ (1954) Self and Other in Moral Judgment. Amer. Sociol. Rev. 19: 249-259.

898. ___ (1954) Value-Conflict in Social Disorganization. Sociol. Soc. Res. 38: 301-308.

899. ___ (1955) Reference Groups of Future-Oriented Men. Soc. Forces 34: 130-136. --Upward mobility strivings related to reference groups and success values, ethical-moral values and "richness of life." Questionnaire data from college students.

900. ___ (1956) Role-Taking, Role Standpoint, and Reference-Group Behavior. Amer. J. Sociol. 61: 316-328. --Role defined as "a set of norms," role-taking and reference-group behavior related to the derivation, validation and implementation of values.

901. +Vedder, Clyde B., Koenig, Samuel and Clark, Robert E. (1953) Criminology; A Book of Readings. New York: Dryden.

902. Warren, Roland L. (1941) Philosophy and Social Science in the Field of Values. J. Phil. 38: 404-409.

903. Wayne, Ivor (1956) American and Soviet Themes and Values; A Content Analysis of Pictures in Popular Magazines. Publ. Opin. Quart. 20: 314-320. --Pictures from Life and Ogonek analyzed by means of content categories based on Spranger's value types; summary table of United States-Soviet differences.

904. Weber, Max (1930) The Protestant Ethic and the Spirit of Capitalism. Trans. by Talcott Parsons. New York: Scribner's. --Classic study of the influence of ethical principles on economic development.

905. +___ (1947) The Theory of Social and Economic Organization. Trans. by A. M. Henderson and Talcott Parsons. New York: Oxford Univ. Press.

906. ___ (1949) The Methodology of the Social Sciences. Trans. by Edward A. Shils and Henry A. Finch. Glencoe, Ill. : Free Press. --See especially: Chs. 1-2, on the meaning of ethical neutrality and the separation of normative from descriptive knowledge.

907. Whyte, William F. , Jr. (1943) A Challenge to Political Scientists. Amer. Pol. Sci. Rev. 37: 692-697. -- An attack on the lack of scientific detachment of political scientists. (See 964, reply; 908 and 965, for continuation.)

908. ___ (1946) Politics and Ethics; A Reply to John H. Hallowell. Amer. Pol. Sci. Rev. 40: 301-307. --Renewal of attack on political scientists for failure to do detached research. (See 907 and 964.)

909. ___ (1956) The Organization Man. New York: Simon and Schuster. --Characteristics, habits, milieu and ideology of the "organization man" in the United States.

910. Wiese, Leopold von (1947) Ethik in der Schauweise der Wissenschaften von Menschen und von der Gesellschaft. Bern: A. Francke. --Criticizes sociological and anthropological theories of the development of morality; develops a theory of the influence of social situations on the formation of ethical theories; examines a variety of ethical theories; proposes universal ethical "oughts. "

911. Wilkening, Eugene A. (1955) Techniques of Assessing Farm Family Values. Rural Sociol. 19: 39- 49. --Comparison of measures of verbal and behavioral values in interviewing.

912. Williams, Robin M. , Jr. (1951) American Society; A Sociological Interpretation. New York: Knopf. --See especially: Institutional Variation; The

-178-

Evasion of Normative Patterns; Value Orientations in American Society, for description and discussion of dominant American values.

913. ___ (1956) Religion, Value-Orientations, and Intergroup Conflict. J. Soc. Issues 12: 12-20. -- Religious conflict interpreted through differences in basic values and beliefs among the main religious groupings in the United States.

914. Willie, Charles V. (1954) Group Relationships of the Elderly in Our Culture. Soc. Casework 35: 206-212. --Impact of group relationships upon behavior of old people, in terms of the aged population's relation to the total social structure, value system and changes with age of roles in family and work groups.

915. +Wolff, Kurt H. (1945) A Methodological Note on the Empirical Establishment of Culture Patterns. Amer. Sociol. Rev. 10: 176-184. --Procedures in the holistic study of a culture.

916. Woods, Sister Frances Jerome (1956) Cultural Values of American Ethnic Groups. New York: Harper. --Theoretical and descriptive treatment of economic and social values, differential age, sex and family roles, and language as a value. Bibliography of 292 items.

917. Wooton, Barbara (1951) Testament for Social Science-- An Essay in the Application of Scientific Method to Human Problems. New York: Norton. --See especially: Discussion of morals and the arts in the framework of contrasting scientific and pre-scientific ways of thinking.

918. +Zelditch, Morris, Jr. (1955) Authority and Solidarity in Three Southwestern Communities. Ph. D. Thesis, Harvard Univ.

919. ___ (1957-58) "Values" Institutionalized in the Family. Antioch Rev. 17: 455-468. --"Family" as a normative concept; application of norms and values to concrete social situations.

920. Znaniecki, Florian (1952) Should Sociologists Be Also Philosophers of Values? Sociol. Soc. Res. 37: 79-84. --Applied social science inevitably becomes involved in evaluative and normative issues, hence applied sociologists should understand the philosophic implications of social problems and learn enough philosophy "to justify their choice of goals."

IV. POLITICAL SCIENCE, PUBLIC ADMINISTRATION AND GOVERNMENT

921. +Aiyar, C. P. Ramaswami (1951) The Philosophical Basis of Indian Legal and Social Systems. IN: Charles A. Moore, ed. Essays in East-West Philosophy. Honolulu: Univ. of Hawaii Press. 336-352.

922. Almond, Gabriel A. (1946) Politics, Science, and Ethics. Amer. Pol. Sci. Rev. 40: 283-293. -- The place of values in political science inquiry.

923. ___ (1950) The American People and Foreign Policy. New York: Harcourt. --Quantitative results of public opinion polls, the concept of American national character and variation of "moods" in reactions to events combined in analysis.

924. Appleby, Paul H. (1949) Policy and Administration. University, Ala.: Univ. of Alabama Press.

925. ___ (1952) Morality and Administration in Democratic Government. Baton Rouge: Louisiana State Univ. Press. --Focussed on the general moral problem of democracy as the protection and promotion of public interest; responsibility shared by administrators, legislators and politicians.

926. +Apter, David (1955) The Gold Coast in Transition. Princeton: Princeton Univ. Press. --Structural-functional analysis of the political transformation of a West African underdeveloped area as the "transfer" of Western institutions.

927. Barker, Ernest (1951) Principles of Social and Political Theory. New York: Oxford Univ.

Press. --A classical political science view of
the foundations of democratic theory.

928. Bayliff, Russell E. et al. (1954) Values and Policy in
American Society. Dubuque, Iowa: Wm. C.
Brown. --The "welfare standard" as a criterion
of ethical value for evaluating social policies.

929. Brecht, Arnold (1947) Beyond Relativism in Political
Theory. Amer. Pol. Sci. Rev. 41: 470-488. --
The place of value commitments in political
science.

930. +Brookings Institution (1955) Research Frontiers in
Politics and Government, Brookings Lectures,
1955. Washington, D. C.: Brookings Institution. --Eight summaries of developments in
theory and method.

931. Brown, D. Mackenzie (1953) The Premises of Indian
Political Thought. Western Pol. Quart. 6:
243-249. --Outline of the political thought of
India prior to Western influence as rooted in
the ethical ideas of the Vedas and other early
writings.

932. Burdeau, Georges (1949-1950) Traité de Science
Politique. Paris: Librairie Générale de Droit
et de Jurisprudence. 3 vols.--Vol. I: Le
Pouvoir politique; Vol. II: L'Etat; Vol. III: Le
Statut du Pouvoir dans l'Etat. Attempts to unify
political science and public law (droit public).

933. Carter, Roy E., Jr. (1956) An Experiment in Value
Measurement. Amer. Sociol. Rev. 21: 156-
163. --Beliefs and values of American,
Filipino and East Indian college students tested
through eliciting approval or disapproval of
national goals for a mythical country.

934. Cole, G. D. H. (1953, 1954, 1956) A History of
Socialist Thought. New York: St. Martin's
Press. --Vol. I: The Forerunners, 1789-
1850; Vol. II: Marxism and Anarchism,
1850-1890; Vol. III: The Second International, 1889-1914, in two parts.

935. ___ (1957) Sociology and Social Policy. Brit. J.
Sociol. 8: 158-171. --Value-free sociology
not useful for formulating social policy; reviews basic values of Western culture.

936. Cook, Thomas I. (1940) Politics, Sociology, and
Values. J. Soc. Phil. 6: 35-46.

937. ___ and Moos, Malcolm (1952) Foreign Policy; The
Realism of Idealism. Amer. Pol. Sci. Rev.
46: 343-356.

938. Dahl, Robert A. (1955) Hierarchy, Democracy, and
Bargaining in Politics and Economics. IN:
Research Frontiers in Politics and Government, Brookings Lectures, 1955. Washington,
D.C.: Brookings Institution. 45-69. --See
especially: Types of Decision-Making Processes; The Problem of Power; The Problem
of the Policy-Maker.

939. ___ (1956) A Preface to Democratic Theory. Chicago:
Univ. of Chicago Press. --Critique of theories
of democracy; proposal for formulating "a satisfactory theory of democratic politics."

940. ___ and Lindblom, Charles E. (1953) Politics, Economics, and Welfare. New York: Harper. --
Uniform vocabulary for the analysis of both
economics and political science.

941. Deutsch, Karl W. (1952) Communication Theory and
Social Science. Amer. J. Orthopsychiat. 22:
469-483. --Cybernetics as an approach to a

theory of self-determination and a theory of growth.

942. ___ (1953) Political Community at the International Level; Problems of Definition and Measurement. Princeton: Princeton Univ. Press.-- Hypotheses and methods for an interdisciplinary approach to political phenomena, values as a part of culture and as an independent, qualitative variable in relation to assimilation and mobilization.

943. Dexter, Lewis A. (1946) Political Processes and Judgments of Value. Amer. Pol. Sci. Rev. 40: 294-301.--The role of values in political science inquiry.

944. Douglas, Paul H. (1952) Ethics in Government. Cambridge: Harvard Univ. Press. Also: Toronto: Reginald Saunders.--A U. S. Senator's lectures on ethical principles and corruption in government; return to simple honesty the best remedy for corruption.

945. Drucker, Peter F. (1939) The End of Economic Man; A Study of the New Totalitarianism. New York: John Day.

946. Duclos, Pierre (1955) De la Démocratie et de ses Styles. Rev. Française de Sci. Pol. 5: 632-640.--Comparative analysis of Western, or classical, and Eastern, or Marxist, democracy.

947. Duguit, Leon (1919) Law in the Modern State. Trans. by Frida and Harold Laski. New York: Huebsch. --An influential analysis.

948. +Duverger, Maurice (1949) Manuel de Droit Constitutionnel et de Sciences Politiques. Rev. ed. Paris: Presses Universitaires de France.-- Combined political science and sociological

approach in the analysis of French political institutions.

949. Easton, David (1950) Harold Lasswell; Policy Scientist for a Democratic Society. J. Pol. 12: 450-477.

950. ___ (1951) The Decline of Modern Political Theory. J. Pol. 13: 36-58.--See especially: II, on the need for value theory as a condition of renewed creativity in political theory.

951. ___ (1953) The Political System; An Inquiry into the State of Political Science. New York: Knopf.-- Urges development of a general systematic theory for the study of political science, with a valuational frame of reference in view of the "inextricable relation of facts and values." See especially: Ch. 9, The Moral Foundations of Theoretical Research.

952. ___ (1955) Shifting Images of Social Science and Values. Antioch Rev. 15: 3-18.--Suggests combination in social science of the synthesizing and socially relevant elements of pre-modern moral philosophy with modern empirical techniques and knowledge.

953. Eulau, Heinz (1958) H. D. Lasswell's Developmental Analysis. Western Pol. Quart 11: 229-242.-- See especially: The Nature of Decision; Facts, Values and Expectations; Developmental Analysis and Policy Science.

954. +___, Eldersveld, Samuel J. and Janowitz, Morris, eds. (1956) Political Behavior; A Reader in Theory and Research. Glencoe, Ill.: Free Press.--See especially: Section III, Orientations Toward the Political Process; Section V, Arenas of Political Decision-Making. Extended bibliography.

955. Fainsod, Merle (1949) Recent Developments in Soviet Public Administration. J. Pol. 11: 679-714. -- Norms, techniques and relationship to party of Soviet public administration.

956. +Ferrero, Guglielmo (1942) The Principles of Power; The Great Political Crises of History. Trans. by Theodore R. Jaeckel. New York: Putnam. -- The conditions of legitimate government approached through political psychology.

957. Field, G. Lowell (1949) Law as an Objective Political Concept. Amer. Pol. Sci. Rev. 43: 229-249. --Detailed analysis of the logic of normative systems, on the assumption "that rigid conceptual clarity in distinguishing norm and fact is necessary for the progress of these [the social science] disciplines."

958. Finer, Herman (1945) Towards a Democratic Theory. Amer. Pol. Sci. Rev. 39: 249-268. --On the necessity of directed action to preserve and enhance democratic government.

959. Friedrich, Carl J. (1946) Constitutional Government and Democracy; Theory and Practice in Europe and America. Boston: Ginn. --Revision of the author's Constitutional Government and Politics, 1937. Extensive bibliography.

960. +___ (1958) Political Philosophy and the Science of Politics. IN: Roland Young, ed. Approaches to the Study of Politics. Evanston: Northwestern Univ. Press. 172-188.

961. ___ and Mason, Edward S., eds. (1941) Public Policy. Cambridge: Harvard Univ. Press.

962. Graham, George A. (1952) Morality in American Politics. New York: Random House. -- Analysis of American moral principles and of

the basic sources of political immorality, using chiefly hearings and reports of the (Douglas)
Committee on Ethical Standards in Government.

963. Gulick, Luther (1937) Science, Values, and Public
Administration. IN: Luther Gulick and L.
Urwick, eds. Papers on the Science of Ad-
ministration. New York: Institute of Public
Administration. 191-195.

964. Hallowell, John H. (1944) Politics and Ethics.
Amer. Pol. Sci. Rev. 38: 639-655. --Criti-
cizes positivist view that scientific inquiry in
unconcerned with ethical and value judgments.
(A reply to Whyte, 907. See also: 965 and
908, for continuation of the controversy.)

965. ___ (1946) Politics and Ethics; A Rejoinder to
William F. Whyte. Amer. Pol. Sci. Rev. 40:
307-312. --The place of value considerations
in political science. (See 907, 908, and 964.)

966. ___ (1954) The Moral Foundation of Democracy.
Chicago: Univ. of Chicago Press. --Democracy
as based on justice, ethical rightness and human nature; centers on Platonic theory.

967. Herring, Pendleton (1940) The Politics of Democracy.
New York: Norton. --Includes treatment of
ethical issues in democratic theory and practice.

968. Hersch, Jeanne (1956) Idéologies et réalité; Essai
d'orientation politique. Paris: Plon. --Five
contemporary European ideologies distinguished
(fascist, communist, liberal-conservative,
progressive democratic and socialist); concludes with a synthesis of political democracy
and economic socialism.

969. Herz, John H. (1951) <u>Political Realism and Political Idealism</u>. Chicago: Univ. of Chicago Press. --Criticism of theories of democracy, proposal of alternative theory.

970. Hillenbrand, Martin J. (1949) <u>Power and Morals</u>. New York: Columbia Univ. Press. --Develops the argument that only valid ethical norms can serve safely as a control on power.

971. Hodson, H. V. (1949) <u>Twientieth Century Empire</u>. London: Faber. --Proposal of policy for colonial administration to adjust the principle of the British Empire system to contemporary conditions.

972. Hofstadter, Richard (1944) <u>Social Darwinism in American Thought, 1860-1915</u>. Philadelphia: Univ. of Pennsylvania Press. Also: London: Milford.

973. ___ and Metzger, Walter P. (1955) <u>The Development of Academic Freedom in the United States</u>. New York: Columbia Univ. Press. --A report of the American Academic Freedom Project of Columbia University.

974. +Holcombe, Arthur N. (1948) <u>Human Rights in the Modern World</u>. New York: New York Univ. Press.

975. Hollister, William W. (1948) <u>Government and the Arts of Obedience</u>. New York: King's Crown Press. --Political philosophy and analysis.

976. Jacobson, Norman (1952) <u>Values and Science in Political Theory</u>. A paper read before the Conference on Reason and Value of the Pacific Coast Committee for the Humanities, A.C.L.S., Mills College, Oakland, California, Sept. 13, 1952. --Criticism of methodologically-oriented

political science theories for their rejection of
value problems.

977. ___ (1958) The Unity of Political Theory; Science,
Morals, and Politics. IN: Roland Young, ed.
Approaches to the Study of Politics. Evanston:
Northwestern Univ. Press. 115-124.

978. Jászi, Oscar and Lewis, John D. (1957) Against the
Tyrant. Glencoe, Ill.: Free Press. --Consti-
tutions as devices against tyrants, related to
shared values in political communities.

979. Jouvenel, Bertrand de (1949) On Power; Its Nature
and the History of Its Growth. New York:
Viking. --Criticism of modern democracy as
developing towards enslavement rather than
freedom; the preservation of freedom better
accomplished by aristocrats.

980. ___ (1951) The Ethics of Redistribution. Cambridge:
Cambridge Univ. Press. --Lectures on redistribution of income and the lost socialist ideal
of equality.

981. ___ (1955) De la Souveraineté; A la recherche du
bien politique. Paris: Editions M. -Th.
Génin, Librairie de Médicis. --Translated into
English as: Sovereignty; An Inquiry into the
Political Good, by J. F. Huntington, Chicago:
Univ. of Chicago Press, 1957. An exploratory
essay in the theory and philosophy of sover-
eignty and public welfare.

982. Kaufman, Herbert (1956) Emerging Conflicts in the
Doctrines of Public Administration. Amer. Pol.
Sci. Rev. 50: 1057-1073. --Historical changes
and contemporary conflict of "three values ...
representativeness, neutral competence, and
executive leadership. "

983. Kecskemeti, Paul (1952) Meaning, Communication, and Value. Chicago: Univ. of Chicago Press. --Ethical assertions, though not scientific, amenable to rational analysis in an appropriate linguistic framework.

984. +Kelsen, Hans (1944) Peace Through Law. Chapel Hill: Univ. of North Carolina Press. --Law as the creator of society and an instrument of peace.

985. ___ (1948) Absolutism and Relativism in Philosophy and Politics. Amer. Pol. Sci. Rev. 42: 906-914.

986. ___ (1951) Science and Politics. Amer. Pol. Sci. Rev. 45: 641-661. --Relationship of facts and values in political science.

987. + ___ (1952) Principles of International Law. New York: Rinehart.

988. ___ (1955) Foundations of Democracy. Ethics 66: 1-101. --Ethical and philosophical principles of Soviet, Rousseauan and other varieties of democracy.

989. Laski, Harold J. (1925) A Grammar of Politics. London: Allen and Unwin. --"A new political philosophy [for] ... a new world." See especially: Ch. 1, The Purpose of Social Organisation; Ch. 3, Rights; Ch. 4, Liberty and Equality; Ch. 8, Political Institutions; Ch. 10, The Judicial Process; Ch. 11, International Organisation.

990. ___ (1936) The Rise of European Liberalism. London: Allen and Unwin.

991. ___ (1943) Reflections on the Revolution of Our Time.
      New York: Viking. --The Second World War
      viewed as part of a long-term revolution, re-
      lated to the problems of preserving and ex-
      tending democratic values and institutions.

992. ___ (1948) The American Democracy; A Commentary
      and an Interpretation. New York: Viking. --
      Description of the American tradition, ideology,
      institutions, culture, religion and social habits.
      See especially: Ch. 14, Americanism as a
      Principle of Civilization, for discussion of the
      "gap between appearance and reality which pro-
      foundly affects the values implicit in Ameri-
      canism."

993. Lasswell, Harold D. (1935) World Politics and Per-
      sonal Insecurity. New York: McGraw-Hill.
      Also: London: Whittlesey House.

994. ___ (1936) Politics; Who Gets What, When and How.
      New York: McGraw-Hill. Also: London:
      Whittlesey House.

995. ___ (1948) The Analysis of Political Behavior; An
      Empirical Approach. London: Kegan Paul,
      Trench, Trubner. --A collection of articles,
      unified by the general theme that the study of
      political behavior involves simultaneously the
      social sciences, ethics and social philosophy.

996. ___ (1948) Power and Personality. New York:
      Norton. --Exploration of scientific data rele-
      vant to the development of an "elite" that
      would promote the interests of freedom in
      society.

997. ___ (1955) Current Studies of the Decision Process;
      Automation vs. Creativity. Western Pol.
      Quart. 8: 381-399.

998. ___ (1956) Impact of Psychoanalytic Thinking on the
Social Sciences. IN: Leonard White, ed. The
State of the Social Sciences. Chicago: Univ.
of Chicago Press. 84-115. --See especially:
discussion of "value disclosure," "man's pursuit of values" and the relation of physician's
and patient's values to the therapeutic
process.

999. ___ (1957) The Normative Impact of the Behavioral
Sciences. Ethics 67: 1-42. --Review of practical effects of activities of behavioral scientists. See especially: 3-8, The Discovery of
Multiple Values, as an improvement over the
single-cause approaches of earlier times.

1000. ___ and Kaplan, Abraham (1950) Power and
Society; A Framework for Political Inquiry.
New Haven: Yale Univ. Press. --Distinguishes
political theory as a set of empirical propositions (political science) from political theory
as value judgments (political doctrine); development of the former. Value conceived as a
"goal event," derived from acts of valuation
and referring to a person's or group's environment rather than to the person or group as
actor.

1001. ___, Lerner, Daniel and Pool, Ithiel de Sola (1952)
The Comparative Study of Symbols; An Introduction. Stanford; Stanford Univ. Press
(Hoover Institute Studies, Series C, Symbols,
1). --Content analysis in comparative study.

1002. Lerner, Max (1940) Ideas Are Weapons; The History and Uses of Ideas. New York: Viking. --
Problems of policy and values treated throughout.

1003. ___ (1941) Ideas for the Ice Age; Studies in a Revo-
lutionary Era. New York: Viking.

1004. Lippmann, Walter (1931) A Preface to Morals. New York: Macmillan. --To attain moral excellence, defined as reasonableness, man can depend only on himself.

1005. ___ (1937) An Inquiry into the Principles of the Good Society. Boston: Little, Brown. --Historical review and author's position on ethical principles in relation to economics and political science.

1006. ___ (1955) Essays in the Public Philosophy. Boston and Toronto: Little, Brown. --Reaffirmation of democratic government, based on anti-relativistic "public philosophy" of confidence in human reason to define justice and determine the public interest.

1007. Livingston, John (1956) Liberalism, Conservatism, and the Role of Reason. Western Pol. Quart. 9: 641-657. --Epistemological and ethical relativism and absolutism in relation to liberalism and conservatism.

1008. March, James G. (1954) Group Norms and the Active Minority. Amer. Sociol. Rev. 19: 733-741. --Towards a theory of group-approval relating group norms to characteristics of active group members.

1009. Marx, Fritz M. (1949) Administrative Ethics and the Rule of Law. Amer. Pol. Sci. Rev. 43: 1119-1144. --Tensions between persons in administrative and legislative positions indicate the need for a general body of ethical rules for administration.

1010. +Maunier, René (1949) The Sociology of the Colonies. Trans. by Mrs. E. O. Lorimer. London: Routledge. 2 vols. --Detailed analysis of colonial administration of European nations, especially in Africa and Asia.

1011. Merriam, Charles E. (1934) <u>Political Power, Its Composition and Incidence</u>. New York: McGraw-Hill. Also: London: Whittlesey House.

1012. +___ (1945) <u>Systematic Politics</u>. Chicago: Univ. of Chicago Press. --Analysis of the political process, including the role of personality and culture and the place of human needs in political systems.

1013. Meyerson, Martin and Banfield, Edward C. (1955) <u>Politics, Planning and the Public Interest</u>. Glencoe, Ill.: Free Press.

1014. Monypenny, Phillip (1953) A Code of Ethics for Public Administration. <u>George Washington Law Rev</u>. 21: 423-444.

1015. Morgenthau, Hans J. (1946) <u>Scientific Man vs. Power Politics</u>. Chicago: Univ. of Chicago Press. --Includes treatment of ethical issues in relation to science and to politics.

1016. ___ (1948) Twilight of International Morality. <u>Ethics</u> 58: 79-99.

1017. ___ (1950) The Mainsprings of American Foreign Policy; The National Interest vs. Moral Abstractions. <u>Amer. Pol. Sci. Rev</u>. 44: 833-854.

1018. ___ (1958) Power as a Political Concept. <u>IN</u>: Roland Young, ed. <u>Approaches to the Study of Politics</u>. Evanston: Northwestern Univ. Press. 66-77. --See especially: III, on the ambivalent moral position of the political scientist in society, IV, on the role of political theory in social change.

1019. Mosca, Gaetano (1939) The Ruling Class. Trans.
by Hannah D. Kahn. Rev. ed. New York and
London: Macmillan. --See especially: Ch. 5,
Juridical Defense, for moral aspects of political rule by an elite.

1020. +Oakeshott, Michael (1943) The Social and Political
Doctrines of Contemporary Europe. New York:
Macmillan. --First British edition, 1939.
Essays and readings in the doctrines of rep-
resentative democracy, communism, fascism
and national socialism.

1021. Oppenheim, Felix E. (1953) Rational Choice. J.
Phil. 50: 341-350.

1022. ___ (1955) In Defense of Relativism. Western Pol.
Quart. 8: 411-417. --Both absolutism and relativism are epistemological theories about the
logical status of intrinsic value judgments in
general rather than ethical theories about the
valuation of particular things; relativists are
less open to the charge of cynicism and nihilism
than are absolutists.

1023. Oppler, Alfred C. (1942) Ethics in Public Administration and Individual Ethics. Cambridge:
Harvard Graduate School of Public Administration, Bureau for Research in Municipal
Government.

1024. Ornstein, Hans (1946) Macht, Moral und Recht;
Studien zur Grundproblematik menschlichen
Zusammenlebens. Berne: Francke. --Philo-
sophical problems and interrelations of social
order, morality, political power and law.

1025. Osgood, Robert Endicott (1953) Ideals and Self-
Interest in America's Foreign Relations; The
Great Transformation of the Twentieth Cen-
tury. Chicago: Univ. of Chicago Press.

1026. Padover, Saul K., with the collaboration of Goguel,
      François, Rosenstock-Franck, Louis and Weil,
      Eric (1954) French Institutions; Values and
      Politics. Stanford: Stanford Univ. Press
      (Hoover Institute Studies, Series E, Institu-
      tions, No. 2). --Socio-political study of French
      institutions, political mores, family life,
      values and foreign policy.

1027. Pauker, Guy J. (1956) A Work Paper on Human
      Values in Social Change in South and Southeast
      Asia and in the United States. Washington,
      D. C.: U.S.G.P.O., 1956. (Department of
      State Publication 6328, International Organi-
      zation and Conference Series 4, UNESCO 31.)

1028. Pennock, J. Roland (1944) Reason, Value Theory,
      and the Theory of Democracy. Amer. Pol.
      Sci. Rev. 38: 855-875. --Defense of democracy
      as the ideally best form of government, based
      on the "supremacy of reason and the objectivity
      of values," modified by consideration of the
      arguments of scepticism and relativism.

1029. ___ (1950) Liberal Democracy; Its Merits and
      Prospects. New York: Rinehart. --Reapprai-
      sal of the ethical basis of democracy.

1030. ___ (1951) Political Science and Political Philoso-
      phy. Amer. Pol. Sci. Rev. 45: 1081-1085. --
      On facts and values in political theory, con-
      cluding with "a plea for both political philo-
      sophers and empirical political scientists to
      mend their ways."

1031. +Pool, Ithiel de Sola (1951) Symbols of Interna-
      tionalism. Stanford: Stanford Univ. Press.

1032. ___ (1952) Symbols of Democracy. Stanford: Stan-
      ford Univ. Press.

1033. +Riemer, Neal (1957) Some Reflections on The
Grand Inquisitor and Modern Democratic
Theory. Ethics 67: 249-256. --Criticism of
arguments favoring authoritarianism.

1034. Rossiter, Clinton (1955) Conservatism in America.
New York: Knopf.

1035. Sabine, George H. (1950) A History of Political
Theory. Rev. ed. New York: Holt. --Written
from the point of view that a "theory of politics requires discrimination between states
of fact, causal connections, formal implications, and the values or ends that a policy is
designed to achieve."

1036. Sayre, Wallace S. (1951) Trends of a Decade in
Administrative Values. Publ. Administration
Rev. 11: 1-9.

1037. Shubik, Martin (1954) Readings in Game Theory and
Political Behavior. Garden City, N. Y.:
Doubleday.

1038. Simon, Herbert A. (1947) Administrative Behavior;
A Study of Decision-Making Processes in Administrative Organizations. New York:
Macmillan. --Social-psychological study of administrative behavior, with a view to formulating an efficient theory of decision-making.
Reissued in 1957, with a new introduction
tracing the effects of the 1947 edition.

1039. ___ (1955) Recent Advances in Organization Theory.
IN: Research Frontiers in Politics and Government, Brookings Lectures, 1955. Washington,
D.C.: Brookings Institution. 23-44. --See especially: The Re-Emergence of Power and
Policy; The Process of Rational Choice; Pro-
grammed and Non-Programmed Decisions.

1040. ___ (1957) Models of Man, Social and Rational. New York: Wiley.--See especially: Ch. 14, A Behavioral Model of Rational Choice (reprinted from Quart. J. Econ., 1955); Ch. 15, Rational Choice and the Structure of the Environment (reprinted from Psychol. Rev., 1956); Ch. 16, A Comparison of Game Theory and Learning Theory (reprinted from Psychometrika, 1956).

1041. +Sington, Derrick and Weidenfeld, Arthur (1943) The Goebbels Experiment; A Study of the Nazi Propaganda Machine. New Haven: Yale Univ. Press.--Documentation and analysis, with bibliography of main sources.

1042. Snyder, Richard C. (1955) Game Theory and the Analysis of Political Behavior. IN: Research Frontiers in Politics and Government, Brookings Lectures, 1955. Washington, D. C.: Brookings Institution. 70-103.

1043. ___ (1958) A Decision-Making Approach to the Study of Political Phenomena. IN: Roland Young, ed. Approaches to the Study of Politics. Evanston: Northwestern Univ. Press. 3-38.

1044. ___, Bruck, H. W. and Sapin, Burton (1954) Decision-Making as an Approach to the Study of International Politics. Princeton: Princeton Univ. Organizational Behavior Section (Foreign Policy Analysis Series No. 3).--Analytical scheme for study of international politics; selective perception and evaluation of information determined by decision-maker's frame of reference; choices derive from situationally and biographically determined preferences.

1045. Srinivasan, N. (1954) Democratic Government in India. Calcutta: World Press.--Analysis of the Indian Constitution and of difficulties in its application resulting from the persistence of undemocratic attitudes.

1046. Strauss, Leo (1957) What Is Political Philosophy?
J. Pol. 3: 343-368. --On the impossibility of
value-free political science.

1047. Tannenbaum, Frank (1945) On Certain Characteristics of American Democracy. Pol. Sci. Quart.
60: 343-350.

1048. Thomson, David (1949) Equality. Cambridge:
Cambridge Univ. Press. --The concept of
equality in democratic theory and practice.

1049. Truman, David B. (1951) The Governmental
Process; Political Interests and Public
Opinion. New York: Knopf.

1050. + ___ (1955) The Impact on Political Science of the
Revolution in the Behavioral Sciences. IN:
Research Frontiers in Politics and Govern-
ment, Brookings Lectures, 1955. Washington,
D. C.: Brookings Institution. 202-231.

1051. Voegelin, Eric (1952) The New Science of Politics;
An Introduction. Chicago: Univ. of Chicago
Press. --Opposition to relativism and to value-
free approach to political science.

1052. Waldo, Dwight (1948) The Administrative State.
New York: Ronald. --Analysis of the value
premises of literature on American public administration. See especially: Part II, ethical
basis of accepted theories.

1053. ___ (1958) "Values" in Political Science. IN:
Roland Young, ed. Approaches to the Study of
Politics. Evanston: Northwestern Univ. Press.
96-111. --Starting from the position that value-
free teaching of political science is impossible,
proceeds to a critical analysis of the fact-value
dichotomy.

1054. Wells, Henry (1955) Ideology and Leadership in
Puerto Rican Politics. Amer. Pol. Sci. Rev.
49: 22-39. --Analysis of the popular democratic program with reference to ideological
and cultural factors.

1055. Williamson, René de Visme (1947) The Challenge
of Political Relativism. J. Pol. 9: 147-177.
--Ethical commitments in political science.

1056. ___ (1949) Culture and Policy, The United States
and the Hispanic World. Knoxville: Univ. of
Tennessee Press. --Analysis of Spanish and
Spanish-American national character in the
interest of intercultural understanding.

1057. Wortley, B. A. (1949) Human Rights. Pol. Quart.
20: 135-145. --Critical analysis of British
proposals for a Bill and Declaration of Human
Rights for the United Nations.

1058. Wright, Quincy (1947) The Relations of Universal
Culture to Power Politics. Symp. Sci. Phil.
Relig. 7: 597-603.

1059. ___ (1947) Specialization and Universal Values in
General International Organization. Symp.
Sci. Phil. Relig. 6: 207-217.

1060. ___ (1954) Moral Standards in Government and
Politics. Ethics 64: 157-168. --On the relation of facts and values, theoretical science
and ethics.

1061. ___ (1954) Problems of Stability and Progress in
International Relations. Berkeley: Univ. of
California Press.

1062. ___ (1955) The Study of International Relations.
New York: Appleton-Century-Crofts. --See
especially: Chs. 29 and 32, for a "six-
dimensional" theory of value.

1063. Young, Roland, ed. (1958) Approaches to the Study
of Politics; Twenty-Two Contemporary Essays
Exploring the Nature of Politics and Methods
by Which It Can Be Studied. Evanston: Northwestern Univ. Press.

V. ECONOMICS

1064. Allen, G. C. (1950) Economic Progress, Retrospect and Prospect. Econ. J. 60: 463-480. --
Psychological, philosophical and economic
factors in economic progress.

1065. Arrow, Kenneth J. (1951) Alternative Approaches to
the Theory of Choice in Risk-Taking Situations.
Econometrica 19: 404-437.

1066. ___ (1951) Social Choice and Individual Values.
New York: Wiley. --Mathematical analysis of
the possibility of "social choice," welfare
economics and treatment of value judgments.
(For criticisms, see 1089 and 1154.)

1067. Ayres, Clarence E. (1918) The Nature of the Relationship Between Ethics and Economics.
Chicago: Univ. of Chicago Press. --A pragmatist position.

1068. ___ (1944) The Theory of Economic Progress.
Chapel Hill: Univ. of North Carolina Press. --
Pragmatist interpretation of economics and
economic values.

1069. ___ (1949) The Value Economy. IN: Ray Lepley,
ed. Value; A Cooperative Inquiry. New York:
Columbia Univ. Press. 43-63.

1070. ___ (1950) The Values of Social Scientists. J. Soc.
Issues 6: 17-20.

1071. Bakke, E. Wight and Kerr, Clark (1948) Unions,
Management and the Public. New York: Harcourt. --A comprehensive collection of readings. See especially: The Interest of the
Community, for questions of policy.

1072. Baran, Paul A. (1954) National Economic Planning. IN: Bernard F. Haley, Ed. A Survey of Contemporary Economics. Homewood, Ill.: Richard D. Irwin. Published for the American Economic Association. 355-407. --Discussion by J. K. Galbraith and Adolph Lowe.

1073. Barnard, Chester I. (1938) The Functions of the Executive. Cambridge: Harvard Univ. Press. --A theory of organization and decision-making.

1074. ___ (1958) Elementary Conditions of Business Morals. Berkeley: Univ. of California Press (Committee on the Barbara Weinstock Lectures).

1075. Benoit-Smullyan, E. (1945) Value Judgments and the Social Sciences. J. Phil. 42: 197-210. -- The social scientist as positivist or moralist.

1076. Bergson, Abram (1949) Socialist Economics. IN: Howard S. Ellis, ed. A Survey of Contemporary Economics. Philadelphia: Blakiston. Published for the American Economic Association. 412-448. --Socialist and welfare economics in relation to planning; the aims of allocating resources.

1077. ___ (1954) On the Concept of Social Welfare. Quart. J. Econ. 68: 233-252.

1078. Bloom, Clark C. (1953) Is a Consistent Governmental Economic Policy Possible? IN: A. Dudley Ward, ed. Goals of Economic Life. New York: Harper. 231-247.

1079. Blum, Fred H. (1955) Action Research--A Scientific Approach. Phil. Sci. 22: 1-7. --Objectivity of pure research seen as spurious; action research, combining facts and values, preferred.

1080. Bonar, James (1927) Philosophy and Political Economy. London: Allen and Unwin.

1081. Boucke, O. Fred (1921) The Development of Economics, 1750-1900. New York: Macmillan. --Includes treatment of moral issues in economic theory.

1082. Boulding, Kenneth E. (1952) Welfare Economics. IN: Bernard F. Haley, ed. A Survey of Contemporary Economics. Homewood, Ill.: Richard D. Irwin. Published for the American Economic Association. 1-38.--Discussion by Melvin W. Reder and Paul A. Samuelson.

1083. ___ (1953) Economic Progress as a Goal of Economic Life. IN: A. Dudley Ward, ed. Goals of Economic Life. New York: Harper. 52-83.

1084. ___ (1953) The Organizational Revolution; A Study in the Ethics of Economic Organization. New York: Harper.--Commentary by Reinhold Niebuhr.

1085. ___ (1956) Some Contributions of Economic to the General Theory of Value. Phil. Sci. 23: 1-14. --Uses field theory to develop an analytic framework for problems involving dynamic systems and choice patterns on the one side and value systems on the other.

1086. Brinkmann, Carl (1935) Economics; Socio-Ethical Schools. IN: Encyclopedia of the Social Sciences, 5. New York: Macmillan. 381-385.

1087. Bronfenbrenner, Martin (1955) Two Concepts of Economic Freedom. Ethics 65: 157-170. -- Six sources of disagreement in defining "freedom"; relationship between values and the problem of defining "freedom."

1088. Buchanan, James M. (1954) Individual Choice in Voting and the Market. J. Pol. Econ. 62: 334-343. --Comparison of individual choice in political voting and in the market process.

1089. ___ (1954) Social Choice, Democracy and Free Markets. J. Pol. Econ. 62: 114-123. -- Criticism of welfare theory and theory of value judgments of Arrow (see 1066).

1090. Buchanan, Norman S. and Ellis, Howard S. (1955) Approaches to Economic Development. New York: Twentieth Century Fund. --An approach to policy for economic development of under-developed countries, including consideration of social institutions, culture and other non-economic factors.

1091. Bye, Raymond T. (1939) The Scope and Definition of Economics. J. Pol. Econ. 47: 623-647. -- Includes treatment of ethical issues.

1092. Carver, Thomas N. (1925) Essays in Social Justice. Cambridge: Harvard Univ. Press.

1093. Chase, Stuart (1951) Roads to Agreement. New York: Harper. --The uses of the social sciences in resolving social and political problems.

1094. Childs, Marquis W. and Cater, Douglass (1954) Ethics in a Business Society. New York: Harper.

1095. Clark, Colin (1957) The Conditions of Economic Progress. 3rd ed. London: Macmillan. -- See especially: Ch. 1, for the thesis that "economics and political science must be subordinate to ethics" and assessment of economic progress through "objectively measurable economic welfare."

1096. Clark, John Maurice (1936) Preface to Social Economics. New York: Farrar and Rinehart. -- See especially: Toward a Concept of Social Value, The Changing Basis of Economic Responsibility.

1097. ___ (1948) Alternative to Serfdom. New York: Knopf. Also: Oxford: Blackwell. --See especially: Ch. 1, Economic Welfare in a Free Society, social philosophy as a part of economics.

1098. ___ (1953) Aims of Economic Life as Seen by Economists. IN: A. Dudley Ward, ed. Goals of Economic Life. New York: Harper. 23-51.

1099. ___ (1957) Economic Institutions and Human Welfare. New York: Knopf. --Essays on the principles of economic policy and ethics.

1100. Commons, John R. (1934) Institutional Economics; Its Place in Political Economy. New York: Macmillan. --Economic theory as analysis of economic problems and guidance of social action; recommends approach to social control through law, ethics, economics and political science.

1101. Cowles Commission for Research in Economics (1951) Rational Decision-Making and Economic Behavior, 19th Annual Report, 1950-51. Chicago: Univ. of Chicago Press.

1102. Cronin, John F. (1945) Economic Analysis and Problems. New York: American Book.

1103. Cropsey, Joseph (1955) What Is Welfare Economics? Ethics 65: 116-125. --A summary for laymen.

1104. Danhof, Clarence H. (1953) Economic Values in
      Cultural Perspective. IN: A. Dudley Ward,
      ed. Goals of Economic Life. New York:
      Harper. 84-117.

1105. Devas, Charles S. (1897) The Restoration of
      Economics to Ethics. Internatl. J. Ethics 7:
      191-204.

1106. Dorfman, Joseph (1946, 1949) The Economic Mind
      in American Civilization. New York: Viking.
      3 vols. --Detailed historical documentation for
      the thesis that economic theories are relative
      to the value assumptions of the theorists and
      the conditions of the times in which the theories
      were formulated.

1107. Ellis, Howard S., assisted by the Research Staff of
      the Council on Foreign Relations (1950) The
      Economics of Freedom. New York: Harper. --
      Proposals for policies of economic and politi-
      cal development under the European Recovery
      Program.

1108. Fanfani, Amintore (1935) Catholicism, Protestant-
      ism and Capitalism. London and New York:
      Sheed and Ward. --Roman Catholic critique of
      Max Weber's thesis relating capitalism to the
      Protestant ethic (see 904).

1109. Ferguson, John M. (1938) Landmarks of Economic
      Thought. New York: Longmans, Green. --
      Includes treatment of ethical issues.

1110. Fetter, Frank A. (1925) Value and the Larger
      Economics. J. Pol. Econ. 31: 790-803. --
      Economics as a theory of welfare rather than
      of value.

1111. Fisher, Franklin M. (1956) Income Distribution, Value Judgments, and Welfare. Quart. J. Econ. 70: 380-424. -- See 1135 for correction.

1112. Flubacher, Joseph Francis (1950) The Concept of Ethics in the History of Economics. New York: Vantage.

1113. Friedman, Milton J. (1953) Choice, Chance, and the Personal Distribution of Income. J. Pol. Econ. 61: 277-292. --A mathematical model for choice, rather than chance, as a determinant of discrepancies in income.

1114. ___ (1954) Essays in Positive Economics. Chicago: Univ. of Chicago Press. --See especially: Introductory essay, distinguishing positive from normative economics, locating in the former the source of disagreements among economists.

1115. ___ and Savage, L. J. (1948) The Utility Analysis of Choices Involving Risk. J. Pol. Econ. 61: 279-304.

1116. Galbraith, John K. (1952) American Capitalism; The Concept of Countervailing Power. Boston: Houghton, Mifflin. --Includes treatment of some moral issues of the American economy.

1117. Georgescu-Roegen, Nicholas (1954) Choice, Expectations and Measurability. Quart. J. Econ. 68: 503-534. --The concept of psychological threshhold as basis for general theory of choices. Bibliography of 59 items.

1118. Ginzberg, Eli et al. (1951) Occupational Choice-- An Approach to a General Theory. --Includes treatment of goals and values as factors of occupational choice.

1119. Graham, Frank D. (1942) Social Goals and Economic Institutions. Princeton: Princeton Univ. Press. --Ethics, politics and economics drawn upon for proposals of realistic goals.

1120. Gray, Alexander (1946) The Socialist Tradition; Moses to Lenin. New York: Longmans, Green.

1121. Haavelmo, Trygve (1950) The Notion of Involuntary Economic Decision. Econometrica 18: 1-8.

1122. Hamilton, Walton (1953) The Law, the Economy, and Moral Values. IN: A. Dudley Ward, ed. Goals of Economic Life. New York: Harper. 248-276.

1123. Haney, Lewis H. (1939) Value and Distribution. New York: Appleton-Century. --Development of philosophical aspects of economic theory is dependent on social science descriptions of economic, ethical and political values.

1124. Harsanyi, John C. (1955) Cardinal Welfare, Individualistic Ethics, and Interpersonal Comparisons of Utility. J. Pol. Econ. 63: 309-321. -- Critical analysis of some difficulties in welfare theory.

1125. Hayek, Friedrich August von (1944) The Road to Serfdom. Chicago: Univ. of Chicago Press. -- Individualism as the preferred principle of economic organization.

1126. ___ (1948) Individualism and Economic Order. Chicago: Univ. of Chicago Press. --An attack on economic planning, on the ground that individuals seeking their own ends produce optimal conditions in society.

1127. Heimann, Eduard (1945) History of Economic Doctrines. New York: Oxford Univ. Press. -- Includes treatment of ethical issues.

1128. ___ (1947) Freedom and Order; Lessons from the War. New York: Scribner's. --Conflict between individual liberty and political order as the chief problem of Western democracies; European totalitarian states a point of reference in the analysis.

1129. ___ (1953) Comparative Economic Systems. IN: A. Dudley Ward, ed. Goals of Economic Life. New York: Harper. 118-147.

1130. Hickman, C. Addison and Kuhn, Manford H. (1956) Individuals, Groups, and Economic Behavior. New York: Dryden. --Social-psychological approach to managerial motivation, welfare economics and economic planning.

1131. Hobson, John A. (1927) Economics and Ethics. IN: W. F. Ogburn and E. A. Goldenweiser, eds. The Social Sciences and Their Interrelations. Boston: Houghton, Mifflin. --Ethical values as elements in economic processes.

1132. ___ (1929) Economics and Ethics; A Study in Social Values. Boston: Heath. --On welfare economics; ethical values involved in economic processes.

1133. Homan, Paul T. (1928) Contemporary Economic Thought. New York: Harper. --Includes discussion of conflicting views on philosophical and ethical assumptions of economic theories.

1134. Innis, Harold A. (1951) Industrialism and Cultural Values. IN: The Bias of Communication. Toronto: Univ. of Toronto Press. 132-141. -- Brief economic-historical survey of how changes in the technology of communication determine changes in cultural values.

—— Katona, George. See Psychology.

1135. Kenen, Peter B. and Fisher, Franklin M. (1957)
Income Distribution, Value Judgments, and
Welfare; A Correction. Quart. J. Econ. 71:
322-324. -- See 1111.

1136. Keynes, John Maynard (1933) Essays in Biography.
New York: Harcourt. --Contains discussions
of moral and ethical philosophies of classical
economists and of the author.

1137. +Kirby, E. Stuart, ed. (1955-1956) Contemporary
China. Hong Kong: Hong Kong Univ. Press.
Also: London and New York: Oxford Univ.
Press. --First of a series of economic and
social studies of contemporary China.

1138. Knight, Frank H. (1935) The Ethics of Competition
and Other Papers. New York and London:
Harper. --Humanistic and social science approach to economic science and problems.

1139. ___ (1941) Social Science. Ethics 51: 127-143. --
On the normative problem in social scientific
inquiry.

1140. ___ (1942) Fact and Value in Social Science. IN:
R. N. Anshen, ed. Science and Man. New
York: Harcourt. 325-345. --An argument
against scientific manipulation and coercion
and for "a free meeting of free minds."

1141. ___ (1947) Freedom and Reform; Essays in Economics and Social Philosophy. New York and
London: Harper. --A collection of previously
published articles, largely on freedom and
democracy.

1142. ___ (1953) Conflict of Values; Freedom and Justice. IN: A. Dudley Ward, ed. Goals of Economic Life. New York: Harper. 204-230.

1143. ___ (1956) On the History and Method of Economics; Selected Essays. Chicago: Univ. of Chicago Press. --See especially: Ch. 2, The Ricardian Theory of Production and Distribution; Ch. 7, "What Is Truth" in Economics?; Ch. 10, Salvation by Science; The Gospel According to Professor Lundberg (see 787); Ch. 11, The Role of Principles in Economics and Politics; Ch. 12, Free Society; Its Basic Nature and Problem.

1144. ___ et al. (1922) Round Table Conference on the Relation Between Economics and Ethics. Amer. Econ. Rev. 12, Suppl.: 192-201. -- Conference of the American Economic Association, 1921. Participants favoring economists' concern with ethical problems of economic data: Frank H. Knight, A. B. Wolfe, Jacob Viner, H. Gordon Hayes; opposed: G. A. Kleene and Willford I. King.

1145. Koivisto, William A. (1953) Value, Theory and Fact in Industrial Sociology. Amer. J. Sociol. 58: 564-572. --Criticizes the premise implicit in industrial sociology that cooperation and productive efficiency are necessarily concomitant; recommends that value judgments be made explicit and value conflicts in industrial situations be studied.

1146. ___ (1955) Moral Judgments and Value Conflict. Phil. Sci. 22: 54-57. --Reply to Hartung (see 745), "in defense of cultural relativism."

1147. Laidler, Harry W. (1945) Social-Economic Movements. New York: Crowell.

1148. Lamb, Helen (In Press) The Indian Merchant. J. Amer. Folklore. --Summary of the values of a major caste-group of India.

1149. Lauterbach, Albert (1954) Man, Motives and Money; Psychological Frontiers of Economics. Ithaca: Cornell Univ. Press. --See especially: Ch. 4, Economic Reform and the Human Mind; American values treated passim.

1150. Lerner, Abba P. (1944) The Economics of Control. New York: Macmillan. --Towards a theory to reconcile liberalism with socialism.

1151. Levin, Harvey J. (1956) Standards of Welfare in Economic Thought. Quart. J. Econ. 70: 117-138. --A review of major theorists in welfare economics.

1152. Lewis, W. Arthur (1949) The Principles of Economic Planning. London: George Allen and Unwin. Also: Dennis Dobson, for the Fabian Society. --A Fabian Socialist position.

1153. Little, Ian M. D. (1950) A Critique of Welfare Economics. Oxford: Clarendon Press. --See especially: Chs. 1-5, summaries of economic theories of value, with concise, logical attacks upon all of them. Bibliography.

1154. ___ (1952) Review of K. Arrow, "Social Choice and Individual Values." J. Pol. Econ. 60: 422-432. --Criticism of Arrow's theory (see 1066).

1155. Macfie, Alec L. (1943) Economic Efficiency and Social Welfare. London: Oxford Univ. Press.

1156. ___ (1953) Choice in Psychology and as an Economic Assumption. Econ. J. 63: 352-367.

1157. Marshak, Jacob (1950) Rational Behavior, Uncertain Prospects, and Measurable Utility. Econometrica 18: 111-141.--A formal model.

1158. Marshall, Alfred (1936) Principles of Economics. 8th ed. London: Macmillan.--Includes evaluation of moral theories of historically important economic theorists and the effects of their theories on the course of events.

1159. Mayo, Elton (1933) The Human Problems of an Industrial Civilization. New York: Macmillan. --Report of the Hawthorne experiment, discussion of moral and social integration in the modern economic order.

1160. Meade, J. E. (1955) Trade and Welfare. London: Oxford Univ. Press.--Welfare economics extended to international economic policy.

1161. Mises, Ludwig von (1949) Human Action; A Treatise on Economics. New Haven: Yale Univ. Press. --Methodology in the tradition of Max Weber, with critical analysis of the ideologies of modern industrial society.

1162. Mitchell, Wesley C. (1944) Facts and Values in Economics. J. Phil. 41: 212-219.--Susceptibility of social scientists greater than that of natural scientists to allowing value premises to affect factual conclusions.

1163. ___ (1949) Lecture Notes on Types of Economic Theory; As Delivered by Professor Wesley C. Mitchell. J. M. Gould and A. M. Kelley, eds. New York: Turtle Bay Bookshop. 2 vols. -- Includes detailed treatment of social and political philosophies of the economic theorists reviewed in the history.

1164. Moos, S. (1945) Laissez-Faire, Planning and Ethics. Econ. J. 55: 17-27.

1165. Morrow, Glenn R. (1923) The Ethical and Economic Theories of Adam Smith. New York: Longmans, Green.

1166. Musgrave, Richard A. (In Press) The Theory of Public Finance. New York: McGraw-Hill. -- Includes treatment of moral and value issues of government expenditure.

1167. Myint, Hla (1948) Theories of Welfare Economics. London: Longmans, Green and the London School of Economics and Political Science. -- Survey of theory and value premises of welfare economics from Adam Smith; an attempt to judge the types of welfare economics most likely to be practically useful in relation to policy. See especially: Part III, ethical and other philosophical aspects of economic theory.

1168. Myrdal, Gunnar (1944) An American Dilemma. New York: Harper. --Theoretic scheme including values used to analyze the position of the Negro in the United States. See also, appendices: A Methodological Note on Valuations and Beliefs and A Methodological Note on Facts and Valuations in Social Science.

1169. ___ (1953) The Political Element in the Development of Economic Theory. Trans. by Paul Streeten. London: Routledge and Kegan Paul. Also: Cambridge: Harvard Univ. Press, 1954. -- First appeared in Swedish in 1929. An examination of economic theory, with detailed attention to political value judgments and to the general problem of the relation of facts and values in economics.

1170. ___ (1956) An International Economy; Problems and
    Prospects. New York: Harper. --See especially:
    Ch. 2, The Viewpoint; Ch. 14, The World
    Adrift; Appendix, Methodological Note on the
    Concepts and the Value Premises. Bibliography
    on economic change and underdeveloped coun-
    tries.

1171. Noyes, G. Reinold (1948) Economic Man in Relation
    to His Natural Environment. Vol. I. New York:
    Columbia Univ. Press. Also: London:
    Geoffrey Cumberlege. --Detailed biological and
    psychological description of man, concluding,
    "We do not have economic and non-economic
    wants. We merely satisfy our wants in eco-
    nomic and non-economic ways." See especially:
    Ch. 7, Means and Their Estimation; Ch. 8,
    Subjective Valuation, arguing for a theory of
    subjective valuation as the indispensable basis
    of economic science.

1172. Oliver, Henry M., Jr. (1954) A Critique of Socio-
    economic Goals. Bloomington: Indiana Univ.
    Press. --On the relationship between economic
    policies and ethical ideas.

1173. ___ (1958) Economic Value Theory as a Policy
    Guide. Ethics 68: 186-193. --Examines re-
    lations of economic value theory to questions
    of earned income for a utilitarian and liber-
    tarian guide.

1174. Papandreou, Andreas G. (1952) Some Basic Prob-
    lems in the Theory of the Firm. IN: Bernard
    F. Haley, ed. A Survey of Contemporary
    Economics. Homewood, Ill.: Richard D.
    Irwin. Published for the American Economic
    Association. 183-222. --Includes treatment
    of organization goals as value premises of
    relevant theory. Discussion by R. B. Hefle-
    bower and E. S. Mason.

1175. Pareto, Vilfredo (1935) The Mind and Society. Trans. by Arthur Livingston and Andrew Bongiorno. New York: Harcourt. 4 vols. -- See especially: Vols. 2 and 3, positivist view of values as susceptible of descriptive study but not of objective formulation.

1176. Parsons, Kenneth H. (1942) John R. Commons' Point of View. J. Land and Public Utility Econ. 18: 245-266. --Special attention to the ethical aspect of Commons' institutional economic theory.

1177. Peacock, Alan T., ed. (1954) Income Redistribution and Social Policy. London: Jonathan Cape.

1178. Pigou, A. C. (1932) The Economics of Welfare. 4th ed. London: Macmillan. --See especially: Ch. 1, Welfare and Economic Welfare, social betterment as the main motive of economic inquiry.

1179. ___ (1951) Some Aspects of Welfare Economics. Amer. Econ. Rev. 41: 287-302. --Reviews fundamental issues of economic welfare as "the part of welfare that is associated with the economic aspects of life."

1180. Polak, Fred L. (1948) Kennen en Keuren in de Sociale Wetenschappen, (Knowledge and Value in the Social Sciences). Leiden: H. E. Steufert Kroese. --Analyzes the "objective" and "subjective" orders of the economy, with a criticism of Max Weber (see 904 and 905).

1181. Ranadive, B. T. (1953) India's Five-Year Plan; What It Offers. Bombay: Current Book House. --A Marxist critique.

1182. Reder, Melvin W. (1947) Studies in the Theory of Welfare Economics. New York: Columbia Univ. Press. Also: London: Geoffrey Cumberlege.

1183. Robbins, Lionel (1932) An Essay on the Nature and Significance of Economic Science. London: Macmillan. --Argues for excluding value judgments from scientific economics.

1184. ___ (1952) The Theory of Economic Policy. London: Macmillan. --Includes criticism of classical economists' ethical assumptions.

1185. Roll, Eric (1946) A History of Economic Thought. New York: Prentice-Hall. --Oriented towards a labor theory of value; traces the development of a theory of value as fundamental to economics.

1186. Ross, Arthur M. (1948) Trade Union Wage Policy. Berkeley: Univ. of California Press. --Includes treatment of policy-making and relationship between trade union functioning and democracy.

1187. Rostow, W. W. (1958) The American National Style. Daedalus, Spring: 110-144 (Issued as vol. 87, no. 2, Proc. Amer. Acad. Arts and Sci.). -- Historical, unifying function of American ideal concepts, efficacy of "classic American idealism" and values in meeting contemporary problems.

1188. ___, ed. (In Press) The American Style; Essays in Value and Performance. New York: Harper. -- Essays and comments covering in full a conference, supported by the Carnegie Corporation at Dedham, Mass., May 23-27, 1957.

1189. Ruml, Beardsley (1943) Government, Business and Values. New York and London: Harper.

1190. Ryan, John A., Msgr. (1942) Distributive Justice. New York: Macmillan. --A Roman Catholic interpretation of the goals of economic activity.

1191. ___ (1942) Two Objectives for Catholic Economists. Rev. Soc. Econ. 1: 1-5.

1192. Samuelson, Paul A. (1947) Foundations of Economic Analysis. Cambridge: Harvard Univ. Press (Harvard Econ. Stud., 80). --See especially: Ch. 8, Welfare Economics, ethical assumptions of competition and other economic principles; value linked to preference.

1193. Schoeffler, Sidney (1955) The Failures of Economics; A Diagnostic Study. Cambridge: Harvard Univ. Press. --Chiefly methodological analysis, with recommendations for changes, e.g., to relate economic decision theory to decision theory in other fields and to separate and define policy-making as such without pretense to science.

1194. Schumpeter, Joseph A. (1949) Science and Ideology. Amer. Econ. Rev. 39: 345-369. --On the cooperation of science and value judgments in economics.

1195. ___ (1951) On the Concept of Social Value. IN: Richard V. Clemence, ed. Essays. Cambridge: Addison-Wesley Press. 1-20.

1196. Scitovsky, Tibor (1951) The State of Welfare Economics. Amer. Econ. Rev. 41: 303-315. -- Welfare economics as "that part of the general body of economic theory which is concerned primarily with policy."

1197. Selekman, Benjamin M. (1947) Labor Relations and Human Relations. New York: McGraw-Hill. -- Practical suggestions for handling labor problems, analyzed in economic, sociological and psychological terms.

1198. Shackle, G. L. S. (1949) Expectation in Economics. Cambridge: Cambridge University Press. -- "Potential Surprise" and other factors in decision-making.

1199. Simons, Henry C. (1948) Economic Policy for a Free Society. Chicago: Univ. of Chicago Press.

1200. Singh, Baljit (1953) Economic Planning in India, 1951-1956. Bombay: Kitabs. --Description and analysis of the program and policy.

1201. Slichter, Sumner H. (1948) The American Economy. New York: Knopf. --Includes treatment of policy problems in industrial relations and in international economics.

1202. Smart, William (1931) An Introduction to the Theory of Value on the Lines of Menger, Wieser, and Böhm-Bawerk. London: Macmillan.

1203. Spengler, Joseph J. and Duncan, Otis D. , eds. (1957) Population Theory and Policy. Glencoe, Ill.: Free Press. --Readings from economists and sociologists, with a classified bibliography.

1204. Stark, Werner (1944) The Ideal Foundations of Economic Thought. New York: Oxford Press.

1205. Stigler, George J. (1949) The Economists and Equality. IN: Five Lectures on Economic Problems. London: Longmans, Green and The London School of Economics and Political Science. --Equality and output as elements in the philosophical systems of the classical economists, of which "individual development" is found to be the ultimate goal.

1206. ___ (1950) The Development of Utility Theory. J. Pol. Econ. 58: 307-327, 373-396. --A historical review.

1207. ___ (1958) The Goals of Economic Policy. Chicago: Univ. of Chicago Law School. --Reprinted J. Business, 1958. On "maximum output, substantial growth and minimum inequality of income" as ideal but not fully realizable goals, and as the "justifications for every important innovation in economic policy."

1208. Strayer, Paul J. (1949) Public Expenditure Policy. Amer. Econ. Rev. 39: 383-404. --Problems of policy and theory in governmental economic activity.

1209. Taeusch, Carl F. (1940) Policy and Ethics in Business. New York: McGraw-Hill.

1210. Taussig, Frank W. (1939) Principles of Economics. New York: Macmillan. --See especially: Vol. I, Monopolistic Competition, for the view that economics should not be concerned with moral questions.

1211. Taylor, O. H. (1955) Economics and Liberalism; Collected Papers. Cambridge: Harvard Univ. Press (Harvard Econ. Stud., 96). --Essays in economics, social science and morality, the latter the predominant concern.

1212. ___ (1957) Economic Science Only--Or Political Economy? Quart. J. Econ. 71: 1-18. --An argument for "human-social-and-moral studies" in economics.

1213. Tinbergen, J. (1956) Economic Policy; Principles
and Design. Amsterdam: North-Holland Publishing. --Mathematical models for policy
analysis.

1214. ___ and Polak, J. J. (1950) The Dynamics of the
Business Cycle. London: Routledge and Kegan
Paul. --See especially: Part III, on policy.

1215. Veblen, Thorstein (1919) The Place of Science in
Modern Civilization and Other Essays. New
York: Huebsch. --Critical view of the values
of industrial society.

1216. Vickrey, William (1953) Goals of Economic Life;
An Exchange of Questions Between Economics
and Philosophy. IN: A. Dudley Ward, ed.
Goals of Economic Life. New York: Harper.
148-180.

1217. Viner, Jacob (1953) International Trade and Economic Development. Oxford: Clarendon. --
Includes treatment of policy issues.

1218. Wagner, Donald O. (1934) Social Reformers, Adam
Smith to John Dewey. New York: Macmillan.

1219. Walker, E. Ronald (1943) From Economic Theory
to Policy. Chicago: Univ. of Chicago Press.

1220. Wasserman, Paul (1957) Bibliography on Decision-
Making. Cornell Univ. Graduate School of
Business and Public Administration. Dittoed.
--Includes sections on values in decision-
making; organization for decision-making;
leadership; small-group research; communication and information; mathematics and statistics,
including game theory; and operations research.

1221. Webb, Sidney and Webb, Beatrice (1936) Soviet
        Communism; A New Civilisation? New York:
        Scribner's. 2 vols. --A Socialist view.

1222. Weisskopf, Walter A. (1951) Hidden Value Conflicts
        in Economic Thought. Ethics 61: 195-204.

1223. ___(1952) The Ethical Role of Psychodynamics.
        Ethics 62: 184-190. --The psychodynamic con-
        cept of man marks the emergence of a new
        ethic and new value system to replace the old
        rationalistic, systematic, competitive value
        systems.

1224. White, Edwin E. (1957) Economics and Public
        Policy. Amer. Econ. Rev. 47: 1-21. --Calls
        upon economists to concern themselves more
        actively with government and policy.

1225. Wieser, Friedrich von (1930) Natural Value. Trans.
        by Christian A. Malloch. New York: Stechert.
        --Contains a historical review of the theory of
        value in economics.

1226. Wolfe, Albert B. (1944) Economy and Democracy.
        Amer. Econ. Rev. 34: 1-20. --Economics as a
        normative science.

1227. Wright, David McCord (1947) The Economics of
        Disturbance. New York and London: Mac-
        millan. --Comprehensive analysis of difficul-
        ties connected with economic planning.

1228. +___, ed. (1951) The Impact of the Union; Eight
        Economic Theorists Evaluate the Labor Union
        Movement. New York: Harcourt. --Contribu-
        tors: J. M. Clark, G. Haberler, F. H.
        Knight, K. E. Boulding, E. H. Chamberlin, M.
        Friedman, D. McC. Wright and P. A. Samuel-
        son.

1229. Zinkin, Maurice (1956) Development for Free Asia. Fair Lawn, N. J. : Essential Books, for The Institute of Pacific Relations. Also: London: Chatto and Windus. --Social, economic and political problems of India's planning for development.

VI. PHILOSOPHY

1230. Ackoff, Russell L. (1949) On a Science of Ethics. Phil. Phen. Res. 9: 663-672. --Pragmatist-experimentalist approach.

1231. +—— (1956) The Development of Operations Research as a Science. Operations Res. 4: 265-295.

1232. Adler, Mortimer J. (1938) Saint Thomas and the Gentiles. Milwaukee: Marquette Univ. Press. --A Thomistic analysis.

1233. ___ (1941) A Dialectic of Morals. Notre Dame: The Revue of Politics, University of Notre Dame. --Thomist ethics, using a "new dialectic" starting from the fact that men have preferences.

1234. Aiken, Henry D. (1945) Definitions of Value and the Moral Ideal. J. Phil. 42: 337-352.

1235. —— (1951) A Pluralistic Analysis of the Ethical 'Ought.' J. Phil. 48: 497-505.

1236. —— (1952) The Authority of Moral Judgments. Phil. Phen. Res. 12: 513-525.

1237. —— (1953) Moral Reasoning. Ethics 64: 24-37.

1238. —— (1953) The Spectra of Value Predications. Phil. Phen. Res. 14: 97-104.

1239. —— (1958) God and Evil: A Study of Some Relations Between Faith and Morals. Ethics 68: 77-97. --The "problem of evil" in relation to doubts of the existence of God.

1240. Aiyar, Sir P. S. Sivāsvāmi (1935) Evolution of
       Hindu Moral Ideals. Calcutta: Calcutta Univ.
       Press.

1241. Albert, Ethel M. (1954) Theory Construction for
       the Comparative Study of Values in Five Cul-
       tures; A Report on the Values Study. Harvard
       Values Study. Dittoed. --Definition, classifi-
       cation and theory for the description and com-
       parison of cultural value systems.

1242. —— (1956) The Classification of Values; A Method
       and Illustration. Amer. Anthrop. 58: 221-248.
       --Cultural value system classified according to
       levels of generalization; illustrated with Ramah
       Navaho data.

1243. —— (1957) Value Sentences and Empirical Research.
       Phil. Phen. Res. 17: 331-338. --Empirical re-
       search and contextual analysis to determine
       emotive or cognitive character of value judg-
       ments.

1244. —— (1957-58) Social-Science Facts and Philosophical
       Values. Antioch Rev. 17: 406-420. --Cultural
       and ethical relativism in the light of recent
       anthropological studies of values.

1245. —— (1958) "First Principles" in Logic and Ethics.
       Bucknell Rev. 7: 133-143. --Anthropological
       data to show that ethical values are less relative
       and logical principles less absolute than
       claimed by emotivists in ethics.

1246. —— (In Press) Une Etude de Valeurs en Urundi. Cahiers
       des Etudes africaines (Paris). --A fatalistic world-
       view and value system described.

1247. —— and Cazeneuve, Jean (1956) La Philosophie des
       Indiens Zuñis. Rev. Psychol. des Peuples
       (Paris) 2me Trimestre: 1-12.

1248. ——, Denise, Theodore C. and Peterfreund, Sheldon
P. (1953) Great Traditions in Ethics. New
York: American Book. --Selections, from Plato
to positivism, edited and explained.

1249. Alexander, Samuel (1889) Moral Order and Progress;
An Analysis of Ethical Conceptions. London:
Trübner. --Emergent evolutionist interpreta-
tion.

1250. —— (1927) Artistic Creation and Cosmic Creation.
London: H. Milford.

1251. —— (1933) Beauty and Other Forms of Value.
London: Macmillan.

1252. Anderson, Alan R. and Moore, Omar Khayyam
(1957) The Formal Analysis of Normative
Concepts. Amer. Sociol. Rev. 22: 9-17.

1253. Asmus, V. (1945) Basic Traits of the Classical
Russian Esthetics. Trans. by Henry F. Mins,
Jr. Phil. Phen. Res. 6: 195-211.

1254. Austen, J. L. (1946) Other Minds. Proc. Aristotelian Soc. Supplement 20: 148-187. --See
especially: 169-174, ethical sentences as
"performatory utterances."

1255. Ayer, Alfred J. (1946) Freedom and Necessity.
Polemic 1: 36-44.

1256. —— (1949) Critique of Ethics and Theology. IN:
Language, Truth and Logic. London: Gollancz.
102-120. --Extreme emotive theory of ethics;
ethical judgments "literal non-sense."

1257. —— (1954) Philosophical Essays. London: Macmillan. --Withdrawal from earlier extreme position; ethical judgments "literal non-sense"
but "expressive."

1258. Bagolini, Luigi (1951) Value Judgments in Ethics and in Law. Phil. Quart. 1: 423-432. --Distinguishes moral value judgments as having "natural" sanctions from legal value judgments as having "artificial" sanctions, both "only historical and relative"; only the values of a religious ethic are absolute.

1259. Baier, Kurt (1954) The Point of View of Morality. Australasian J. Phil. 32: 104-135. --To reduce ethical scepticism, suggests restriction of so-called ethical terms to strictly moral usages and exclusion of non-ethical uses of ethical words.

1260. —— (1958) The Moral Point of View; A Rational Basis of Ethics. Ithaca: Cornell Univ. Press.

1261. Bain, Alexander (1869) Moral Science; A Compendium of Ethics. New York: Appleton. --Early radical empiricist. Morality based on the compulsive power of social organization, "conscience" the product of the unpleasant effects of social disapproval. Traditional moral categories denied validity.

1262. Bakan, Mildred B. (1952) Current Issues of Importance in American Sociology and Related Disciplines: Part II. Rev. Metaphysics 6: 301-314. --Conceptions of "value" of Weber, Parsons and others; the impact of the study of man on valuation.

1263. Balz, Albert G. A. (1937) The State of Nature and the Social Sciences. J. Phil. 34: 505-515. --Social science as normative science.

1264. —— (1943) The Value Doctrine of Marx. New York: King's Crown Press.

1265. Bartlett, Ethel M. (1937) Types of Aesthetic Judgment. London: Allen and Unwin.

1266. Bayer, R. (1956) Traité d'Esthétique. Paris:
Armand Colin. --Questions the feasibility of
scientific esthetics, as contingent upon a non-
existent science of quality applicable to judgment and taste.

1267. Beauvoir, Simone de (1948) Ethics of Ambiguity.
Trans. by Bernard Frechtman. New York:
Philosophical Library. --Existentialist ethics.

1268. Bergmann, Gustav (1951) Logical Atomism, Ele-
mentarism and the Analysis of Value. Phil.
Stud. 2: 85-92.

1269. Bergson, Henri (1911) Laughter; An Essay on the
Meaning of the Comic. Trans. by Cloudesley
Brereton and Fred Rothwell. London and New
York: Macmillan.

1270. —— (1935) The Two Sources of Morality and Religion. Trans. by R. Ashley Audra, Cloudesley Brereton and W. Horsfall Carter. New
York: Holt. --The compulsion of social instinct
and the inspiration of creative genius account
for "universal acceptance of law" and "common
imitation of a model. "

1271. Bertocci, Peter A. (1945) A Reinterpretation of
Moral Obligation. Phil. Phen. Res. 6: 270-
283. --The experience of moral obligation dis-
sociated from cognition of values and from the
Freudian "internalized monitor"; "oughtness"
a non-cognitive and non-conative psychological
imperative not involving moral knowledge; by
contrast to obligations (oughts), values have
content and are subject to cultural influences
and change.

1272. Bhattacharyya, Krishnachandra (1956) Studies in Philosophy. Vol. I. Calcutta: Progressive Publishers. --See especially: Pain as Evil and The Concept of Rasa, on the negative feelings associated with philosophical speculation.

1273. +Bidney, David (1950) The Concept of Myth and the Problem of Psychocultural Evolution. Amer. Anthrop. 52: 16-26. --The concepts of myth and belief as used by anthropologists in the study of primitive and modern cultures.

1274. —— (1953) The Concept of Value in Modern Anthropology. IN: Alfred L. Kroeber, ed. Anthropology Today. Chicago: Univ. of Chicago Press. 682-699. --Historical review of evaluation in anthropology, an attack on ethical relativism, and a plea for social action and progressive, rational ideals in anthropology.

1275. —— (1953) The Problem of Freedom and Authority in Cultural Perspective. Symp. Sci. Phil. Relig. 12: 289-307.

1276. —— (1953) Theoretical Anthropology. New York: Columbia Univ. Press. --Propaedeutic to a normative anthropology, to be based on the creative element of a universal human nature which has (restricted) freedom of will. (For criticism, see 1734.)

1277. Black, Max (1958) The Moral Point of View. Ithaca: Cornell Univ. Press. --Major problems of ethics, from a linguistic point of view.

1278. Blackham, Harold John (1951) Six Existentialist Thinkers. London: Routledge and Kegan Paul.

1279. Blanshard, Brand (1955) The Impasse in Ethics and a Way Out. Howison Lecture, 1954. Berkeley: Univ. of California Press (University of

California Publications in Philosophy 28: 93-
112). --Criticism of three dominant schools of
recent philosophic ethics, to clear the way for
a return to the more vital stream of traditional
ethics.

1280. Boas, George (1939) Habit, Fact and Value. J.
Phil. 36: 526-530. --Habit as a bridge between
fact and value.

1281. Bollnow, Otto Friedrich (1953) Deutsche Existenzphilosophie. (Bibliographische Einführungen in
das Studium der Philosophie. Heft 23.) Bern:
Bochenski. --Full listing of adherents to Existenzphilosophie, including H. Lipps, P. L.
Landsberg, L. Binswanger, and H. Kunz.

1282. Bosanquet, Bernard (1912) The Principle of Individuality and Value. Gifford Lectures for 1911.
London: Macmillan. --Neo-Hegelian view.

1283. —— (1913) The Value and Destiny of the Individual.
Gifford Lectures for 1912. London: Macmillan.

1284. —— (1918) Some Suggestions in Ethics. London:
Macmillan. --Self-realization as self-abandon-
ment to the Absolute; evil contributes to overall perfection and serves as a source of
catharsis.

1285. —— (1923) Three Lectures on Aesthetic. London:
Macmillan.

1286. Bouwsma, O. K. (1950) The Expression Theory of
Art. IN: Max Black, ed. Philosophical
Analysis. Ithaca: Cornell Univ. Press. 75-
101.

1287. Bowdery, George J. (1941) Conventions and Norms.
Phil. Sci. 8: 493-505. --Criteria to identify
conventions and define their properties in relation to scientific inquiry.

1288. Bradley, Francis H. (1876) Ethical Studies. London: H. S. King. --Attack on hedonistic ethics; modified Hegelianism expounded and defended (by the "dialectician extraordinary of British philosophy").

1289. Braithwaite, R. B. (1946) Belief and Action. Proc. Aristotelian Soc. Supplement 20: 1-19. -- Pragmatist-experimentalist ethics.

1290. —— (1950) Moral Principles and Inductive Policies. London: Brit. Acad. Proc. 36: 51-68.

1291. —— (1955) Theory of Games as a Tool for the Moral Philosopher. An Inaugural Lecture Delivered in Cambridge on 2 December 1954. Cambridge and New York: Cambridge Univ. Press. -- Principles of game strategy and utility functions in decision-making applied to a hypothetical moral dilemma; the method does not "suppose that one code of values is better than any other."

1292. Brandt, Richard B. (1944) The Significance of Differences of Ethical Opinion in Ethical Rationalism. Phil. Phen. Res. 4: 469-494.

1293. —— (1952) The Status of Empirical Assertion Theories in Ethics. Mind 61: 458-479.

1294. —— (1954) Hopi Ethics; A Theoretical Analysis. Chicago: Univ. of Chicago Press. --Hopi ethical attitudes, concepts, ideals and norms; based on the author's fieldwork.

1295. —— (1955) The Definition of an "Ideal Observer" Theory in Ethics. Phil. Phen. Res. 15: 407-413.

1296. —— (1957) Some Puzzles for Attitude Theories of
Value. IN: Ray Lepley, ed. The Language of
Value. New York: Columbia Univ. Press.
153-177.

1297. —— (In progress) Ethical Theory. New York:
Prentice-Hall. --Metaethical and normative
questions of ethics, with references to anthropological and psychological theory.

1298. Bréhler, Émile (1939) Doutes Sur la Philosophie
des Valeurs. Rev. de Métaphysique et de
Morale 46: 399-414.

1299. Brentano, Franz (1902) The Origin of the Knowledge
of Right and Wrong. Trans. by C. Hague.
Westminster: Constable. --Realist-intuitionist
ethical theory, part of the author's general
psychological theory of "acts" and "intentions."
Value considered as self-evident.

1300. Brightman, Edgar S. (1943) The Problem of an Objective Basis for Value Judgments. Symp. Sci.
Phil. Relig. 3: 1-6.

1301. —— (1945) Nature and Values. New York: Abing-
don-Cokesbury. --Personal idealism; persons
the only intrinsic value; a Supreme Mind recon-
ciles nature and value, both manifestations of
the Supreme Mind.

1302. Britton, Karl (1939) Communication; A Philosophical Study of Language. London: Kegan Paul,
Trench, Trübner. --See especially: Chs. 9 and
10, on values and morals.

1303. Broad, Charlie Dunbar (1930) Five Types of
Ethical Theory. London: Kegan Paul, Trench
Trübner. Also: New York: Harcourt. --Ex-
haustive critical analyses of the ethical systems of Spinoza, Butler, Hume, Kant and Sidgwick.

1304. —— (1934) Determinism, Indeterminism and Libertarianism. Cambridge: Cambridge Univ. Press.

1305. —— (1946) Some of the Main Problems of Ethics. Philosophy 21: 99-117. Also in: Herbert Feigl and Wilfrid Sellars, eds. Readings in Philosophical Analysis. New York: Appleton-Century-Crofts, 1949. 547-563.

1306. —— (1952) Ethics and the History of Philosophy. London: Routledge and Kegan Paul. --Deontology modified by concessions to utilitarianism; analysis of moral judgments, moral emotion and moral volition.

1307. Brodbeck, May (1951) Towards a Naturalistic "Non-Naturalistic" Ethic. Phil. Stud. 2: 7-11.

1308. Brogan, Albert P. (1919) The Fundamental Value Universal. J. Phil. 16: 96-104. --"Value" held indefinable; "better" more fundamental than "good." Suggests scientific study of actual value preferences to illuminate ethical problems.

1309. Brown, Harold Chapman (1937) Ethics from the Viewpoint of Modern Science. J. Phil. 34: 113-121. --Moral codes contingent upon social and economic conditions; study of ethics requires knowledge of social science; the "reform of man" comes only through "reform" of social institutions.

1310. Burtt, Edwin A., ed. (1939) The English Philosophers from Bacon to Mill. New York: Modern Library.

1311. Campbell, Charles A. (1935) Moral and Non-Moral Values; A Study in the First Principles of Axiology. Mind 44: 273-299. --Limitations of subjectivistic approach to ethics.

1312. —— (1948) Moral Intuition and the Principle of Self-Realization. London: Brit. Acad. Proc. 34: 23-56. --Self-realization as the ultimate moral principle and "genuine object of intuition."

1313. Caponigri, A. Robert (1951) Italian Philosophy, 1943-50. Phil. Phen. Res. 11: 489-509.

1314. Carritt, Edgar F. (1935) Morals and Politics. Oxford: Clarendon Press. --Intuited rightness the basis of ethics; political obligation derived from general obligation to our fellow men; social science, not ethics, should answer basic questions of conduct, choice and similar problems.

1315. —— (1947) Ethical and Political Thinking. Oxford: Clarendon Press.

1316. +Cassirer, Ernst (1944) An Essay on Man; An Introduction to a Philosophy of Human Culture. New Haven: Yale Univ. Press. --Summarizes Philosophie der Symbolischen Formen, 3 vols., 1923-1928-1929, Berlin. Neo-Kantian analysis of symbolic behavior in religion, myth, art, science and history.

1317. +—— (1946) Language and Myth. Trans. by Susanne K. Langer. New York: Harper.

1318. Cavell, Stanley and Sesonske, Alexander (1952) Moral Theory, Ethical Judgments, and Empiricism. Mind 61: 543-563. --Towards reconciliation of cognitivist (pragmatist) and emotivist (positivist) ethical theories.

—— Cazeneuve, Jean. See Anthropology.

1319. Cerf, Walter (1951) Value Decisions. Phil. Sci. 18: 26-34. --On estimating the relative values of different ideals.

1320. Chapman, John Jay (1901) The Unity of Human Nature. Internatl. J. Ethics 11: 158-167.

1321. Churchman, Charles West (1948) Theory of Experimental Inference. New York: Macmillan. --
See especially: Chs. 15 and 16, experimentalist-
pragmatist value theory.

1322. —— (1956) Science and Decision Making. Phil. Sci.
23: 247-249. --A reply to Jeffrey on "Valuation
and Acceptance of Scientific Hypotheses" (see
1954), suggesting that the scientist "is a decision maker with multiple aims, and the criteria
of optimal decision making depend on the values
of these aims."

1323. —— and Ackoff, Russell L. (1950) Methods of Inquiry; An Introduction to Philosophy and Scientific Method. St. Louis: Educational Publishers. --See especially: Ch. 15, a statistical
science of value, modeled on industrial quality
control.

1324. —— (1954) An Approximate Measure of Value.
Operations Res. 2: 172-187.

1325. +——, Ackoff and Arnoff, E. Leonard (1957) Introduction to Operations Research. New York: Wiley.

1326. Clapp, James G. (1948) Freedom as Fulfillment.
IN: Philosophy of Freedom, Symposium. Phil.
Phen. Res. 8: 522-531.

1327. Clark, Gordon H. and Smith, Thomas V., eds.
(1931) Readings in Ethics. New York: Appleton-Century-Crofts.

1328. Cobb, John B. (1954) The Possibility of a Universal
Normative Ethics. Ethics 55: 55-71. --Reply
to Asher Moore's argument (see 1608) that the
concept of a universal normative ethic is impossible because self-contradictory.

1329. Cohen, Morris R. (1944) Values, Norms and
      Science. IN: A Preface to Logic. New York:
      Holt. 155-178. --Rebuttal of two arguments that
      deny the possibility of a normative science.

1330. Collingwood, Robin G. (1938) The Principles of Art.
      Oxford: Clarendon Press.

1331. Copi, Irving M. (1955) A Note on Representation in
      Art. J. Phil. 52: 346-349. --On the esthetic
      relevance of content in works of art.

1332. Corkey, R. (1954) Basic Intrinsic Ethical Values.
      Philosophy 29: 321-331.

1333. Creegan, Robert F. (1955) Recent Trends in the
      Psychology of Values. IN: A. A. Roback, ed.
      Present-Day Psychology. New York: Philo-
      sophical Library. 949-960. --Phenomenological
      and existential approach to the problem of
      values.

1334. Crissman, Paul (1942) Temporal Change and Sexual
      Difference in Moral Judgments. J. Soc.
      Psychol. 16: 29-38.

1335. Croce, Benedetto (1913) The Philosophy of the
      Practical; Economic and Ethic. Trans. by
      Douglas Ainslie. London: Macmillan. --Logic
      and esthetics theoretical, economics and
      morals practical activities.

1336. —— (1921) The Essence of Aesthetic. Trans. by
      Douglas Ainslie. London: Heinemann.

1337. —— (1922) Aesthetic as Science of Expression and
      General Linguistic. Trans. by Douglas Ainslie.
      London: Macmillan. Also: New York: Noon-
      day Press. --Intuition the locus of esthetic val-
      ue and the base on which spirit experiences all
      else; art is independent of logic, morals,
      pleasure, utility, or matter: art is form.

1338. —— (1929) Aesthetic. Trans. by Douglas Ainslie. London: Macmillan.

1339. —— (1945) Politics and Morals. Trans. by Salvatore J. Castiglione. New York: Philosophical Library. --Theoretical dogmas and abstractions must not be allowed to replace spontaneous, creative individual thinking in specific situations of politics and ethics.

1340. Czezowski, Tadeusz (1953) Ethics as an Empirical Science. Phil. Phen. Res. 14: 163-171.

1341. Danto, Arthur C. and Morgenbesser, Sidney (1957) Character and Free Will. J. Phil. 54: 493-505. --Towards resolving the free will controversy, an exploration of "what sort of evidence [one] . . . would require . . . to concede defeat."

1342. Davidson, Donald, McKinsey, J. C. C., and Suppes, Patrick (1955) Outlines of a Formal Theory of Value, I. Phil. Sci. 22: 140-160. --Formal conditions for rational choice (Rational Preference Ranking) among valued entities, a methodological device.

1343. +——, Suppes, Patrick and Siegel, Sidney (1957) Decision-Making; An Experimental Approach. Stanford: Stanford Univ. Press. --Models for measuring subjective probability, experimentally tested.

1344. de Laguna, Grace A. (1942) Cultural Relativism and Science. Phil. Rev. 51: 141-166. --Analysis of "relativism" and "knowledge," concluding that science forms ethical universals that transcend cultural relativism.

1345. —— (1949) Culture and Rationality. Amer. Anthrop.
51: 379-391. --Rationality a function of personality achieved through idealized (valued),
objective culture.

1346. Demos, Raphael (1945) Moral Value as Irreducible, Objective, and Cognizable. Phil. Phen.
Res. 6: 163-193.

1347. Dennes, William R. (1946) Conflict. Phil. Rev. 55:
343-376.

1348. —— (1954) Knowledge and Values. Symp. Sci.
Phil. Relig. 13: 603-618.

1349. —— (In Press) Some Dilemmas of Naturalism.
Woodbridge Lectures, Sixth Series, 1958.
New York: Columbia Univ. Press. --See especially: The Naturalistic Fallacy, Reason
and Moral Obligation.

1350. Dessoir, Max (1906) Aesthetik und Allgemeine
Kunstwissenschaft. Stuttgart: F. Enke. --
Esthetics as a science.

1351. —— (1926) Aesthetics and the Philosophy of Art in
Contemporary Germany. Monist 36: 299-
310. --The science of esthetics requires study
of materials, social aspects, particular arts
and their production and the artist.

1352. Dewey, John (1903) The Logical Conditions of a
Scientific Treatment of Morality. Chicago:
Univ. of Chicago Press. --An early exploratory
essay.

1353. —— (1915) The Logic of Judgments of Practice. J.
Phil. Psychol. Sci. Method 12: 505-523; 533-
543. --Intelligence, equated with scientific
method and applied to conduct, basic to a dynamic morality; ethics must change as the

conditions of life change, adapting to biological, sociological and cultural conditions.

1354.　——　(1922)　Human Nature and Conduct; An Introduction to Social Psychology.　New York: Holt. --General value theory. "Satisfactoriness" as integration or harmony in the resolution of unsettled situations; value theory a scientific enterprise.

1355.　——　(1929)　The Construction of the Good.　IN: Quest for Certainty.　New York: Putnam. --Proposes integrating ethics with everyday activities, means with ends, theory with practice.

1356.　——　(1933)　Art as Experience.　New York: Minton, Balch. --Pragmatic view of art as needing to be integrated in everyday life; artists can influence society and be a part of it.

1357.　——　(1939)　Theory of Valuation.　Chicago: Univ. of Chicago Press (International Encyclopaedia of Unified Science 2, 4). --Brief exposition of pragmatist-instrumentalist ethics; value judgments verifiable as scientific judgments; criticizes emotivist position.

1358.　——　(1944)　Some Questions about Value.　J. Phil. 41: 449-455. --Discussion of "prizing," "evaluating" and the application of scientific method to testing value judgments.

1359.　——　and Tufts, James H. (1932)　Ethics.　Rev. ed. New York: Holt. --Detailed program for unifying ethical theory and practice.

1360.　Dickinson, Goldsworthy L. (1907)　The Meaning of Good; A Dialogue.　4th ed.　London: Brimley Johnson and Ince.　Also: New York: McClure, Phillips.

1361. Diggs, Bernard J. (1957) Ethics and Experimental Theories of Motivation and Learning. Ethics 67: 100-118. --To clarify issues in the dispute between "naturalistic" and "linguistic" views of ethical theory in contemporary philosophy, examines current psychological theories to modernize psychological basis of moral philosophy.

1362. Dilthey, Wilhelm (1906) Das Erlebnis und die Dichtung. Leipsig: Teubner. --Lebensphilophie in relation to poetry.

1363. —— (1911) Die Typen der Weltanschauung und ihre Ausbildung in den Metaphysischen Systemen. Berlin: Verlag Reichl. --The doctrine of Verstehungs-Psychologie as basic to understanding social goals and values.

1364. Dryer, Douglas P. (1953) Ethical Reasoning. IN: Academic Freedom, Logic and Religion, Symposium. American Philosophical Association, Eastern Division, 2. Philadelphia: Univ. of Pennsylvania Press. 143-157. --Practical reasoning and ethical reasoning analyzed and distinguished.

1365. Ducasse, Curt J. (1929) The Philosophy of Art. New York: Dial Press.

1366. ___ (1940) The Nature and Function of Theory in Ethics. Ethics 51: 22-37. --A metaethical inquiry, outlining conditions necessary for rational choice.

1367. ___ (1953) Scientific Method in Ethics. Phil. Phen. Res. 14: 72-88. --Humanistic interpretation of ethics as guided by rational-scientific inquiry.

1368. Duncan-Jones, Austin E. (1933) Ethical Words and Ethical Facts. Mind 42: 473-500.

-241-

1369. ___ (1938-1939) Freedom; An Illustrative Puzzle. Proc. Aristotelian Soc. 39: 99-120.

1370. Duncker, Karl (1939) Ethical Relativity? (An Enquiry into the Psychology of Ethics). Mind 48: 39-57.

1371. Dunham, Barrows (1947) Man Against Myth. Boston: Little, Brown. --In a popular style, critical analysis of popular fallacies relevant to values, ethics, beliefs and attitudes towards empirical knowledge and social change.

1372. Eaton, Howard O. (1930) The Austrian Philosophy of Value. Norman: Univ. of Oklahoma Press. -- Wertphilosophie of Brentano, Meinong and Ehrenfels.

1373. Edel, Abraham (1944) Naturalism and Ethical Theory. IN: Yervant H. Krikorian, ed. Naturalism and the Human Spirit. New York: Columbia Univ. Press. 65-95. --Outline of a science of ethics.

1374. ─── (1945) The Evaluation of Ideals. J. Phil. 42: 561-577.

1375. ─── (1948) Coordinates of Criticism in Ethical Theory. Phil. Phen. Res. 7: 543-577.

1376. ─── (1953) Concept of Values in Contemporary Philosophical Value Theory. Phil. Sci. 20: 198-207. --Value theory as a search for unity of value in human history.

1377. ─── (1953) Ethical Reasoning. IN: Academic Freedom, Logic and Religion, Symposium. American Philosophical Association, Eastern Division, 2. Philadelphia: Univ. of Pennsylvania Press. 127-142. --Criticizes attempts to introduce new validity models into ethical theory, the scientific model already available considered adequate. Reviews briefly linguistic theories in ethics.

1378. —— (1953) Some Relations of Philosophy and Anthropology. Amer. Anthrop. 55: 649-660. -- "Morality" and "ethical pattern" as ethnographic categories; the relevance of cross-cultural evidence to problems in ethical theory.

1379. —— (1955) Ethical Judgment; The Use of Science in Ethics. Glencoe, Ill.: Free Press. --The use of the human sciences to reduce indeterminacy in ethics; analyses of the main problems of relating science to ethics.

1380. Edman, Irwin (1928) The World, the Arts and the Artist. New York: Norton.

1381. —— (1939) Arts and the Man. New York: Norton.

1382. Edwards, Paul (1955) The Logic of Moral Discourse. Glencoe, Ill.: Free Press. --Emotivist ethics redefined in the direction of naturalism and defended.

1383. —— and Pap, Arthur, eds. (1957) Moral Judgments. IN: A Modern Introduction to Philosophy; Readings from Classical and Contemporary Sources. Part VI. Glencoe, Ill.: Free Press.

1384. Elliot, Hugh S. R. (1922) Human Character. London and New York: Longmans, Green. -- Naturalistic, anti-teleological approach to human behavior.

1385. Elton, William, ed. (1954) Aesthetics and Language. New York: Philosophical Library. --Essays by Cambridge and Oxford philosophical analysts and others of a similar tendency.

1386. Ewing, Alfred C. (1939) A Suggested Non-Naturalistic Analysis of Good. Mind 48: 1-22.

1387. —— (1947) The Definition of Good. New York: Macmillan. --Metalinguistic analysis.

1388. —— (1953) Ethics. New York: Macmillan. -- Arguments against subjectivistic and naturalistic ethical theories; detailed analysis of "good" and "ought."

1389. Falk, W. D. (1953) Goading and Guiding. Mind 62: 145-171. --Value terms as instruments of goading and guiding.

1390. —— (1956) Moral Perplexity. Ethics 66: 123-131. --Contemporary uncertainty about morals located at both practical and philosophical levels, reflecting need to make the difficult choice between freedom and social welfare.

1391. Farber, Marvin, ed. (1943) The Foundation of Phenomenology; Edmund Husserl and the Quest for a Rigorous Science of Philosophy. Cambridge: Harvard Univ. Press. --In a phenomenological framework, maintains the theoretical intertranslatability of facts, values and actions.

1392. Farrell, B. A. (1946) An Appraisal of Therapeutic Positivism. Mind 55: 25-48.

1393. Feibleman, James K. (1949) Aesthetics; A Study of the Fine Arts in Theory and Practice. New York: Duell, Sloan and Pearce. --An organistic theory of art.

1394. —— (1953) Freedom and Authority in the Structure of Cultures. Symp. Sci. Phil. Relig. 12: 309-316.

1395. —— (1954) Toward an Analysis of the Basic Value System. Amer. Anthrop. 56: 421-432. --An ontological theory of values, intended as a philosophical rendering of the anthropological theory that cultures have patterns pervasive through time and common to their individual members.

1396. —— (1955) Introduction to an Objective, Empirical Ethics. Ethics 55: 102-115.

1397. Feigl, Herbert (1943) Logical Empiricism. IN: Dagobert Runes, ed. Twentiety Century Philosophy. New York: Philosophical Library. 371-416. --Moral rules, values and the categorical imperative expressible only in emotive language, therefore neither true nor false.

1398. —— (1950) De Principiis Non Disputandum? IN: Max Black, ed. Philosophical Analysis. Ithaca: Cornell Univ. Press. 119-156. --Reprinted with changes as: Validation and Vindication; An Analysis of the Nature and Limits of Ethical Argument. IN: Wilfrid Sellars and John Hospers, eds. Readings in Ethical Theory. Appleton-Century-Crofts, 1952. 667-680. The limits to rational justification of assertions in ethics and in science.

1399. —— (1950) The Difference Between Knowledge and Valuation. J. Soc. Issues 6: 39-44.

1400. Ferm, Vergilius, ed. (1956) Encyclopedia of Morals. New York: Philosophical Library. -- 52 contributions on moral theory and practice, from anthropology, philosophy, religion, political science and oriental studies.

1401. Feuer, Lewis S. (1955) Psychoanalysis and Ethics. Springfield, Ill.: Thomas. --Psychoanalysis as an aid in reducing anxiety, freeing individuals

for fuller self-realization; ultimate value statements verifiable through evidence produced by
psychoanalytic methods; criticism of Freud's
philosophy of civilization.

1402. Findlay, J. N. (1944) Morality by Convention.
Mind 54: 142-169.

1403. Fingarette, Herbert (1957) The Judgment Functions
of Moral Language. IN: Ray Lepley, ed. The
Language of Value. New York: Columbia
Univ. Press. 131-152.

1404. Firth, Roderick (1952) Ethical Absolutism and the
Ideal Observer. Phil. Phen. Res. 12: 317-
345.

1405. Fitch, Robert E. (1936) The Two Methods of Ethics.
J. Phil. 33: 318-324. --Careful methodology
to reduce disagreements in ethics a necessary
step towards a science of ethics.

1406. Flew, Anthony (1954) The Justification of Punishment. Philosophy 29: 291-307.

1407. Flewelling, Ralph T. (1915) Personalism and the
Problems of Philosophy. New York and Cin-
cinnati: Methodist Book Concern.

1408. —— (1935) Reflections on the Basic Ideas of East
and West. Peiping, China: College of Chinese
Studies, California College in China.

1409. —— (1951) Conflict and Conciliation of Cultures.
Stockton, Calif.: College of the Pacific
Press. --Personalist philosophy extended to a
cross-cultural study of philosophy and values.

1410. Frankel, Charles (1953) Empiricism and Moral
Imperatives. J. Phil. 50: 257-269.

1411. —— (1955) The Case for Modern Man. New York: Harper. --Prolegomena to a social philosophy, reasserting confidence in human reason and human ability to fulfill the ideals of liberalism.

1412. —— (1957) Explanation and Interpretation in History. Phil. Sci. 24: 137-155. --Inquiries into the ways a historian's values may affect his interpretation of causal connections.

1413. Frankena, William K. (1939) The Naturalistic Fallacy. Mind 48: 464-477. --Critique and amendment of G. E. Moore's views on the indefinability of the word, "good."

1414. —— (1950) Obligation and Ability. IN: Max Black, ed. Philosophical Analysis. Ithaca: Cornell Univ. Press. 157-175.

1415. —— (1951) Moral Philosophy at Mid-Century. Phil. Rev. 60: 44-55. --Comprehensive review of American and European sources.

1416. —— (1952) The Concept of Universal Human Rights. IN: Science, Language and Human Rights, Symposium. American Philosophical Association, Eastern Division, 1. Philadelphia: Univ. of Pennsylvania Press. 189-207. --Logico-linguistic analysis of utterances asserting universal human rights.

1417. Friedmann, Frederick G. (1953) The World of "La Miseria." Partisan Rev. 20: 218-231. --Philosophy and values of Italian peasants.

1418. Garnett, Arthur Campbell (1937) Reality and Value. London: Allen and Unwin. Also: New Haven: Yale Univ. Press. --Deontological ethics.

1419. —— (1940) Deontology and Self-Realization. Ethics 51: 419-438.

1420. —— (1949) Intrinsic Good; Its Definition and Referent. IN: Ray Lepley, ed. Value; A Cooperative Inquiry. New York: Columbia Univ. Press. 78-92.

1421. —— (1952) The Moral Nature of Man; A Critical Evaluation of Ethical Principles. New York: Ronald. --Deontology and teleology synthesized in a modified intuitionistic utilitarianism; criticisms of naturalistic reductionism in contemporary ethics. In Ch. 2, contrasts between primitive and civilized morality.

1422. —— (1957) A Non-Normative Definition of "Good." IN: Ray Lepley, ed. The Language of Value. New York: Columbia Univ. Press. 122-130.

1423. Garvin, Lucius (1947) The Paradox of Aesthetic Meaning. Phil. Phen. Res. 8: 99-106.

1424. —— (1958) Emotivism, Expression, and Symbolic Meaning. J. Phil. 55: 111-118. --An emotivist theory of esthetics.

1425. +Gehlen, Arnold (1942) Zur Systematik der Anthropologie. IN: Nicolai Hartmann, ed. Systematische Philosophie. Stuttgart and Berlin: W. Kohlhammer. --Traditional philosophical anthropology, an inquiry into human nature.

1426. +—— (1950) Der Mensch, Seine Natur und Seine Stellung in der Welt. 4th ed. Bonn: Athenäum-Verlag. --First ed., Berlin, 1940.

1427. Geiger, George R. (1938) Towards an Objective Ethics. Yellow Springs, Ohio: Antioch Press. --Pragmatist position.

1428. —— (1947) Philosophy and the Social Order; An Introductory Approach. Boston and New York: Houghton, Mifflin. --Value theory in relation to social institutions.

1429. —— (1949) Values and Inquiry. IN: Ray Lepley, ed. Value; A Cooperative Inquiry. New York: Columbia Univ. Press. 93-111.

1430. —— (1950) Values and Social Sciences. J. Soc. Issues 6: 8-16.--Interrelations of ethics and the social sciences.

1431. Gentile, Giovanni (1931) La Filosofia dell'Arte. Milano: Fratelli Treves.

1432. Gewirth, Alan (1954) Can Men Change Laws of Social Science? Phil. Sci. 21: 229-241. -- "Man through his awareness of the impact of the laws of social science on his values may intervene . . . to remove some of those laws from actual operation . . . " and to create new ones.

1433. Gilbert, Katherine E. (1927) Studies in Recent Aesthetic. Chapel Hill: Univ. of North Carolina Press.

1434. —— and Kuhn, Helmut (1939) A History of Esthetics. Bloomington: Indiana Univ. Press.

1435. Gilman, Eric (1954) Objectivity in Conduct. Philosophy 29: 308-320.

1436. Gilson, Etienne (1931) Moral Values and the Moral Life; The System of St. Thomas Aquinas. Trans. by Leo Richard Ward. St. Louis: Herder.

1437. Goheen, John (1941) Whitehead's Theory of Value. IN: Paul A. Schilpp, ed. The Philosophy of Alfred North Whitehead. New York: Tudor. 437-459.

1438. Golightly, Cornelius L. (1947) Race, Values and Guilt. Soc. Forces 26: 125-139.--Americans rationalize discrimination against Negroes through a dual system of caste values and democratic ideals.

1439. —— (1947) Social Science and Normative Ethics. J. Phil. 44: 505-516. --Scientific determination of ultimate values the province of social scientists.

1440. —— (1956) Value as a Scientific Concept. J. Phil. 53: 233-245.

1441. Gomperz, H. (1937) Some Simple Thoughts on Freedom and Responsibility. Philosophy 12: 61-76.

1442. —— (1943) When Does the End Sanctify the Means? Ethics 53: 173-183.

1443. Goodwin, William F. (1955) Ethics and Value in Indian Philosophy. Phil. East and West (Honolulu) 4: 321-344.

1444. —— (1956) Mysticism and Ethics; An Examination of Radhakrishnan's Reply to Schweitzer's Critique of Indian Thought. Ethics 67: 25-41. --On the question whether Indian "abstract mysticism" entails the rejection of ethics. (See 1698 and 1903.)

1445. Gotesky, Rubin (1952) The Nature of Myth and Society. Amer. Anthrop. 54: 523-531.-- Critique of Bidney's concept of myth (see 1273) and an examination of the meaning of "myth" in relation to values, beliefs and scientific knowledge.

1446. Gotshalk, Dilman W. (1947) Art and the Social Order. Chicago: Univ. of Chicago Press. -- Pragmatist view of the integration of art and experience.

1447. —— (1952) Value Science. Phil. Sci. 19: 183-192. --Pragmatist view.

1448. Grave, S. A. (1958) Are the Analyses of Moral Concepts Morally Neutral? J. Phil. 55: 455-460. --Doubts the freedom from moral consequences of contemporary ethical analyses.

1449. Greene, Theodore M. (1940) The Arts and the Art of Criticism. Princeton: Princeton Univ. Press. --An organistic theory of art.

1450. —— (1953) Secular Values and Religious Faith. IN: A. Dudley Ward, ed. Goals of Economic Life. New York: Harper. 365-396.

1451. —— (1955) The Symbolic Vehicles of Our Cultural Values. Symp. Sci. Phil. Relig. 14: 229-282.

1452. —— (1958) Moral, Aesthetic, and Religious Insight. New Brunswick: Rutgers Univ. Press.

1453. Grene, Marjorie (1948) Dreadful Freedom, a Critique of Existentialism. Chicago: Univ. of Chicago Press.

1454. Grinnell, Robert (1949) Franciscan Philosophy and Gothic Art. IN: F. S. C. Northrop, ed. Ideological Differences and World Order. New Haven: Yale Univ. Press. 117-136. -- Philosophic values expressed in medieval art.

1455. Hahn, Lewis E. (1949) A Contextualist Looks at Values. IN: Ray Lepley, ed. Value; A Cooperative Inquiry. New York: Columbia Univ. Press. 112-124.

1456. Hall, Everett W. (1947) A Categorial Analysis of Value. Phil. Sci. 14: 333-344.

1457. —— (1952) What Is Value? An Essay in Philosophical Analysis. London: Humanities Press. -- Extended logico-linguistic analysis of value judgments; value terms a means to analyzing experience.

1458. —— (1956) Modern Science and Human Values; A Study in the History of Ideas. Princeton: Van Nostrand. --Understanding values necessary to survival, but scientific method does not give knowledge of values but only of the facts of the physical world. (See 1471, for criticism.)

1459. Halldén, Sören (1954) Emotive Propositions; A Study of Value. Stockholm: Almqvist and Wiksell. --Variant of emotivist ethical theory.

1460. Hamburg, Carl H. (1956) Psychology and the Ethics of Survival. Phil. Sci. 23: 82-89. --Criticizes thesis that the survival value of behavior practices is the ultimate criterion for moral goodness.

1461. Hammond, William A. (1934) A Bibliography of Aesthetics and of the Philosophy of the Fine Arts from 1900 to 1932. New York: Longmans, Green.

1462. Hampshire, Stuart (1949) Fallacies in Moral Philosophy. Mind 58: 466-482. --For rejoinders and follow-up, see Mind, volumes 59 and 60.

1463. Handy, Rollo (1958) Philosophy's Neglect of the Social Sciences. Phil. Sci. 25: 117-124. -- Reviews philosophers' recent use of social science results in value theory, metaphysics and methodology.

1464. Hare, Richard M. (1952) The Language of Morals. Oxford: Clarendon Press. --Ethics defined as logical examination of the language of morals, ethical judgments as functioning to commend; discussion of the decision-making process.

1465. Hart, H. L. A. (1949) The Ascription of Responsibility and Rights. Proc. Aristotelian Soc. 49: 171-194. Also in: Anthony Flew, ed. Logic and Language. Oxford: Blackwell. Also: New York: Philosophical Library. 145-166. --Ethical judgments as ascribing rights and responsibilities.

1466. Hart, Samuel L. (1949) Treatise on Values. New York: Philosophical Library. --Discusses moral, esthetic and religious values, conceived as generic concepts subject to reason.

1467. —— (1955) The Nature and Objectivity of Ethical Judgments. Phil. Phen. Res. 15: 360-368. -- "Moral rationality is contingent upon the . . . urge to live."

1468. Hartman, Robert S. (1948) The Moral Situation; A Field Theory of Ethics. J. Phil. 45: 292-300. --Asserts the possibility of a science of ethics, with Lewinian field theory as a framework for analysis.

1469. —— (1950) Is a Science of Ethics Possible? Phil. Sci. 17: 238-246.

1470. —— (1957) Value Propositions. IN: Ray Lepley, ed. The Language of Value. New York: Columbia Univ. Press. 197-231. --Cognitivist position.

1471. —— (1958) Value, Fact and Science. Phil. Sci. 25: 97-108. --Criticism of Hall, Modern Science and Human Values (see 1458), rejecting the view that science can give us knowledge of facts but never of values, favoring the pragmatist alternative that scientific study of the phenomena of values is possible and desirable.

1472. Hartmann, Nicolai (1932) Ethics. Trans. by Stanton Coit. London: Allen and Unwin. Also: New York: Macmillan. 3 vols. --Phenomenological approach, concerned with the preconditions of value consciousness and ultimate value hierarchy. Values intuited, objective, self-existent, ideal essences, with a tendency to come into existence.

1473. Havice, Doris Webster (1958) The Need for Sound Type-Theory in Ethical Inquiry. IN: Studies in Ethical Theory. Boulder: Univ. of Colorado Press (University of Colorado Studies, Series in Philosophy 1). 72-82. --An interdisciplinary approach to personality typology would end contemporary confusion and produce a result useful in ethical theory.

1474. Hawkins, David (1958) Ethics and Ethical Experience. IN: Studies in Ethical Theory. Boulder: Univ. of Colorado Press (University of Colorado Studies, Series in Philosophy, 1). 57-71. --Critical analysis of objectivism and subjectivism in ethical theory; behavioral science data relevant to ethics.

1475. Haworth, Lawrence L. and Minas, J. S. (1954) Concerning Value Science. Phil. Sci. 21: 54-61. --"Value science . . . as . . . the science of adjusting social activities relative to the goal of human betterment."

1476. Heidegger, Martin (1929) Von Wesen des Grundes. IN: Festschrift für Edmund Husserl, Halle a. d. S. : Niemeyer. 71-110. --Existentialist ethico-metaphysical view.

1477. ―― (1951) The Age of the World View. Measure 2: 269-284. --Phenomenological and existential analysis of human existence, an attempt to recover man's pristine ability to understand

reality and human existence; exploration of
Sorge as dominant characteristic of human
consciousness.

1478. +Hempel, Carl G. (1949) The Logical Analysis of
Psychology. Trans. by Wilfrid Sellars. IN:
Herbert Feigl and Wilfrid Sellars, eds.
Readings in Philosophical Analysis. New
York: Appleton-Century-Crofts. 373-384. --
Compatibility of physicalistic philosophy and
the study of nonmaterial phenomena.

1479. Henle, Paul (1943) Method in Ethics. Ethics 54:
29-40. --Critical examination of pragmatist
parallels of ethical and epistemological positions.

1480. +Hennemann, Gerhard (1951) Das Bild der Welt und
des Menschen in Ontologischer Sicht. Basel:
Reinhardt (Glauben und Wissen Nr. 8). --
Philosophical anthropology.

1481. Hill, Thomas E. (1950) Contemporary Ethical
Theories. New York: Macmillan. --Readings.

1482. Hilliard, Albert L. (1950) The Forms of Value; The
Extension of a Hedonistic Axiology. New York:
Columbia Univ. Press. --Logical construction
and elaboration of hedonism in ethics, esthetics, economics and epistemology.

1483. Hocking, William E. (1932) Human Nature and Its
Remaking. New Haven: Yale Univ. Press. --
Self-realization the goal of ethics, related to
the unity of human instincts governed by conscience.

1484. Hodges, Donald C. (1955) Human Conduct and
Philosophical Ethics. J. Phil. 52: 309-318. --
Criticism of current analytical methods in
philosophy; recommends "the re-evaluation of

our original intuitions of the good in the light of historical knowledge, logical analysis, and policy decision."

1485. Hofstadter, Albert (1956) The Seriousness of Moral Philosophy. Ethics 66: 284-287. --"Moral theory which neglects moral experiences would be as absurd as . . . physical theory which flouts experimental data . . . ," in criticism of some contemporary ethical theory.

1486. —— (1957) Six Necessities. J. Phil. 54: 597-613. --Distinguishes varieties of necessity: logical, linguistic, ontic, physical, of the hypothetical imperative and of the categorical imperative, with the Humean conclusion that necessity is mental but objectively grounded.

1487. Hollister, William W. (1953) Conduct and the Circle. J. Phil. 50: 57-70. --Utility of the "vicious circle" in explaining behavior and clarifying the relation of ethical principles to social science generalization.

1488. Hook, Sidney (1958) Moral Freedom in a Determined World; Responsibility and Sentimentalism. Commentary 25: 431-443. --Acts can be both determined and morally responsible; "proximate freedom" sufficient, human effort can "re-determine the direction of events even though it cannot determine the conditions which make human effort possible."

1489. Hoop, J. H. van der (1948) Freedom in the Philosophy of East and West. IN: Philosophy of Freedom, Symposium. Phil. Phen. Res. 8: 557-572.

1490. Horsburgh, H. J. N. (1954) The Plurality of Moral Standards. Philosophy 29: 332-346.

1491. Hospers, John (1947) Meaning and Truth in the
Arts. Chapel Hill: Univ. of North Carolina
Press. --Art related to life but transforms
experiences into something novel and intrinsically rewarding; art has no direct social
function, but may be useful to counteract the
contemporary tendency to excessive abstract-
ness in knowledge.

1492. Hourani, George F. (1956) Ethical Value. Ann
Arbor: Univ. of Michigan Press. --Defends a
variant of utilitarianism, related to an analysis of ethical terms as used by ordinary persons.

1493. Huisman, Denis (1954) L'Esthétique. Paris:
Presses Universitaires de France. --The role
of esthetics in philosophy and the future of experimental esthetics; sections on the history of esthetics; philosophy, psychology and sociology of
art; the relation of esthetics to science and
morality; systems and methodology.

1494. Hungerland, Isabel C. (1958) Poetic Discourse.
Berkeley and Los Angeles: Univ. of California Press.

1495. Husserl, Edmund (1931) Ideas; General Introduction to Pure Phenomenology. Trans. by W. R.
Boyce Gibson. London: Allen and Unwin. --
A phenomenological search for truth in science,
ethics, and other fields, free from all presuppositions.

1496. Irving, John A. (1952) Science and Values.
Toronto: Ryerson. --Recommends the use of
social science in philosophic value theory and
the orientation of social philosophy to actual
life conditions.

1497. James, William (1898) The Moral Philosopher and
the Moral Life. IN: The Will to Believe and

Other Essays in Popular Philosophy. New
York: Longmans, Green. 184-215. --"Cash
value" extended to values in general; "the essence of good is simply to satisfy demand."

1498. —— (1907) Pragmatism, a New Name for Some Old
Ways of Thinking. New York: Longmans,
Green.

1499. —— (1910) The Moral Equivalent of War. Popular
Sci. Monthly 77: 400-410.

1500. Jaspers, Karl (1933) Man in the Modern Age.
Trans. by Eden and Cedar Paul. London:
Routledge. --Existentialist view.

1501. —— (1938) Existenzphilosophie. Berlin: de
Gruyter.

1502. —— (1952) Existentialism and Humanism; Three
Essays. Trans. by E. B. Ashton. New York:
Moore. --Analyzes possible attitudes towards
the world, decisions in life's crises and ways
of meeting them. Seeks to overcome the limitations on philosophy imposed by science,
preferring to understand reality through deep
experience and conflicts.

1503. —— (1952) Nature and Ethics. IN: R. N. Anshen,
ed. Moral Principles of Action. New York:
Harper. 48-61.

1504. Jessup, Bertram E. (1943) Relational Value Meanings. Eugene: Univ. of Oregon Press.

1505. —— (1949) On Value. IN: Ray Lepley, ed. Value;
A Cooperative Inquiry. New York: Columbia
Univ. Press. 125-146.

1506. —— (1954) The Comparative Esthetic Judgment.
Phil. Phen. Res. 14: 546-552.

1507. Joad, Cyril E. M. (1921) Common-Sense Ethics.
New York: Dutton. --Ultimate meaning of
moral terms found in life itself; the task of
morals is to give impulse free rein, thus
leading to individual happiness and social good;
Freudian and behavioristic psychology reveal
the irrelevance of traditional ethical systems
to life.

1508. —— (1948) Decadence; A Philosophical Inquiry.
London: Faber and Faber. --Criticism of contemporary life and morals.

1509. Jordan, Elijah (1937) The Aesthetic Object; An Introduction to the Philosophy of Value. Bloomington, Ind.: Principia Press. --The psychology
of esthetic experience; the metaphysics of esthetic value.

1510. —— (1949) The Good Life. Chicago: Univ. of
Chicago Press. --Moral and political philosophy,
based on a conception of the individual as part
of society, organistically conceived.

1511. Jørgensen, Carl (1956) On the Possibility of De-
ducing What Ought To Be from What Is. Ethics
66: 271-278. --In disagreement with Hume's
classical statement, cites four types of situation in which "ought" is correctly deduced from
"is."

1512. Joseph, Horace W. B. (1931) Some Problems in
Ethics. Oxford: Clarendon Press. --Self-
realization theory; rightness, goodness of
consequences and of will depend upon an ideal
form of life shared by men and adopted in the
performance of right acts.

1513. Kadish, Mortimer R. (1951) Evidence and Decision.
J. Phil. 48: 229-242. --Recommends resolving
ethical problems by phrasing them as decision-
making problems.

1514. Kallen, Horace M. (1942) Art and Freedom; A Historical and Biographical Interpretation of the Relations Between the Ideas of Beauty, Use and Freedom in Western Civilization from the Greeks to the Present Day. New York: Duell, Sloan and Pearce. --Pragmatist position; social progress and advancement of art require freedom for the artist; criticism should be directed at standards as well as at works of art.

1515. ___ (1948) The Discipline of Freedom. IN: Philosophy of Freedom, Symposium. Phil. Phen. Res. 8: 508-514.

1516. ___ (1949) The Education of Free Men. New York: Farrar, Straus. --Value a function of resolving human problems; values of freedom and individualism of central importance.

1517. Kaplan, Abraham (1942) Are Moral Judgments Assertions? Phil. Rev. 51: 280-303. --Moral judgments pragmatic in function; behavioral science results useful in ethics.

1518. ___ (1954) Referential Meaning in the Arts. J. Aesthetics and Art Criticism 12: 457-474.

1519. ___ (1955) Obscenity as an Esthetic Category. IN: Robert Kramer, ed. Law and Contemporary Problems. Durham: Duke Univ. Press. 544-559. --The definition of "obscenity" in relation to the censorship of works of art.

1520. ___ (1958) American Ethics and Public Policy. Daedalus, Spring: 48-77 (Issued as vol. 87, no. 2, Proc. Amer. Acad. Arts and Sci.). --The dualism of transcendent ideals and daily experience endangers moral values and degrades political life; objective relativism distinguished from cultural relativism and moral subjectivism.

1521. ___ and Kris, Ernst (1948) Esthetic Ambiguity.
Phil. Phen. Res. 8: 415-435. Also in:
Ernst Kris, ed. Psychoanalytic Explorations
in Art. New York: International Universities
Press, 1952. 243-264. --The creative function
of various types of ambiguity.

1522. Kattsoff, L. O. (1953) Man Is the Measure of All
Things. Phil. Phen. Res. 13: 452-465.

1523. Katz, Joseph (1955) Ethics Without Morality. J.
Phil. 52: 287-291. --Morality is emotive,
ethics is rationally directed emotion; rejects
"moralizing" attitude of certain social psychological studies of authoritarian personality.

1524. Kaufmann, Felix (1944) Methodology of the Social
Sciences. New York: Oxford Univ. Press. --
See especially: Chs. 9, 15, 16, phenomenological analysis of value judgments as analytic
propositions dependent on axiological rules,
analogous to scientific propositions. Value
judgments, properly understood, may safely
be made in social science.

1525. Knox, Israel (1936) The Aesthetic Theories of Kant,
Hegel, and Schopenhauer. New York: Colum-
bia Univ. Press.

1526. Koch, Adrienne (1953) Power and Morals and the
Founding Fathers; Jefferson. Rev. Pol. 15:
470-490. --Morality of "founding fathers" in
relation to contemporary political problems.

1527. ___ (1958) The Status of Values and Democratic
Political Theory. Ethics 68: 166-185. --Sur-
veys, in relation to political inquiry, three
theories of the status of value judgments.

1528. Krusé, Cornelius (1937) Cognition and Value
Reëxamined. J. Phil. 34: 225-234. --

Cognition related to values through the process
of valuation.

1529. ___ (1951) Western Theories of Value. IN: Charles
A. Moore, ed. Essays in East-West Philosophy.
Honolulu: Univ. of Hawaii Press. 383-397.

1530. Kuhn, Helmut (1942) Fact and Value in Ethics. Phil.
Phen. Res. 2: 501-510.

1531. Kunz, Hans (1946) Die Anthropologische Bedeutung
der Phantasie. Basel: Recht und Gesellschaft
AG. (Studia Philosophica, Supplements 3 and
4, 2 vols.)

1532. ___ (1954) Zur Frage Nach dem Wesen der Norm.
Psyche (Heidelberg) 8: 241-271. --The normative a function of the alternatives open to men.

1533. Kurtz, Paul W. (1952) The Problems of Value Theory.
New York: Journal of Philosophy Press. --Sur-
vey of recent ethical theory.

1534. ___ (1956) Human Nature, Homeostasis, and Value.
Phil. Phen. Res. 17: 36-55. --The value principle of "maximized actualization of life" de-
rivable from a dynamic theory of human nature.

1535. Ladd, John (1952) Ethics and Explanation. J. Phil.
49: 499-504. --Critique of metaethical analysis, calling attention to the vagueness of the
distinction between object-language and meta-
language.

1536. ___ (1953) Reason and Practice. IN: John Wild, ed.
The Return to Reason. Chicago: Regnery. --
The nature and relations of reason and practice
in ethics.

1537. ___ (1956) The Structure of a Moral Code; A Philosophical Analysis of Ethical Discourse Applied

to the Ethics of the Navaho Indians. Cambridge:
Harvard Univ. Press. --Extended philosophical
analysis of aims and methods of descriptive
ethics and of the structure of ethical discourse,
followed by a detailed account of the ethical system of a Navaho headman.

1538. Lafleur, Lawrence J. (1942) Biological Evidence in
Aesthetics. Phil. Rev. 51: 587-595. --
Towards an objective esthetics.

1539. ___ (1954) The Meanings of Good. Phil. Phen. Res.
15: 210-221. --Brief review of various concepts
of good, directed to possible meaning for
"summum bonum."

1540. ___ (1955) A Semi-Statistical Approach to a Problem in Aesthetics. J. Phil. 52: 281-287. --On
"the objectivity of an aesthetic element and ...
the objectivity of beauty."

1541. Laird, John (1935) An Enquiry into Moral Notions.
London: Allen and Unwin. --Intuitionist theory
of the possibility of an ethic of maximum good,
including goodness of acts and agents as well
as of consequences.

1542. Lamont, Corliss (1949) Humanism as a Philosophy.
New York: Philosophical Library. --See especially: Part VI, human happiness, freedom
and progress as the composite goal of humanistic ethical theory.

1543. Lamont, William D. (1946) The Principles of Moral
Judgment. Oxford: Clarendon Press. --Moral
judgments in relation to scientific research.

1544. ___ (1955) The Value Judgment. New York: Philosophical Library. --Valuation as conative choice;
the economic order the locus of "value," dis-
tinct from the juridical order as the locus of
moral obligation.

1545. Langer, Susanne K. (1953) Feeling and Form; A Theory of Art Developed from "Philosophy in a New Key." New York: Scribner's. --Form, specific art materials and symbols the foci of a theory of esthetic and of art, oriented to the view that "art is the creation of forms symbolic of human feeling."

1546. Lanz, Henry (1947) Aesthetic Relativity. Stanford: Stanford Univ. Press.

1547. Laserson, Max M. (1943) On the Sociology of Ethics. J. Phil. 40: 148-156. --A sociological approach to ethics requires appreciation of the "inner reality of ethics and the laws of its development."

1548. +Lavine, Thelma Z. (1942) Sociological Analysis of Cognitive Norms. J. Phil. 39: 342-356.

1549. Lechner, Robert (1953) The Aesthetic Experience. Chicago: Regnery. --A variant of Thomistic esthetics.

1550. Lee, Harold N. (1938) Perception and Aesthetic Value. New York: Prentice-Hall.

1551. ___ (1949) Methodology of Value Theory. IN: Ray Lepley, ed. Value; A Cooperative Inquiry. New York: Columbia Univ. Press. 147-166.

1552. ___ (1957) The Meaning of "Intrinsic Value." IN: Ray Lepley, ed. The Language of Value. New York: Columbia Univ. Press. 178-196.

1553. Lepley, Ray (1937) The Dawn of Value Theory. J. Phil. 34: 365-372. --Proposes an empirical basis for value theory.

1554. ___ (1940) The Verifiability of Different Kinds of Facts and Values. Phil. Sci. 7: 464-475. --

Scientific, esthetic and moral facts and values
verifiable in substantially the same manner
and degree.

1555. ___, ed. (1949) Value; A Cooperative Inquiry. New
York: Columbia Univ. Press. --A symposium,
reviewing positions and criticisms of pragmatist value theory.

1556. ___, ed. (1957) The Language of Value. New York:
Columbia Univ. Press. --A symposium, the
second part consisting of comments and responses of participants.

1557. Le Senne, René (1942) Traité de Morale Générale.
Paris: Presses Universitaires de France.

1558. Levine, Israel (1924) Reason and Morals. Glasgow:
Maclehose, Jackson. --Behaviorism and Freudianism adapted to a humanistic, rationalistic
ethical theory; reason defined as man's ability
to conform to reality; to be moral is to be reasonable.

1559. Lewis, Clarence Irving (1946) An Analysis of Knowledge and Valuation. La Salle, Indiana: Open
Court. --Complex, detailed analysis of epistemology to support the thesis that valuation is
a form of empirical knowledge.

1560. ___ (1955) The Ground and Nature of the Right. New
York: Columbia Univ. Press. --Relation between
"valuable" and "right" consists in consideration
of the value-consequences of deliberated acts or
choices involving either term.

1561. Leys, Wayne A. R. (1938) Types of Moral Values
and Moral Inconsistency. J. Phil. 35: 66-73.

1562. ___ (1952) Ethics for Policy Decisions. New York:
Prentice-Hall. --The decision-making process

as a fruitful approach to formulating ethical
questions.

1563. ___ (1953) Human Values in the Atomic Age.
Annals Amer. Acad. Pol. Soc. Sci. 290: 127-
133.

1564. Lipman, Matthew (1954) The Relation of Critical
Functions and Critical Decisions to Art Inquiry.
J. Phil. 51: 653-667.

1565. Lipps, Hans (1941) Die Menschliche Natur. Frank-
furt a. M.: Klostermann (Frankfurter wissen-
schaftliche Beiträge. Kulturwissenschaftliche
Riehe. 8). --Existentialist analysis.

1566. Lipps, Theodor (1904-1905) Weiteres zur "Ein-
fühling." Archiv für die Gesamte Psychologie
4: 465-519. --Esthetic experience as empathy
of the self with the not-self of artistic form.

1567. Loewenberg, Jacob (1949) Dialogues from Delphi.
Berkeley: Univ. of California Press. --Funda-
mentals of esthetic philosophy.

1568. Macbeath, Alexander (1946) Is Anthropology Relevant to Ethics? Proc. Aristotelian Soc. Supplement 20: 94-121.

1569. ___ (1949) The Relationship Between Primitive
Morality and Religion. Frazer Lecture. Glasgow: Univ. of Glasgow.

1570. ___ (1952) Experiments in Living; A Study of the
Nature and Foundation of Ethics or Morals in
the Light of Recent Work in Social Anthropology.
London: Macmillan. --Concepts and data of
social anthropology used for an analysis of the
structure of moral life and in support of intuitionist, utilitarian ethics.

1571. MacDonald, Margaret (1950) Ethics and the Cere-
      monial Use of Language. IN: Max Black, ed.
      Philosophical Analysis. Ithaca: Cornell Univ.
      Press. 211-229. --Ethical utterances compared
      with and partly reduced to ceremonial utter-
      ances.

1572. McGill, Vivian J. (1943) Types of Men and Their
      Relation to Ethics. Phil. Phen. Res. 3: 424-
      448.

1573. ___ (1948) Two Concepts of Freedom. IN: Philos-
      ophy of Freedom, Symposium. Phil. Phen.
      Res. 8: 515-521.

1574. McGilvary, Evander Bradley (1915) The Warfare of
      Moral Ideals. Hibbert J. 14: 43-64. --Conflict
      of ethical systems as the process of human de-
      velopment.

1575. McGreal, Ian (1949) A Naturalistic Analysis of
      Value Terms. Phil. Phen. Res. 10: 73-84.

1576. McKeon, Richard (1936) Literary Criticism and the
      Concept of Imitation in Antiquity. Modern
      Philology 34: 1-35.

1577. ___ (1948) A Philosophy for UNESCO. IN: Philos-
      ophy of Freedom, Symposium. Phil. Phen.
      Res. 8: 573-586.

1578. ___ (1950) Conflicts of Values in a Community of
      Cultures. J. Phil. 47: 197-210.

1579. ___ (1958) Power and the Language of Power.
      Ethics 68: 98-115. --The heritage of value-
      laden terms in modern political theory.

1580. ___ et al. (1953) Interrelations of Cultures; Their
      Contribution to International Understanding.
      New York: Columbia Univ. Press. Also:

Paris: UNESCO. --Essays from different disciplines and cultures, converging on the view
that intercultural understanding depends on
common values that underlie cultural diversity.
Sketches of Hindu, Spanish, African and Chinese
value systems.

1581. Mabbott, J. D. (1946) Is Anthropology Relevant to
Ethics? Proc. Aristotelian Soc. Supplement
20: 85-93.

1582. Magid, Henry M. (1955) A Critique of Easton on the
Moral Foundations of Theoretical Research in
Political Science (Discussion). Ethics 65: 201-
205. --See 951.

1583. Mahadevan, T. M. P. (1951) The Basis of Social,
Ethical, and Spiritual Values in Indian Philos-
ophy. IN: Charles A. Moore, ed. Essays in
East-West Philosophy. Honolulu: Univ. of
Hawaii Press. 317-335.

1584. Mandelbaum, Maurice H. (1955) The Phenomenology
of Moral Experience. Glencoe, Ill.: Free
Press. --Phenomenological analysis of moral
judgments; current ethical theories tested by
a standard of "fittingness"; principles of Ges-
talt psychology utilized.

1585. Marcel, Gabriel (1955) The Decline of Wisdom.
New York: Philosophical Library. --Religious
existentialist philosophy as a cure for the
"spirit of abstraction" which hinders contemporary human fulfillment.

1586. Maritain, Jacques (1930) Art and Scholasticism.
Trans. by J. F. Scanlan. New York: Scribner's. --A variant of Thomist esthetics.

1587. ___ (1940) Science and Wisdom. Trans. by Bernard
Wall. New York: Scribner's. --In a Thomistic,

humanistic framework, suggests a spiritual and personal approach in morals and politics; social science, like all other knowledge, dependent on ethics which, in turn, depends on theology and knowledge of the natural world.

1588. ___ (1943) The Rights of Man and Natural Law. Trans. by Doris Anson. New York: Scribner's. --Natural law as the demand of man's nature and source of the basic rights of existence, freedom and pursuit of eternal life and of regard for others.

1589. ___ (1952) Natural Law and Moral Law. IN: R. N. Anshen, ed. Moral Principles of Action. New York: Harper. 62-76.

1590. Marshall, Henry R. (1894) Pain, Pleasure and Aesthetics. London: Macmillan.

1591. Mead, George H. (1908) The Philosophical Basis of Ethics. Internatl. J. Ethics 18: 311-323. -- Adaptation of Deweyean pragmatism.

1592. ___ (1923) Scientific Method and the Moral Sciences. Internatl. J. Ethics 33: 229-247.

1593. ___ (1934) Mind, Self and Society. Charles W. Morris, ed. Chicago: Univ. of Chicago Press.

1594. ___ (1938) Philosophy of the Act. Charles W. Morris, ed. Chicago: Univ. of Chicago Press. --Ties between individuals and society basic to ethics; individual moral betterment dependent on social betterment; to guide social progress, institutions and values must be functionally interrelated.

1595. Mead, Hunter (1952) An Introduction to Esthetics. New York: Ronald.

1596. Mei, Y. P. (1951) The Basis of Social, Ethical, and
      Spiritual Values in Chinese Philosophy. IN:
      Charles A. Moore, ed. Essays in East-West
      Philosophy. Honolulu: Univ. of Hawaii Press.
      301-316.

1597. Meinong, Alexius von (1894) Psychologisch-ethisch
      Untersuchungen zur Wert-Theorie. Graz:
      Leuschner and Lubensky. --Influential in the
      development of general theory of value; value
      as a property arising from "feeling" about an
      object; an intuitionist, phenomenological posi-
      tion.

1598. Melden, Abraham I. (1948) On the Method of Ethics.
      J. Phil. 45: 169-181.

1599. ___ (1950) Ethical Theories; A Book of Readings.
      New York: Prentice-Hall. --Selections from
      classics in moral philosophy.

1600. ___ (1952) The Concept of Universal Human Rights.
      IN: Science, Language and Human Rights,
      Symposium. American Philosophical Associa-
      tion, Eastern Division, Philadelphia, 1. Univ.
      of Pennsylvania Press. 167-188. --Criticizes
      philosophers' derogation of appeals to human
      rights; reformulates the concept to meet some
      of the objections urged against it.

1601. Messner, Johannes (1949) Social Ethics; Natural
      Law in the Modern World. Trans. by J. J.
      Doherty. St. Louis: Herder. --Thomist
      analysis.

1602. ___ (1954) Kulturethik; Mit Grundlegung durch
      Prinzipienethik und Persönlichkeitsethik.
      Innsbruck: Tyrolia-Verlag. --Thomist posi-
      tion. Bibliography of French, German and
      English sources.

1603. Mesthene, Emmanuel G. (1947) On the Need for a
Scientific Ethic. Phil. Sci. 14: 96-101.

1604. Meyerhoff, Hans (1951) Emotive and Existentialist
Theories of Ethics. J. Phil. 48: 769-783.

1605. Miller, David L. (1951) Norms, Values and the
Social Sciences. S.W. Soc. Sci. Quart. 32:
137-149. --Social problems involve conflicting
norms; resolution of conflicts necessary to
fulfill common values.

1606. Mitchell, E. T. (1949) Values, Valuing, and Evaluation. IN: Ray Lepley, ed. Value; A Cooperative Inquiry. New York: Columbia Univ.
Press. 190-210.

1607. Monro, D. H. (1955) Anthropology and Ethics.
Australasian J. Phil. 33: 160-176. --Centers
on examination of Malinowski's position, concluding that ethics has little to gain from
anthropology.

1608. Moore, Asher (1953) A Categorical Imperative?
Ethics 63: 235-250. --The concept of ethical
absolutes is self-contradictory, hence a universal normative ethic impossible. (For
criticism, see 1328.)

1609. Moore, Charles A., ed. (1951) Essays in East-
West Philosophy. Honolulu: Univ. of Hawaii
Press. --A collection of essays on Western
and Asian legal and ethical concepts.

1610. ___ (1951) Metaphysics and Ethics in East and
West. IN: Charles A. Moore, ed. Essays in
East-West Philosophy. Honolulu: Univ. of
Hawaii Press. 398-424.

1611. Moore, George E. (1903) Principia Ethica. London:
Cambridge Univ. Press. --A "prolegomena to

any future ethics that can possibly pretend to be
scientific," introducing the "analytic" method
of much twentieth century ethical theory. In
moral philosophy, an intuitionist position, with
"good" indefinable but intuitable.

1612. ___ (1942) A Reply to My Critics. IN: Paul A.
Schilpp, ed. The Philosophy of G. E. Moore.
Evanston: Northwestern Univ. Press. 535-
677. --Restatement and elaboration of analytic
method and non-naturalist, intuitionist ethical
theory.

1613. Moore, Willis (1957) The Language of Values. IN:
Ray Lepley, ed. The Language of Values.
New York: Columbia Univ. Press. 9-28.

1614. Morgenbesser, Sidney (1954) On the Justification
of Beliefs and Attitudes. J. Phil. 51: 565-
576. --Criticizes the view that the justification of attitudes is more difficult than the
justification of beliefs.

1615. Morris, Bertram (1940) Intention and Fulfillment
in Art. Phil. Phen. Res. 1: 127-153. --An
organistic theory.

1616. ___ (1941) The Art-Process and the Aesthetic
Fact in Whitehead's Philosophy. IN: Paul A.
Schilpp, ed. The Philosophy of Alfred North
Whitehead. New York: Tudor. 463-486.

1617. ___ (1943) The Aesthetic Process. Evanston:
Northwestern Univ. Press.

1618. ___ (1958) Ethics and Human Nature. IN: Studies
in Ethical Theory. Boulder: Univ. of Colorado Press (University of Colorado Studies,
Series in Philosophy, 1). 1-16. --Reviews
literature on relation between theories in
ethics and conceptions of human nature,

concluding that, "A morality which ignores society is bound to be a morality which ignores that which is distinctively human."

1619. Morris, Charles W. (1942) Paths of Life; Preface to a World Religion. New York: Harper. -- Seven basic value-orientations and their relevance for the orientation of contemporary man.

1620. ___ (1948) The Open Self. New York: Prentice-Hall. --Elaboration of behavioristic pragmatism.

1621. ___ (1949) Axiology as the Science of Preferential Behavior. IN: Ray Lepley, ed. Value; A Cooperative Inquiry. New York: Columbia Univ. Press. 211-222.

1622. ___ (1951) Comparative Strength of Life Ideals in Eastern and Western Cultures. IN: Charles A. Moore, ed. Essays in East-West Philosophy. Honolulu: Univ. of Hawaii Press. 353-370.

1623. ___ (1951) The Science of Man and Unified Science. IN: Contributions to the Analysis and Synthesis of Knowledge; A Symposium. Proc. Amer. Acad. Arts and Sci. 80: 37-44. --Values can be studied scientifically with a biologically-based theory of signs.

1624. ___ (1953) Significance, Signification and Painting. Methodos 5: 87-102. Also in Ray Lepley, ed. The Language of Value. New York: Columbia Univ. Press, 1957. 58-76.

1625. ___ (1956) Varieties of Human Value. Chicago: Univ. of Chicago Press. --Aspects of philosophy, psychology, social science theory and the methods of factor analysis, joined in a study of questionnaire data from several thousand college students of China, Japan, India, Canada, United States and Norway.

1626. ___ and Jones, Lyle V. (1955) Value Scales and Dimensions. J. Abnorm. Soc. Psychol. 51: 523-535. --Compares five cultures, using psychological scaling methods and factor analysis.

1627. Mothershead, John L., Jr. (1955) Ethics; Modern Conceptions of the Principles of Right. New York: Holt.

1628. Mounier, Emmanuel (1949) Existentialist Philosophies. Trans. by Eric Blau. New York: Macmillan. --Review and discussion.

1629. Munro, Thomas (1956) Toward Science in Aesthetics; Selected Essays. New York: Liberal Arts Press. --Aim and methods of scientific esthetics not "an effort to measure beauty, or to dissect art," or a search for mystical absolute laws of beauty and good taste, but "empiricism and naturalistic humanism" utilizing the social sciences.

1630. Münsterberg, Hugo (1909) The Eternal Values. Boston: Houghton, Mifflin. --Idealistic ethics, values residing in persons and in the fulfillment of personality.

1631. Murphy, Arthur E. (1939) Conscience, Tolerance, and Moral Discrimination. Ethics 69: 286-308. --"Good Will and good judgment, applied to the discovery of what ought to be done, are precisely what our (conscience) 'moral faculty' consists in . . . ."

1632. ___ (1943) The Uses of Reason. New York: Macmillan. --A variant of pragmatism.

1633. ___ (1956) The Artist as Creator; An Essay of Human Freedom. Baltimore: Johns Hopkins Press.

1634. Nahm, Milton C. et al. (1940) Form in Art; The
Function of Art. IN: Art; A Bryn Mawr Symposium. Bryn Mawr: Bryn Mawr College.
275-311; 312-350. --Art as a source of courage
for facing life and of energy for numerous goals.

1635. ___ et al. (1946) Aesthetic Experience and Its Presuppositions. New York: Harper.

1636. Nakamura, Hajime (1954) The Changing Value of
Man in Modern India. Symp. Sci. Phil. Relig.
13: 701-731.

1637. ___ (1956) The Vitality of Religion in Asia. IN:
Cultural Freedom in Asia. Rutland, Vt. and
Tokyo, Japan: Charles E. Tuttle. (Proc. of
the Congress for Cultural Freedom, Feb. 1955.)
53-66. --Religion in relation to cultural freedom and economic development, discussed
largely in terms of values.

1638. Negley, Glenn (1953) Legal Imperative and Moral
Authority. Symp. Sci. Phil. Relig. 12: 237-
251.

1639. Nelson, John O. (1958) Philosophical Ethics and
Morality. IN: Studies in Ethical Theory.
Boulder: Univ. of Colorado Press (University
of Colorado Studies, Series in Philosophy, 1).
26-44. --The philosopher's task is in ethical
theory, not in making moral judgments.

1640. Nelson, Leonard (1956) System of Ethics. Trans.
by Norbert Guterman. New Haven: Yale Univ.
Press. --Kantian analysis; ethics concerned
with moral duty, not with happiness or satisfaction.

1641. Nicol, Eduard (1948) Liberty as a Fact, Freedom
as a Right. IN: Philosophy of Freedom,
Symposium. Phil. Phen. Res. 8: 532-537.

1642. Nielsen, Kai (1957) Reason and Morality. J. Higher Educ. 28: 265-275. --The modern moral predicament requires realization that morality is practical; rational moral choice requires scientific knowledge of human nature.

1643. Nikam, N. A., ed. (1956) Human Relations and International Obligations. Mysore, India: N. A. Nikam for Indian Philosophical Congress (A Report of the UNESCO-Indian Philosophical Congress Symposium Held at Ceylon, December 1954). --Official report and proceedings of an international symposium, showing agreements and differences among philosophers on basic moral issues.

1644. Nikhilananda, Swami (1952) Hindu Ethics. IN: R. N. Anshen, ed. Moral Principles of Action. New York: Harper. 616-644.

1645. Northrop, F. S. C. (1946) The Meeting of East and West. New York: Macmillan.

1646. ___ (1947) The Physical Sciences, Philosophy, and Human Values. IN: E. P. Wigner, ed. Physical Science and Human Values. Princeton: Princeton Univ. Press. 98-113.

1647. ___ (1949) Ideological Man in His Relation to Scientifically Known Natural Man. IN: F. S. C. Northrop, ed. Ideological Differences and World Order. New Haven: Yale Univ. Press. 407-428.

1648. ___ (1951) The Theory of Types and the Verification of Ethical Theories. IN: Charles A. Moore, ed. Essays in East-West Philosophy. Honolulu: Univ. of Hawaii Press. 371-382.

1649. ___ (1952) Criterion of Universal Ethical and Legal Norms. IN: R. N. Anshen, ed. Moral

Principles of Action. New York: Harper.
122-139.

1650. ___ (1952) The Question of Values. Wenner-Gren
Inventory Paper 36. --Objective moral norms
can be obtained through disinterested physical
scientific data; science can bring economic
and technical conditions into conformity with
human needs.

1651. ___ (1955) Ethical Relativism in the Light of Recent
Legal Science. J. Phil. 52: 649-662. --Denies
"that all philosophical and ethical judgments
are culturally relative," explicates natural law
ethics and jurisprudence as empirically verifiable evaluation.

1652. Nowell-Smith, Patrick H. (1954) Ethics. London:
Penguin. Also: New York: Philosophical
Library, 1957. --Analysis of the ethical lan-
guage of ordinary discourse.

1653. ___ (1954) Psycho-Analysis and Moral Language.
Rationalist Annual: 36-45. --Psychoanalysis
cannot be ethically neutral; psychoanalytic
theory reveals the limits of freedom and responsibility but allows retention of the language
of freedom.

1654. Ofstad, Harald (1951) Objectivity of Norms and
Value-Judgments According to Recent Scandi-
navian Philosophy. Phil. Phen. Res. 12: 42-
68.

1655. Osborne, Harold (1933) Foundations of the Philos-
phy of Value. London: Cambridge Univ.
Press. --Idealistic value theory; "ought" prior
to "value."

1656. ___ (1953) Theory of Beauty. New York: Philosophical Library. --Search for an objective, non-

relational basis for esthetics; requirements for a "science of esthetics"; the psychology of appreciation; the nature of a work of art and of mathematical norms in esthetics.

1657. Otto, Max C. (1949) Science and the Moral Life. New York: New American Library. --Scientific humanism as the solution to modern problems, following Dewey in outline and details.

1658. Pap, Arthur (1946) The Verifiability of Value Judgments. Ethics 56: 178-185.

1659. ___ (1949) Elements of Analytic Philosophy. New York: Macmillan. --See especially: Chs. 1 and 2, ethics concerned with defining ethical terms and related problems; an emotivist position, but verifiability of conditional ethical judgments accepted.

1660. Parker, DeWitt H. (1920) The Principles of Aesthetics. New York: Silver, Burdett.

1661. ___ (1930) Value as Any Object of Any Interest. Internatl. J. Ethics 40: 465-495.

1662. ___ (1931) Human Values. New York and London: Harper. --Modification of R. B. Perry's interest theory of values (see 1679); value resident in satisfaction of interests in objects; harmonious satisfaction the supreme good.

1663. ___ (1946) Reflections on the Crisis in Theory of Value. Part I. Mostly Critical. Ethics 56: 193-207.

1664. ___ (1947) Aesthetics. IN: Dagobert Runes, ed. Twentieth Century Philosophy. New York: Philosophical Library, 39-50.

1665. ___ (1957) The Philosophy of Value. Ann Arbor:
       Univ. of Michigan Press. --A posthumous pub-
       lication, prepared by W. K. Frankena. A
       theory of values based on psychology to be
       suitable for dealing with human experience.

1666. Partridge, P. H. (1956) Value Judgments and the
       Social Sciences. Australian J. Pol. and History
       1: 210-222.

1667. Peirce, Charles S. (1958) Values in a Universe of
       Chance. Stanford: Stanford Univ. Press.
       Also: New York: Doubleday Anchor. --Selec-
       tions from the works of the originator of prag-
       matism.

1668. Pepper, Stephen C. (1923) The Equivocation of
       Value. Berkeley: Univ. of California Press
       (University of California Publications in
       Philosophy 4: 107-132). --There are different
       kinds of value, hence it is misleading to speak
       as though they constituted a homogeneous class.

1669. ___ (1938) Aesthetic Quality; A Contextualistic
       Theory of Beauty. New York: Scribner's.

1670. ___ (1947) A Digest of Purposive Values. Berkeley:
       Univ. of California Press. --Purposive values
       rooted in appetitive and aversive strivings.

1671. ___ (1949) Observations on Value from an Analysis
       of a Simple Appetition. IN: Ray Lepley, ed.
       Value; A Cooperative Inquiry. New York:
       Columbia Univ. Press. 245-260.

1672. ___ (1950) A Brief History of General Theory of
       Value. IN: Vergilius Ferm, ed. A History of
       Philosophical Systems. New York: Philosophi-
       cal Library. 493-503.

1673. ___ (1957) Evaluation and Discourse. IN: Ray Lepley, ed. The Language of Value. New York: Columbia Univ. Press. 77-93.

1674. ___ (1958) The Sources of Value. Berkeley: Univ. of California Press. --Psychological, anthropological and philosophical concepts combined to elaborate the nature and relations of different kinds of values.

1675. Perry, Charner M. (1933) Bases, Arbitrary and Otherwise for Morality: A Critique Criticized; The Arbitrary as a Basis for Rational Morality. Internatl. J. Ethics 43: 127-166. --Belief in objectivity of value judgments produces uncertainty, belief in subjectivity of value judgments produces definite and useful moral principles; agreement in social morals a sound basis for ethical choice.

1676. ___ (1939) Principles of Value and the Problem of Ethics. Rev. Internationale de Philosophie 1: 666-683. --Rejects possibility of universal principles acceptable to all reasonable men; arbitrariness in value judgments is avoided because men's actual choices are made in the context of actual facts.

1677. ___ (1945) Sound Ethics and Confused Language. Ethics 55: 209-215. --Critical review of Stevenson's Ethics and Language (see 1768).

1678. ___ (1948) Proposed Sources of Practical Wisdom. Ethics 58: 262-274. --Review of Ewing's The Definition of Good (see 1387).

1679. Perry, Ralph Barton (1926) The General Theory of Value. New York: Longmans, Green. --Value as "any object of any interest," with a calculus of values using concepts from social science; "harmony of inclusive interests" the ideal goal of morality. Probably the most complete and systematic treatment of general value in the English language.

1680. ___ (1954) Realms of Value; A Critique of Human Civilization. Cambridge: Harvard Univ. Press.

1681. Plessner, Helmuth (1950) Lachen und Weinen; Eine Untersuchung nach den Grenzen Menschlichen Verhaltens. München: Lehnen.

1682. +___ (1953) Zwischen Philosophie und Gesellschaft. Bern: Francke.

1683. Polin, Raymond (1944) La Création des Valeurs. 2nd ed. Paris: Presses Universitaires de France. --Phenomenological method applied to values.

1684. ___ (1950) The Philosophy of Values in France. IN: Marvin Farber, ed. Philosophic Thought in France and the United States. Buffalo: Univ. of Buffalo Publications in Philosophy. 203-218. --Analysis and explanation of the French philosophers' preference for specific value areas over general value theory.

1685. Popper, Karl (1945) The Open Society and Its Enemies. London: Routledge. --Attack on Plato and Hegel as inspirers of closed societies.

1686. Portnoy, Julius (1942) A Psychology of Art Creation. Philadelphia: Univ. of Pennsylvania Press.

1687. Pos, Hendrik J. et al. (1948) Philosophy of Freedom, Symposium. Phil. Phen. Res. 8: 491-586.

1688. Prall, David W. (1921) A Study in the Theory of
Value. Berkeley: Univ. of California Press
(University of California Publications in
Philosophy 3 : 179-290). --An early emotivist;
values rooted in the "instinctive life of impulse," value basically esthetic, i. e., felt but
not thought.

1689. ___ (1925) Naturalism and Norms. Berkeley: Univ.
of California Press (University of California
Publications in Philosophy 7: 51-86).

1690. ___ (1929) Aesthetic Judgment. New York: Crowell.

1691. ___ (1936) Aesthetic Analysis. New York: Crowell.

1692. Pratt, James B. (1949) Reason in the Art of Living.
New York: Macmillan. --Rationality in the pursuit of values the essence of morality; value a
property of anything that "some sentient being
likes ... when he gets it; or would like it if he
got it."

1693. Prichard, Harold A. (1912) Does Moral Philosophy
Rest upon a Mistake? Mind n. s. 21: 21-37. --
Influential paper asserting that moral philosophy
is by definition concerned with obligation, not
with inclination; "goodness" belongs in ethics but
not in morality.

1694. ___ (1950) Moral Obligation. New York: Oxford
Univ. Press.

1695. Prior, Arthur N. (1949) Logic and the Basis of
Ethics. Oxford: Clarendon Press.

1696. Rader, Melvin M. (1935) A Modern Book of Esthetics; An Anthology. New York: Holt.

1697. Radhakrishnan, Sarvepalli (1927) The Hindu View
of Life. Upton Lectures Delivered at Manchester College, Oxford, 1926. London:
Allen and Unwin. Also: New York: Macmillan. --On "the central motives of the Hindu
faith and . . . its way of approach to some of
the pressing problems of the day."

1698. ___ (1940) Eastern Religions and Western Thought.
London: Oxford Univ. Press. --See especially:
Ch. 3, Mysticism and Ethics in Hindu Thought,
a reply to Albert Schweitzer's criticism of
Indian philosophy (see 1903) as life-denying
rather than life-affirming.

1699. Rand, Benjamin (1909) The Classical Moralists.
Boston: Houghton, Mifflin. --An excellent
sourcebook in classical moral philosophy.

1700. Reichenbach, Hans (1951) The Rise of Scientific
Philosophy. Berkeley: Univ. of California
Press. --See especially: 276-302, The Nature
of Ethics, emotivist analysis; ethics based on
volitional attitudes and individual moral imperatives.

1701. Reid, John R. (1938) A Theory of Value. New
York: Scribner's. --Detailed examination of
the physiological basis of valuing, value as a
unique affective quality; the logic of value
judgments equated with the logic of other kinds
of judgment.

1702. Reininger, Robert (1939) Wertphilosophie und Ethik;
Die Frage nach dem Sinn des Lebens als Grund-
lage einer Wertordnung. Wien: W. Braumüller.

1703. Reiser, Oliver L. (1949) Scientific Humanism as
Creative Morality. Girard, Kansas: Halde-
man-Julius Publications. --Creative self-evolu-
tion and progressive social evolution as the
goals of scientific humanism.

1704. Reulet, Anibal Sánches, ed. (1954) Contemporary Latin-American Philosophy. Trans. by Willard R. Trask. Albuquerque: Univ. of New Mexico Press.

1705. Rice, Philip Blair (1944) Toward a Syntax of Evaluation. J. Phil. 41: 309-320.

1706. ___ (1949) Science, Humanism, and the Good. IN: Ray Lepley, ed. Value; A Cooperative Inquiry. New York: Columbia Univ. Press. 261-290.

1707. ___ (1955) On the Knowledge of Good and Evil. New York: Random House. --Critical introduction to twentieth century ethical theories, with frequent reference to psychology and social thought.

1708. Robinson, Edward S. (1957) The Languages of Sign Theory and Value Theory. IN: Ray Lepley, ed. The Language of Value. New York: Columbia Univ. Press. 29-57.

1709. Romanell, Patrick (1947) The Background of Contemporary Mexican Thought. Phil. Phen. Res. 8: 256-265.

1710. ___ (1955) Does Biology Afford a Sufficient Basis for Ethics? Sci. Monthly 81: 138-146.

1711. Rome, Sydney C. (1954) Some Formulae for Aesthetic Analysis. Rev. Metaphysics 8: 357-365.

1712. Roshwald, M. (1955) Value-Judgments in the Social Sciences. Brit. J. Phil. Sci. 6: 186-208. -- Examines various arguments for ethical neutrality; concludes they do not justify logically the abandonment of moral judgment.

1713. Ross, William D. (1930) The Right and the Good. Oxford: Clarendon Press. --Both "right" and "good" necessary and irreducible elements in moral life, but "right" the more important moral concept.

1714. ___ (1939) Foundations of Ethics. Oxford: Clarendon Press.

1715. Royce, Josiah (1924) The Philosophy of Loyalty. New York: Macmillan. --Neo-Hegelian idealism. "Loyalty" the identification of the self with larger and ever-widening meaning; "loyalty to loyalty" the basis and essence of human virtue.

1716. Rudner, Richard (1950) The Ontological Status of the Esthetic Object. Phil. Phen. Res. 10: 380-388.

1717. ___ (1953) The Scientist Qua Scientist Makes Value Judgments. Phil. Sci. 20: 1-6. --An experimentalist-pragmatist view that evaluation is intrinsic to scientific judgments.

1718. ___ (1957) Some Problems of Non-Semiotic Aesthetic Theories. J. Aesthetics and Art Criticism 15: 298-310. --Attempts to show that a non-semiotic esthetic theory can account for "expressive," "literary" and "symbolic" elements in art without giving up its basic tenet of esthetic immanence and intrinsicality.

1719. Russell, Bertrand (1910) The Elements of Ethics. IN: Philosophical Essays. London: Longmans, Green. 1-58. --One of the author's early attempts to formulate a view of ethics.

1720. ___ (1935) Religion and Science. New York: Holt. --See especially: Ch. 9, human society in ethics and politics.

1721. ___ (1946) Good and Bad. Polemic 1: 2-8. --Value judgments optative, i. e. , expressing wishes or desires; analysis of current social problems.

1722. ___ (1954) Human Society in Ethics and Politics. London: Allen and Unwin. --Modification of earlier position; considers the possibility of objective knowledge in ethics, concluding that this "will take us from personal ethics into the sphere of politics . . . . "

1723. Russell, L. J. (1946) Is Anthropology Relevant to Ethics? Proc. Aristotelian Soc. Supplement 20: 61-84.

1724. Ruyer, Raymond (1948) Le Monde des Valeurs. Paris: Aubier.

1725. ___ (1952) Philosophie de la Valeur. Paris. Collection Armand Colin. --Analyzes various theories of values.

1726. Ryle, Gilbert (1954) Dilemmas. New York: Cambridge Univ. Press. --Discussion of determinism and freedom, science and everyday life and other conflicting and paradoxical views.

1727. Rynin, David (1948) Definitions of "Value" and the Logic of Value Judgments. J. Phil. 45: 281-292. --Points out the inadequacy of some definitions of value, suggests a conception of value for which social verification of value judgments is possible.

1728. ___ (1957) The Autonomy of Morals. Mind 66: 308-317. --Reopens the question of the reducibility of normative to factual statements, in relation to the assertion of the autonomy of morals.

1729. Sacksteder, William (1958) Human Nature, Science, and Philosophy. IN: Studies in Ethical Theory.

Boulder: Univ. of Colorado Press (University
of Colorado Studies, Series in Philosophy, 1).
83-98. --On some relationships between factual
and philosophical materials.

1730. Santayana, George (1896) The Sense of Beauty.
New York: Scribner's.

1731. ___ (1905) The Life of Reason. Vol. IV. Reason
in Art. New York: Scribner's. --Materials,
form and representation the elements of works
of art; beauty appears when the pleasure of
sense is objectified, concentrated on the formal relations of the art work as the object of
contemplation. Ethical and esthetic values
similar.

1732. ___ (1920) Character and Opinion in the United
States. New York: Scribner's. --Reissued in
1956.

1733. ___ (1923) Scepticism and Animal Faith. New York:
Scribner's. --The moral life as fusing impulse
and reflection.

1734. +Saran, A. K. (1956) Theoretical Anthropology and
the Cult of Man. Ethics 66: 198-208. --"The
problem of man" the principal problem of contemporary anthropology; criticizes Bidney's
Theoretical Anthropology (see 1276) for failure
to develop properly the needed concepts.

1735. Sartre, Jean-Paul (1950) L'Être et le Néant.
Paris: Gallimard. --Non-theological existentialism; an ethical system derived from metaphysics, psychology, epistemology and literary
criticism, directing men to create their own
values.

1736. Schanck, Richard L. (1954) The Permanent Revolution in Science. New York: Philosophical

Library. --Considers the emergence of a common method in the physical and social sciences; evaluates attempts towards a science of ethics.

1737. Scheffler, Israel (1953) Anti-Naturalist Restrictions in Ethics. J. Phil. 50: 457-466. --Criticism of arguments which use restrictive definitions to "protect" various domains of ethical language from analysis.

1738. Scheler, Max F. (1919) Vom Umsturz der Werte. Leipzig: Der Neue Geist. --Phenomenological position.

1739. ___ (1928) Die Stellung des Menschen im Kosmos. Darmstadt: O. Reichl. --Influential phenomenologist, concerned with the value-qualities of being and proposing a hierarchy of concrete values.

1740. Schlick, Moritz (1939) Problems of Ethics. Trans. by David Rynin. New York: Prentice-Hall. --One of the Vienna Circle; denies verifiability of ethical statements and possibility of normative science; ethics must be applicable to actual life problems; recommends descriptive study of psychology of morality.

1741. Schmidt, Paul F. (1955) Some Criticisms of Cultural Relativism. J. Phil. 52: 780-791. --Distinguishes descriptive fact of cultural relativism, long recognized in philosophy, from relativism in philosophical ethics.

1742. Schuetz, Alfred (1951) Choosing among Projects of Action. Phil. Phen. Res. 12: 161-184. --A phenomenological approach.

1743. Schuster, Cynthia A. (1953) Rapprochement in Value Theory. J. Phil. 50: 653-662.

1744. Selby-Bigge, L. A. (1897) British Moralists. Oxford: Clarendon Press. --Selections and commentary.

1745. Sellars, Roy Wood (1953) Ethics and Politics. Symp. Sci. Phil. Relig. 12: 191-199.

1746. Sellars, Wilfrid S. (1950) Language, Rules and Behavior. IN: Sidney Hook, ed. John Dewey; Philosopher of Science and Freedom. New York: Dial Press. 289-315.

1747. ___ and Hospers, John, eds. (1952) Readings in Ethical Theory. New York: Appleton-Century-Crofts. --Selections dealing with contemporary problems of philosophical ethical theory, with special emphasis on philosophical analysis. Bibliography.

1748. Selsam, Howard (1943) Socialism and Ethics. New York: International Publishers. --Marxist analysis.

1749. Sesonske, Alexander (1957) Value and Obligation; Empiricist Foundations for Ethics. Berkeley: Univ. of California Press (University of California Publications in Philosophy).

1750. Sharp, Frank Chapman (1908) A Study of the Influence of Custom on the Moral Judgment. Madison: Univ. of Wisconsin Bulletin 236. --One of the first American ethicists to deal directly with anthropological data in ethical theory; recommends starting from actual ethical judgments and moral experiences and working towards ethical theory; customs held less influential than thought in moral judgments, utility the principal factor.

1751. ___ (1950) Good Will and Ill Will; A Study of Moral Judgments. Chicago: Univ. of Chicago Press.

-289-

1752. Sheldon, W. H. (1914) An Empirical Definition of Value. J. Phil. Psychol. and Sci. Method 11: 113-124. --Review of sensuous, economic, esthetic, moral, religious and intellectual values, concluding "the value of an object consists in its helping to complete or fulfill some tendency already present."

1753. Sidgwick, Henry (1922) The Methods of Ethics. London: Macmillan. --Intuitionist utilitarianism; minds perceive directly self-evident moral axioms, e.g., "Other things being equal, one must never prefer his own lesser good to the greater good of another."

1754. Singer, Edgar A. (1934) Beyond Mechanism and Vitalism. Phil. Sci. 1: 273-295.

1755. ___ (1936) Esthetic and the Rational Ideal. IN: On the Contented Life. New York: Holt. 3-58.

── Singer, Milton. See Anthropology.

1756. Smith, James Ward (1946) Should General Theory of Value Be Abandoned? Ethics 57: 274-288.

1757. Smith, Thomas Vernor (1931) Ethics. IN: Edwin R. A. Seligman, ed. Encyclopaedia of the Social Sciences 5. New York: Macmillan: 602-606. --Brief account of Western ethical philosophies from the Greeks to Dewey.

1758. ___ (1934) Beyond Conscience. New York: McGraw-Hill. --Ethical scepticism as an instrument of tolerance and liberalism.

1759. ___ (1948) Constructive Ethics, with Contemporary Readings. New York: Appleton-Century-Crofts. --Actualities of contemporary morality treated in theoretical essays, supplemented by selections from other writers. Proposes

experimental equalitarianism as a curb to the
power impulse and to encourage tolerance and
harmony.

1760. Smith, Wendell Bristow (1945) Ethics and the
Aesthetic; An Essay on Value. Phil. Phen.
Res. 6: 87-107.

1761. Sontag, Frederick (1957) The Decline of British
Ethical Theory; 1903-1951. Phil. Phen. Res.
18: 219-227. --Observations on the progressive
removal from living moral issues of British
moral philosophy, as seen in Sellars and Hospers, Readings in Ethical Theory (see 1747).

1762. Spiegelberg, Herbert (1947) What Makes Good Things
Good? An Inquiry into the Grounds of Value.
Phil. Phen. Res. 7: 578-610. --A phenomeno-
logical analysis.

1763. Sprott, W. J. H. (1948) Psychology and the Moral
Problems of Our Time. Philosophy 23: 227-
238. --Contemporary moral problems result
from the multiplicity of choices available;
urges research into the ways people face these
choices.

1764. Stace, Walter T. (1929) The Meaning of Beauty, a
Theory of Aesthetics. London: Richards and
Toulmin.

1765. ___ (1937) The Concept of Morals. New York and
London: Macmillan. --Asserts a universal
moral law based on utilitarianism, held to be
factually verifiable.

1766. ___ (1950) What Are Our Values? Lincoln: Univ.
of Nebraska Press. --Popular lectures.
Freedom, equality and individualism described
as universal values, not peculiar to western
European and American democratic culture.

1767. Stebbing, L. Susan (1944) Men and Moral Princi-
      ples. London: Oxford Univ. Press (L. T. Hob-
      house Memorial Trust Lectures, No. 13). Also
      in: Hobhouse Memorial Lectures, 1941-1950.
      London: Oxford Univ. Press, 1952. --Ideals
      tend to be partial; choice is often between in-
      compatible goods.

1768. Stevenson, Charles L. (1944) Ethics and Language.
      New Haven: Yale Univ. Press. --Disagreements
      in science held to be logically resolvable, those
      in ethics not so; extended discussion of non-
      scientific rational and persuasive methods for
      resolving disagreements in ethics. (For criti-
      cism, see 1677.)

1769. ___ (1949) The Nature of Ethical Disagreement. IN:
      Herbert Feigl and Wilfrid Sellars, eds. Read-
      ings in Philosophical Analysis. New York:
      Appleton-Century-Crofts. 587-593.

1770. ___ (1950) Interpretation and Evaluation in Aesthe-
      tics. IN: Max Black, ed. Philosophical Analy-
      sis. Ithaca: Cornell Univ. Press. 341-383.

1771. ___ (1957) On "What Is a Poem?" Phil. Rev. 66:
      329-362.

1772. ___ (1958) On the "Analysis" of a Work of Art.
      Phil. Rev. 67: 33-51.

1773. Stolnitz, M. Jerome (1950) On Ugliness in Art.
      Phil. Phen. Res. 11: 1-24.

1774. ___ (1952) On the Formal Structure of Esthetic
      Theory. Phil. Phen. Res. 12: 346-364.

1775. ___ (1958) Notes on Ethical Indeterminacy. J.
      Phil. 55: 353-366. --". . . An ethical system
      which is empirical, situational, and pluralis-
      tic will be relatively free of . . . theoretical

obscurantism and practical inefficacy, but . . .
situational analysis will disclose indeterminacy
which runs very deep . . . ."

1776. Storer, Thomas (1946) The Logic of Value Imperatives. Phil. Sci. 13: 25-40.

1777. Stout, A. K. (1936-1937) Free Will and Responsibility. Proc. Aristotelian Soc. 37: 213-230.

1778. Studies in Ethical Theory (1958) Boulder: Univ. of
Colorado Press (University of Colorado Studies, Series in Philosophy, 1). --A series of
articles, chiefly on the relation of conceptions
of human nature to ethics.

1779. Suppes, Patrick (1957) Two Formal Models for
Moral Principles. Technical Report No. 15,
for Office of Naval Research. Stanford: Applied Mathematics and Statistics Laboratory,
Stanford University.

1780. Suzuki, Daisetz Teitaro (1952) Ethics and Zen
Buddhism. IN: R. N. Anshen, ed. Moral
Principles of Action. New York: Harper.
606-615.

1781. Swabey, William C. (1942) Westermarckian Relativity. Ethics 52: 222-230. --See 293-294.

1782. Taylor, Paul W. (1954) Four Types of Ethical Relativism. Phil. Rev. 63: 500-516.

1783. +Taylor, Richard (1950) Comments on a Mechanistic Conception of Purposefulness. Phil. Sci.
17: 310-317. --See 1970.

1784. +___ (1950) Purposeful and Non-Purposeful Behavior; A Rejoinder. Phil. Sci. 17: 327-332.
--See 1969.

1785. Taylor, William Stephens (1941) Changing Attitudes in a Conflict of Cultures. Character and Pers. 10: 87-108.

1786. ___ (1948) Basic Personality in Hindu Culture Patterns. J. Abnorm. Soc. Psychol. 43: 3-13.

1787. Tillich, Paul (1944) Existential Philosophy. J. History of Ideas 5: 44-70. --Traces the development of existentialism.

1788. ___ (1952) The Courage to Be. New Haven: Yale Univ. Press. --Modified religious existentialism.

1789. Tomas, Vincent (1958) Creativity in Art. Phil. Rev. 67: 1-15. --The relation of logical necessity to esthetic necessity.

1790. Toulmin, Stephen E. (1950) An Examination of the Place of Reason in Ethics. Cambridge: Cambridge Univ. Press. --Defense of the logical possibility of practical reasoning in ethics; criticism of positivism.

1791. ___ (1950) Knowledge of Right and Wrong. Proc. Aristotelian Soc. 50: 139-156.

1792. ___ (1956) Principles of Morality. Philosophy 31: 142-153.

1793. Tsanoff, R. A. (1947) The Moral Ideals of Our Civilization. New York: Harper. --Personalist, idealist ethics.

1794. Tsurumi, Shunsuke (1951) An Experiment in Common Man's Philosophy. Phil. Phen. Res. 12: 246-263. --Analysis of the value systems of Japanese philosophers and popular novelists, concluding that the latter is more satisfactory.

1795. Tufts, James H. (1917) The Moral Life and the Construction of Values and Standards. IN: Creative Intelligence; Essays in the Pragmatic Attitude. New York: Holt. 354-408.

1796. University of California Associates (1938) The Freedom of the Will. IN: Knowledge and Society. New York: Appleton-Century. 148-177. Reprinted in: Herbert Feigl and Wilfrid Sellars, eds. Readings in Philosophical Analysis. New York: Appleton-Century-Crofts, 1949. 594-615. --Historical background and logical difficulties of the free will-determinism problem, with suggested resolution.

1797. Urban, Wilbur M. (1909) Valuation; Its Nature and Laws. London: Swan, Sonnenschein. Also: New York: Macmillan. --One of the first American philosophers to adopt the concept of "value" in moral philosophy.

1798. ___ (1930) Fundamentals of Ethics. New York: Holt. --Valuation defined as having cognitive, affective and volitional elements; value conceived as a claim upon existence; moral value, as value for man, defined as spiritual self-realization.

1799. Ushenko, Andrew P. (1953) Dynamics of Art. Bloomington: Indiana Univ. Press.

1800. Uyeda, S. (1956) Language, Meaning and Value. Tokyo.

1801. Vaihinger, Hans (1924) Philosophy of "As If." Trans. by C. K. Ogden. New York: Harcourt. --"Fictionalism" as the explanatory principle of science, philosophy, religion and ethics.

1802. Veatch, Henry (1945) Concerning the Distinction Between Descriptive and Normative Sciences. Phil. Phen. Res. 6: 284-306.

1803. Vivas, Eliseo (1944) A Natural History of the Aesthetic Transaction. IN: Yervant Krikorian, ed. Naturalism and the Human Spirit. New York: Columbia Univ. Press. 96-120.

1804. ___ (1950) The Moral Life and the Ethical Life. Chicago: Univ. of Chicago Press. --An appeal for a return to common human feelings, as against science and intellect, to discover values; values as antecedently real entities carrying imperatives. Social science materials employed.

1805. ___ (1955) Creation and Discovery; Essays in Criticism and Aesthetics. New York: Noonday Press. --Collection of the author's articles, concerned largely with the poet's function as discovering "the meanings and values of a society through the act of creation."

1806. ___ and Krieger, Murray, eds. (1953) The Problems of Aesthetics; A Book of Readings. New York: Rinehart.

1807. Volkelt, Johannes (1925-1927) System der Aesthetik. Munich: Beck. --Empathy with the art object as the essence of esthetic experience.

1808. von Wright, George H. (1951) Deontic Logic. Mind 60: 1-15.

1809. ___ (1951) An Essay in Modal Logic. Amsterdam: North-Holland Publishing Co. --The logic of imperatives.

1810. Wahl, Jean (1948) Freedom and Existence in Some Recent Philosophies. IN: Philosophy of

Freedom, Symposium. Phil. Phen. Res. 8: 538-556. --An existentialist view.

1811. Warren, W. Preston (1950) Philosophy and the Quest for Prime Integratives. Lewisburg: Bucknell Univ. Press (Bucknell University Studies 2: 1-23). --Naturalistic ethics relating individual and social good, emphasizing responsibility and integration.

1812. Weiss, Paul (1942) Morality and Ethics. J. Phil. 39: 381-385. --Distinguishes morality, as socially defined, from ethics, as conformance to ideal good.

1813. Wells, Donald A. (1955) Phenomenology and Value Theory. J. Phil. 52: 64-70. --The value theory of a "presuppositionless" philosophy.

1814. Werkmeister, W. H. (1954) Prolegomena to Value Theory. Phil. Phen. Res. 14: 293-307.

1815. White, Morton G. (1949) Value and Obligation in Dewey and Lewis. Phil. Rev. 58: 321-329. --Pragmatists agree about "value," but not about "obligation" and "justice."

1816. ___ (1956) Toward Reunion in Philosophy. Cambridge: Harvard Univ. Press. --See especially: Part III, critical review of contemporary philosophical issues raised by philosophical analysis and positivism; arguments in justification of decisions are parallel to those for the justification of beliefs.

1817. Whitehead, Alfred North (1925) Science and the Modern World. Lowell Institute Lectures, 1925. New York: Macmillan. Also: Cambridge: Cambridge Univ. Press. --Value as "the intrinsic reality of an event," pattern as necessary but not sufficient to establish value.

1818. ___ (1929) Process and Reality. Gifford Lectures, 1927-28. New York: Macmillan. Also: Cambridge: Cambridge Univ. Press. --An analysis of experience, the esthetic factor elaborated.

1819. ___ (1933) Adventures of Ideas. New York: Macmillan. Also: Cambridge: Cambridge Univ. Press. --Includes a theory of valuation and an analysis of beauty; moral and esthetic values not essentially different.

1820. ___ (1941) Mathematics and the Good. IN: Paul A. Schilpp, ed. The Philosophy of Alfred North Whitehead. New York: Tudor. 666-681. -- Form and event as fundamental in analyzing value.

1821. Wieman, Henry N. (1950) Science in Service of Values. J. Soc. Issues 6: 33-38.

1822. Wild, John (1953) The Return to Reason. Chicago: Regnery. --Collection of papers, largely analytic, opposing to positivism arguments for the possibility of reasoning in ethics.

1823. Williams, Donald C. (1937) The Meaning of 'Good.' Phil. Rev. 46: 416-423.

1824. Williams, Gardner (1951) Humanistic Ethics. New York: Philosophical Library.

1825. Wisdom, John (1953) Philosophy and Psycho-Analysis. New York: Philosophical Library. --Essays on the influence of Freud on philosophy; concludes that philosophical analysis is futile though harmless, qualities desired by its practitioners; attempts to reconcile religion and psychoanalysis.

1826. Wood, Ledger (1937) Cognition and Moral Value. J. Phil. 34: 234-239. --Attacks the notion that moral beliefs can be derived from sociological and psychological materials.

1827. Woodbridge, Frederick J. E. (1911) Natural Teleology. IN: Essays on Modern Theology. New York: Scribner's. 307-326. --Reprinted in: Nature and Mind. New York: Columbia Univ. Press, 1937. "Natural teleology" as a basis for ethics; morality as adjustment, not theory or system; moral meanings from natural, cosmic process to be supplemented by the higher moral meanings constructed by men.

1828. ___ (1931) The Preface to Morals. Yale Rev. 20: 691-704. --Reprinted in: Nature and Mind. New York: Columbia Univ. Press, 1937.

1829. Yee, Chiang (1949) The Philosophical Basis of Chinese Painting. IN: F. S. C. Northrop, ed. Ideological Differences and World Order. New Haven: Yale Univ. Press. 35-68.

VII. RELATED SOURCES OUTSIDE THE BEHAVIORAL SCIENCES AND PHILOSOPHY

A. HUMANITIES, HISTORY, LAW AND THEOLOGY

1830. Acton, Lord (1948) Essays on Freedom and Power. Boston: Beacon Press.

1831. Akzin, Benjamin (1936) The Concept of Legislation. Iowa Law Rev. 21: 713-750. Also in: John C. Wahlke and Heinz Eulau, eds. Legislative Behavior. Glencoe, Ill.: Free Press, in press.

1832. Alisjahbana, Takdir (1956) Traditional and Modern Values in Our Culture. IN: Cultural Freedom in Asia. Rutland, Vt. and Tokyo, Japan: Charles E. Tuttle. (Proc. of the Congress for Cultural Freedom, Feb. 1955.) 38-44. --An Indonesian report.

1833. Anshen, Ruth Nanda, ed. (1952) Moral Principles of Action; Man's Ethical Imperative. New York: Harper. --Collection of papers on relativism and absolutism in values, different cultural values, and other aspects of values and ethics.

1834. Babbitt, Irving (1932) On Being Creative. Boston: Houghton, Mifflin. --"Reflective moderation," not spontaneity, the essence of artistic creation; works of art should express universals in particular subjects.

1835. Barbour, Ian (1955) Indeterminacy and Freedom; A Reappraisal. Phil. Sci. 22: 8-20. --On the utility of the indeterminacy concept in physics for understanding moral freedom; reviews the literature and issues.

1836. Barth, Karl (1939) The Knowledge of God and the
        Service of God. Gifford Lectures. Trans. by
        J. L. M. Haire and Ian Henderson. New York:
        Scribner's.--Theological ethics: man depends
        entirely upon God, ethics is necessarily part of
        dogmatics; man-made ethical codes purely rel-
        ative and untrustworthy.

1837. +Beard, Charles A. and Beard, Mary R. (1927 and
        1933) The Rise of American Civilization. New
        York: Macmillan. 2 vols.

1838. Bennett, John C. (1953) A Theological Conception
        of Goals for Economic Life. IN: A. Dudley
        Ward, ed. Goals of Economic Life. New
        York: Harper. 397-432.

1839. Bentley, Arthur F. (1908) The Process of Govern-
        ment. Chicago: Univ. of Chicago Press. --
        An analysis and philosophy becoming influen-
        tial half a century after original presentation.

1840. Berenson, Bernhard (1948) Aesthetics and History
        in the Visual Arts. London: Constable.

1841. ___ (1958) Essays in Perception. New York: Mac-
        millan.

1842. Bond, C. M. (1940) College Student Attitudes
        Toward Some Basic Christian Values.
        Religious Educ. 35: 109-116. --Results of
        questionnaire on the Bible, immortality,
        prayer and Jesus.

1843. Breasted, James Henry (1933) The Dawn of Con-
        science. New York: Scribner's. --Develop-
        ment of moral ideas and emergence of higher
        values viewed as "an unfinished historical
        process," the origins of moral feeling traced
        to the ancient Egyptians.

1844. Brinton, Crane (1959) <u>A History of Western Morals</u>. New York: Harcourt. --Traces briefly, from Greek and Jewish origins to the present, the relations among Western world-views, ethical principles and, so far as evidence is available, actual conduct.

1845. Brubacher, John S. (1957) The Importance of Moral Option in Education. <u>Bull. Res. Inst. Comp. Educ. and Culture.</u> (English Edition 1, Fukuoka, Japan: Kyushu University.) 16-28.

1846. Buber, Martin (1947) <u>Between Man and Man.</u> Trans. by Ronald Gregor Smith. London: Kegan Paul. --A theological ethical theory.

1847. Buchanan, Daniel C. (1954) Japanese Character and Personality as Revealed in Their Culture. IN: William A. Parker, ed. <u>Understanding Other Cultures.</u> Washington, D. C.: American Council of Learned Societies.

1848. Burke, Kenneth (1931) <u>Counter-Statement.</u> New York: Harcourt. Also: Chicago: Univ. of Chicago Press, Phoenix ed., 1957. --Rev. and abridged ed., Los Altos, Calif.: Hermes Publications, 1957. See especially: Psychology and Form.

1849. ___ (1941) <u>The Philosophy of Literary Form; Studies in Symbolic Action.</u> Baton Rouge: Louisiana State Univ. Press. --Rev. ed. New York: Knopf, Vintage Books, 1957.

1850. ___ (1945) <u>A Grammar of Motives.</u> New York: Prentice-Hall. --A theory of linguistic placement, built around an analysis of act, scene, agent, agency and purpose.

1851. ___ (1950) A Rhetoric of Motives. New York:
       Prentice-Hall. --Persuasion and "identifica-
       tion" in rhetoric.

1852. Burlingame, Roger (1957) The American Con-
       science. New York: Knopf. --A study of the
       "body of American public opinion that judges
       behavior in the community."

1853. Capen, Samuel (1948) Reflections on Freedom in
       Education. IN: Philosophy of Freedom, Sym-
       posium. Phil. Phen. Res. 8: 494-507.

1854. Cardozo, Benjamin N. (1932) The Nature of the
       Judicial Process. New Haven: Yale Univ.
       Press.

1855. Cohen, Felix (1933) Ethical Systems and Legal
       Ideals; An Essay on the Foundations of Legal
       Criticism. New York: Falcon Press.

1856. Cohen, Julius (1954) The Value of Value Symbols
       in Law. Symp. Sci. Phil. Relig. 13: 433-440.

1857. ___, Robson, Reginald A. H. and Bates, Alan
       (1955) Ascertaining the Moral Sense of the
       Community. J. Legal Educ. 8: 137-149. --
       Joint effort of sociologists and lawyers to
       ascertain the moral and ethical beliefs of
       citizens of Nebraska.

1858. Collier, John (1955) Values and the Introduction of
       Change. Merrill-Palmer Quart. 1: 148-157.

1859. Commager, Henry S. (1950) The American Mind.
       New Haven: Yale Univ. Press.

1860. Congress for Cultural Freedom (1956) Cultural
       Freedom in Asia. Rutland, Vt., and Tokyo,
       Japan: Charles E. Tuttle (Proceedings of a
       conference held at Rangoon, Burma on

Feb. 17-20, 1955). --Participants from several
Asian nations.

1861. Cowan, T. A. (1950) Experimental Jurisprudence
and the "Pure Theory of Law." Phil. Phen.
Res. 11: 164-177.

1862. De Selincourt, Oliver (1935) Art and Morality.
London: Methuen. --Primarily discussion of
Art for Art's sake as opposed to Art for
Morality's sake.

1863. Dror, Yehezkel (1957-1958) Values and the Law.
Antioch Rev. 17: 440-454. --Differences and
reciprocal relations between legal norms and
other social norms and values.

1864. Edgerton, Franklin (1957) Dominant Ideas in the
Formation of Indian Culture. IN: Introduction to the Civilization of India. Chicago:
Univ. of Chicago Press, Syllabus Division,
398-403.

1865. Frankfurter, Felix (1930) The Public and Its Government. New Haven: Yale Univ. Press.

1866. Gombrich, E. H. (1954) Visual Metaphors of Value
in Art. Symp. Sci. Phil. Relig. 13: 255-281.

1867. Griswold, Erwin N. (1949) Law and Justice in Contemporary Society. An Address Delivered at
the Congregation of the University of British
Columbia on October 26. Harvard Alumni
Bull. (1950) 52: 298-301. --Judgments of
justice are judgments of value; the relation between law and justice may be the central problem of legal thought.

1868. Hall, Robert King (1949) Shushin, the Ethics of a
Defeated Nation. New York: Columbia Univ.,
Teachers College, Bureau of Publications.

1869. Hand, Learned (1952) The Spirit of Liberty. New
       York: Knopf.

1870. Hildebrand, Dietrich von (1953) Christian Ethics.
       New York: David McKay. --A phenomenological
       interpretation of St. Thomas Aquinas, reaf-
       firming Roman Catholic values against rela-
       tivism, scepticism and similar contemporary
       trends.

1871. Horton, Mildred McAfee et al. (1954) Modern Ed-
       ucation and Human Values. Pittsburgh: Pitts-
       burgh Univ. Press (Pitcairn-Crabbe Foundation
       Lecture Series, 5). --Lectures on: Moral and
       Religious Assumptions in America's Educa-
       tional Heritage; The Most Critical Problem in
       Our American Universities; An Oriental Looks
       at the Modern Western Civilization; The Human
       Values of American History.

1872. Hummel, Arthur W. (1952) Some Basic Moral Prin-
       ciples in Chinese Culture. IN: R. N. Anshen,
       ed. Moral Principles of Action. New York:
       Harper. 598-605.

1873. Hungerland, Helmuth (1954) An Analysis of Some
       Determinants in the Perception of Works of
       Art. J. Aesthetics and Art Criticism 12:
       450-456.

1874. Iino, David N. (1953) Freedom and Authority in the
       Realization of Values. Symp. Sci. Phil. Relig.
       12: 717-732.

1875. Ingalls, Daniel (In Press) The Brahman Tradition.
       J. Amer. Folklore. --A summary of the values
       of a major caste-group of India.

1876. Kahn, Sir Muhammad Zafrullah (1952) Moral Prin-
       ciples as the Basis of Islamic Culture. IN:
       R. N. Anshen, ed. Moral Principles of Action.
       New York: Harper. 559-577.

1877. Kaplan, Mordecai M. (1954) Religion as the Symbolization of the Values of Holiness. Symp. Sci. Phil. Relig. 13: 183-197.

1878. Korzybski, Alfred (1933) Science and Sanity. Lancaster, Pa.: International Non-Aristotelian Publications.--Social ills diagnosed in terms of neurolinguistic maladjustments; semantic therapy the cure for infantilism and "social unsanity."

1879. ___ (1951) The Role of Language in the Perceptual Processes. IN: Robert Blake and Glenn V. Ramsey, eds. Perception, An Approach to Personality. New York: Ronald. 170-205.-- Restatement of the role and importance of the non-Aristotelian approach in perception and evaluation.

1880. Kramrisch, Stella (In Press) Traditions of the Indian Craftsman. J. Amer. Folklore. -- Summary of the values of a major caste-group of India.

1881. Lecky, William Edward Hartpole (1876) History of European Morals from Augustus to Charlemagne. New York: Appleton. 2 vols. -- Classic Victorian study of "the degrees in which, in different ages, recognised virtues have been enjoined and practised."

1882. Lynes, Russell (1954) The Tastemakers. New York: Harper.

1883. Mazlish, Bruce (1958) History and Morality. J. Phil. 55: 230-240. --Historical review of alternatives to F. Schiller's dictum, "The World's History is the World's Court."

1884. Morgan, Kenneth W., ed. (1953) The Religion of the Hindus. New York: Ronald. --A collection

of articles describing for Western readers Hindu
beliefs and moral ideals. Contributors: D. S.
Sarma; J. N. Banerjea; R. Basak; R. N. Dande-
kar; S. Bhattacharyya; S. C. Chatterjee; V.
Raghavan.

1885. Mumford, Lewis (1944) The Condition of Man. New
York: Harcourt. --Current life style can be
brought up to higher standards by using science
and the characteristics of the machine age
beneficially rather than detrimentally.

1886. Niebuhr, H. Richard (1952) The Center of Value.
IN: R. N. Anshen, ed. Moral Principles of
Action. New York: Harper. 162-175. --A
Christian interpretation.

1887. Niebuhr, Reinhold (1939) The Nature and Destiny of
Man; A Christian Interpretation. Gifford Lectures. New York: Scribner's. --Ethics, because rooted in finite human nature, is inevitably relative; only divinely revealed Christian
ethics can provide moral absolutes.

1888. Nostrand, Howard Lee (1954) Needed Contributions
Toward a World Community of Values. Symp.
Sci. Phil. Relig. 13: 657-700.

1889. Ogden, Charles K. and Richards, I. A. (1922) The
Foundations of Aesthetics. London: Allen and
Unwin.

1890. +Parrington, Vernon Louis (1927-30) Main Currents
in American Thought. New York: Harcourt.

1891. Petrazycki, Leon J. (1955) Law and Morality.
Trans. by Hugh W. Babb. Cambridge: Harvard Univ. Press. --Sources of law include
ethical experiences in the minds of individuals
as well as the rules of political society. Particular emphasis placed upon "the importance

of formulating a polity of law to demonstrate
the kind of law essential 'to attain the ideal of
active love.'"

1892. Pope, Arthur (1925) A Quantitative Theory of
Aesthetic Value. IN: Art Studies; Medieval,
Renaissance, and Modern. Vol. III. Cam-
bridge: Harvard Univ. Press.

1893. Potter, David M. (1954) People of Plenty; Economic
Abundance and the American Character.
Chicago: Univ. of Chicago Press.

1894. Pound, Roscoe (1942) Social Control Through Law.
New Haven: Yale Univ. Press. --Interrelations
of law, sociology and control; attempt to define
the elements of law, the ends of law and an adequate measure of values.

1895. Raghavan, V. (1957) Some Leading Ideas of Hindu
Thought. IN: Introduction to the Civilization
of India. Chicago: Univ. of Chicago Press,
Syllabus Division. 390-397.

1896. ___ (1957) Variety and Integration in the Pattern of
Indian Culture. IN: Introduction to the Civiliza-
tion of India. Chicago: Univ. of Chicago Press,
Syllabus Division. 381-389.

1897. Ratner, Sidney (1957) Facts and Values in History.
Humanist 17: 31-38.

1898. Read, Herbert E. (1952) The Philosophy of Modern
Art; Collected Essays. London: Faber and
Faber.

1899. Richards, I. A. (1942) Theory of Poetic Value.
Lakeville, Conn.: Institute of General Semantics (General Semantics Monographs, 3).

1900. Roy, Ellen and Ray, Sibnarayan (1948) In Man's Own
Image. Calcutta: Renaissance Publishers. --A
philosophical essay, outlining the "New Humanism" for India.

1901. Schnier, Jacques (1957) The Function and Origin of
Form; A Preliminary Communication on the
Psychology of Aesthetics. J. Aesthetics and
Art Criticism 16: 66-75. --Psychoanalytic interpretation of the origin and function of esthetic
form as restitutive; through the work of art, "the
unconscious baneful impulses of infancy are ex-
piated" and "the objects originally destroyed in
fantasy are brought back to life."

1902. Schweitzer, Albert (1923) Civilization and Ethics.
Trans. by John Naish, London: Black (Revised
by Mrs. Charles E. B. Russell, 1946). --Not
"world-view" but "life-view" the proper basis
of ethics; "good consists in maintaining, assist-
ing, and enhancing life," evil is whatever destroys life; reverence for life links men with
the Eternal.

1903. ____ (1936) Indian Thought and Its Development.
Trans. by Mrs. Charles E. B. Russell. London: Hodder and Stoughton. Also: New York:
Holt; Boston: Beacon Press. --Characterizes
Hindu philosophy as life-denying, rather than
life-affirming and as negating ethics. (See
1698 and 1444.)

1904. Sharp, Malcolm (1947) Aggression; A Study of
Values and Law. Ethics 57: 1-39.

1905. Siches, Luis Recaséns et al. (1948) Latin-American
Legal Philosophy. Trans. by Gordon Ireland
et al. Cambridge: Harvard Univ. Press.

1906. Stone, Julius (1946) Province and Function of Law
as Logic, Justice and Social Control. Sydney,
Australia: Associated General Publishers.

1907. Tanaka, Kotaro (1957) Educational Values from the Viewpoint of Integral Humanism. Bull. Res. Inst. Comp. Educ. and Culture (English Ed. 1, Fukuoka, Japan: Kyushu University): 1-15.

1908. Telling, Irving (1953) Ramah, New Mexico, 1876-1900; An Historical Episode with Some Value Analysis. Utah Historical Quart.: 117-136.

1909. Tempels, R. P. Placidus (1949) La philosophie bantoue (trans. from Dutch by A. Rubbens). Paris: Collection Présence Africaine. --Defends the study of African ideas by missionaries and others as both theoretically and practically valuable; reconstructs Bantu ontology, wisdom, psychology and ethics, all unified by the Bantu concept of deity as "cosmic living strength."

1910. Trilling, Lionel (1950) Manners, Morals and the Novel. IN: The Liberal Imagination; Essays on Literature and Society. New York: Viking. 205-222.

1911. +Trimborn, Hermann (1949) Das Menschliche ist Gleich im Urgrund aller Kulturen. Braunschweig: Verlag Albert Limbach (Beitrage zum Geschichtsunterricht, No. 9). --Universal characteristics of human nature as the ground of culture.

1912. von Fritz, Kurt (1952) Relative and Absolute Values. IN: R. N. Anshen, ed. Moral Principles of Action. New York: Harper. 94-121.

1913. Waggoner, Hyatt H. (1951) The Heel of Elohim; Science and Values in Modern American Poetry. Norman: Univ. of Oklahoma Press.

1914. Ward, A. Dudley, ed. (1953) Goals of Economic Life. New York: Harper. --An interdisciplinary approach to the problem of the goals of economic life.

1915. Weitz, Morris (1943) Does Art Tell the Truth? Phil. Phen. Res. 3: 338-348.

1916. +Wright, Arthur F., ed. (1953) Studies in Chinese Thought. Chicago: Univ. of Chicago Press. Also in: Robert Redfield and Milton Singer, eds. Comparative Studies of Cultures and Civilizations, No. 1. (American Anthropological Association, Memoir 75).

1917. ___ (1954) Struggle versus Harmony; Symbols of Competing Values in Modern China. Symp. Sci. Phil. Relig. 13: 589-602.

1918. Wright, Willard Huntington (1916) The Creative Will; Studies in the Philosophy and the Syntax of Aesthetics. New York: John Lane.

1919. Wyzanski, Charles Edward, Jr. (1955) Process and Pattern; The Search for Standards in the Law. Indiana Law J. 30: 133-151.

1920. +Anderson, Theodore W., Jr. (1954) Probability
Models for Analyzing Time Changes in Attitudes. IN: Paul F. Lazarsfeld, ed. Mathematical Thinking in the Social Sciences. Glencoe, Ill.: Free Press.

1921. +Bates, James (1954) A Model for the Science of
Decision. Phil. Sci. 21: 326-339.

1922. +Blackwell, David and Girshick, M. A. (1954)
Theory of Games and Statistical Decisions.
New York: Wiley. --Theorems and proofs in
statistical games, with detailed discussion of
strategy spaces and payoff functions.

1923. Bohnert, Herbert G. (1945) The Semiotic Status of
Commands. Phil. Sci. 12: 302-315.

1924. +___ (1954) The Logical Structure of the Utility
Concept. IN: Robert M. Thrall, Clyde H.
Coombs and Robert L. Davis, eds. Decision
Processes. New York: Wiley. --A critical,
logical analysis of traditional and current
treatments of the utility concept, both rational
and empirical.

1925. Brickner, Richard M. (1944) Man and His Values
Considered Neurologically. J. Phil. 41: 225-
243. --"Neurology would try to study the actual
performance of the brain in producing values...."

1926. Bridgman, Percy W. (1938) The Intelligent Individual
and Society. New York: Macmillan. --Ideals of
operationism and science as social philosophy.

1927. ___ (1947) New Vistas for Intelligence. IN: E. P.
Wigner, ed. Physical Science and Human Values,

a Symposium. Princeton: Princeton Univ. Press. 144-156.

1928. ___ (1954) The Task before Us. Proc. Amer. Acad. Arts and Sci. 83: 97-112.

1929. Bronowski, J. (1956) Science and Human Values. Nation 183: 550-566. --Adoption of science's values of creativity, truth and human dignity, together with scientific technology, will humanize broader societal values; both science and ethics are testable systems of concepts.

1930. ___ (1958) Science and Human Values. New York: Julian Messner. --See especially: 52-56, 65-94, discussion of scientific method in ethics, necessity for change in values to suit the times and proposed resolution of the "is-ought" dilemma by shifting from an individual to a social context.

1931. Bush, Vannevar (1949) Modern Arms and Free Men; A Discussion of the Role of Science in Preserving Democracy. New York: Simon and Schuster.

1932. Canguilhem, Georges (1945) Essai sur Quelques Problèmes Concernant le Normal et le Pathologique. Clermont-Ferrand: Imprimerie "La Montagne" (Publications de la Faculté des Lettres de l'Université de Strasbourg, Fasicule 100). --Every empirical concept of illness is linked with an axiological concept of illness; research can be objective but its aim must be conceived and constructed with reference to values as well as facts.

1933. Conklin, Edwin G. (1939) Does Science Afford a Basis for Ethics? Sci. Monthly 49: 295-303. --Lower forms of life, perhaps matter itself, contain rudiments of freedom and purpose;

ethics for man must use the universal principles that make life possible.

1934. Driesch, Hans (1927) Ethical Principles in Theory
and Practice. Trans. by W. H. Johnston.
New York: Norton. --The philosophy of vitalism
applied to ethics, with evolutionistic development
("super-personal phylogenetic entelechy") the
dominant idea.

1935. Emerson, Alfred E. (1953) The Biological Founda-
tions of Ethics and Social Progress. IN: A.
Dudley Ward, ed. Goals of Economic Life.
New York: Harper. 277-304.

1936. ___ (1954) Dynamic Homeostasis; A Unifying Principle in Organic, Social, and Ethical Evolution.
Sci. Monthly 78: 67-85.

1937. Evans, Griffith C. (1954) Subjective Values and
Value Symbols in Economics. Symp. Sci.
Phil. Relig. 13: 745-757.

1938. Fehr, Howard D. (1955) Values and the Study of
Mathematics. Scripta Mathematica 21: 49-
53. --Relates values to the personal satisfac-
tions derived from the acquisition of knowledge,
contending that "values are not apart from
science but are continuously interacting with
science itself." Describes values in the study
of mathematics.

1939. Frank, Philipp (1943) The Relativity of Truth and
the Objectivity of Values. Symp. Sci. Phil.
Relig. 3: 12-27.

1940. ___ (1950) Relativity, a Richer Truth. Boston:
Beacon Press. --Humanistic positivism, the
unity of science and the use of science for
social betterment.

1941. ___ (1950) Relativity, Truth and Values. Symp.
Sci. Phil. Relig. 10: 203-214.

1942. ___ (1951) The Logical and Sociological Aspects of
Science. IN: Contributions to the Analysis
and Synthesis of Knowledge. Proc. Amer.
Acad. Arts and Sci. 80: 16-30. --Socio-ethical
considerations can play a part in guiding scientific research; suprascientific methods are to
be avoided even when science is not decisive;
decision must wait until a scientific answer is
found.

1943. Gerard, Ralph W. (1942) A Biological Basis for
Ethics. Phil. Sci. 9: 92-120. --Reply to the
charge that science destroys values; scientific
ethics can be based on evolutionary development and specialization of selfish and altruistic impulses, the latter gaining in recent animal history.

1944. ___ (1955) The Biology of Ethics. IN: Iago Gald-
ston, ed. Society and Medicine. New York
Acad. Med. Lectures to the Laity, No. XVII.
New York: International Universities Press.
--Science and religion, though intrinsically
opposite, are equally important; both are concerned with goals and purposes.

1945. +Girshick, Meyer A. (1954) An Elementary Survey
of Statistical Decision Theory. Rev. Educ.
Res. 24: 448-466.

1946. Haldane, John B. S. (1928) Science and Ethics.
London: Watts. --Science can remake ethics
through a conception of a "Great Being" con-
stituted of individuals.

1947. Herrick, Charles J. (1939) A Neurologist Makes Up
His Mind. Sci. Monthly 49: 99-110. --Relates
"survival" to ethics.

1948. ___ (1956) The Evolution of Human Nature. Austin: Univ. of Texas Press. --See especially: Ch. 12, The Evolution of Value.

1949. Holmes, Samuel J. (1939) Darwinian Ethics and Its Practical Applications. Science 90: 117-123.

1950. ___ (1941) The Ethics of Enmity in Social Evolution. Jacques Cattell, ed. Biological Symposia 2, Part 3. Lancaster, Pa.: Jacques Cattell Press. 193-201. --From a Darwinian ethical theory, draws implications for appropriate changes in practical ethics.

1951. Huxley, Julian S. (1947) Evolutionary Ethics; Romanes Lecture, 1943. London: Pilot Press. Also: New York: Harper. American ed.: Touchstone for Ethics. --Ethics a part of evolution, not opposed to it (see 1953). A proto-ethical mechanism in man, supplemented by experience, leads towards objective reality and an ultimate principle of the fullest development of individuality and society.

1952. ___ (1950) New Bottles for New Wine; Ideology and Scientific Knowledge. J. Royal Anthrop. Inst. 80: 7-23. --General discussion of belief systems in an evolutionary context and a plea for a new, unifying ideology.

1953. Huxley, Thomas H. (1893) Evolution and Ethics. New York and London: Macmillan. --Reacting against Nietzsche and others who interpreted evolutionary theory as justifying an ethic of "survival of the fittest," separates ethics from evolution: man should not imitate but should combat nature.

1954. Jeffrey, Richard C. (1956) Valuation and Acceptance of Scientific Hypotheses. Phil. Sci. 23: 237-246. --The activity proper to the scientist

is not to make value judgments by accepting or
rejecting hypotheses but to assign probabilities
to hypotheses. (See 1717.)

1955. Keith, Sir Arthur (1947) Evolution and Ethics. New
York: Putnam's. --Published in England as:
Essays on Human Evolution.

1956. Leake, Chauncey D. and Romanell, Patrick (1950)
Can We Agree? A Scientist and a Philosopher
Argue about Ethics. Austin: Univ. of Texas
Press.

1957. Littauer, Sebastian B. (1954) Social Aspects of
Scientific Method in Industrial Production.
Phil. Sci. 21: 93-100. --Pragmatic-experi-
mentalist application of concepts from industrial statistical quality control to a "science of
ethics."

1958. +Luce, R. Duncan and Raiffa, Howard (1957) Games
and Decisions; Introduction and Critical Survey.
New York: Wiley. Also: London: Chapman
and Hall. --For non-mathematicians, a critical
review and exposition of the theory of games
and decision-making models.

1959. McCulloch, Warren S. (1945) A Heterarchy of
Values Determined by the Topology of Nervous
Nets. Bull. Math. Biophysics 7: 89-93. --
Apparent inconsistency of preference indicates
an order of consistency too high to permit construction of a scale of values but permits finite
topological analysis.

1960. +___ and Pitts, Walter (1947) How We Know Universals; The Perception of Auditory and Visual
Forms. Bull. Math. Biophysics 9: 127-147.

1961. Margenau, Henry (1950) Ethical Science. Symp.
Sci. Phil. Relig. 10: 185-202.

—— Mosteller, Frederick. See <u>Sociology</u>.

1962. Muller, H. J. (1958) Human Values in Relation to
Evolution. <u>Science</u> 127: 625-629. --Values
genetically based and culturally elaborated,
functioning teleologically to insure the survival
and extension of the group.

1963. Nissen, Henry (1955) Problems of Mental Evolution
in the Primates. IN: James A. Gavin, ed.
<u>The Non-Human Primates and Human Evolution</u>.
Detroit: Wayne Univ. Press. --Includes discussion of values in the primates.

1964. Noüy, Pierre Lecomte du (1947) <u>Human Destiny; An
Interpretation of Evolution and a Theory of
Man's Place in the Universe.</u> New York:
Longmans, Green.

1965. Rapoport, Anatol (1950) <u>Science and the Goals of
Man; A Study in Semantic Orientation.</u> New
York: Harper. --In support of the proposition
that science generates a particular ethic.

1966. ___ (1951) How Relative Are Values? <u>Etc.</u> 8: 180-
192. --Distinguishes derivative needs and relative values from universal invariants of human
needs; by the nature of its central value premises and goals, science is justified in evaluating
values and cultures.

1967. ___ (1953) <u>Operational Philosophy; Integrating Knowledge and Action.</u> New York: Harper. --The
basic goals of man fixed by the invariants of
human needs, scientific ethics a means to these
ends, through the inherent scientific values of
self-insight, freedom of choice and knowledge of
consequences.

1968. ___ (1957) Scientific Approach to Ethics. <u>Science</u>
125: 796-799. --The ethics of science can be

-318-

generalized to a complete ethical system suitable for all humanity.

1969. +Rosenblueth, Arturo and Wiener, Norbert (1950) Purposeful and Non-Purposeful Behavior. Phil. Sci. 17: 318-326. --A reply to Taylor (see 1783).

1970. +___ and Bigelow, Julian (1943) Behavior, Purpose, and Teleology. Phil. Sci. 10: 18-24. --Purpose in organisms compared to engineering feedback and contrasted with random behavior.

1971. Russell, H. N. (1947) The Ivory Tower and the Ivory Gate. IN: E. P. Wigner, ed. Physical Science and Human Values. Princeton: Princeton Univ. Press. 165-176.

1972. Sarton, George (1952) Science and Morality. IN: R. N. Anshen, ed. Moral Principles of Action. New York: Harper. 436-452.

1973. Schroedinger, Erwin (1951) Science and Humanism. Cambridge: Cambridge Univ. Press.

1974. Shapley, Harlow (1947) The Uses and Hopes of Scientific Societies. IN: E. P. Wigner, ed. Physical Science and Human Values. Princeton: Princeton Univ. Press. 74-83.

1975. Sherrington, Sir Charles (1940) Man on His Nature. The Gifford Lectures, 1937-38. Cambridge: Cambridge Univ. Press.

1976. ___ (1954) An Essay on the Relation of Science to Human Values. IN: Donald P. Geddes, ed. An Analysis of the Kinsey Reports on Sexual Behavior in the Human Male and Female. New York: Dutton (Mentor).

1977. Simpson, George Gaylord (1949) The Meaning of
       Evolution; A Study of the History of Life and
       of Its Significance for Man. London: Oxford
       Univ. Press. Also: New Haven: Yale Univ.
       Press. --See especially: Part II, Ch. 10, The
       Problem of Problems--"What forces have been
       acting throughout the history of life?"--an in-
       terpretation of evolution; Part III, Evolution,
       Humanity and Ethics, a positive interpretation
       of evolution and the unity of biological and
       social science as a basis for values.

1978. Smith, Nicholas M., Jr. (1956) A Calculus for
       Ethics; A Theory of the Structure of Value.
       Parts 1 and 2. Behavioral Science 1: 111-
       142; 186-211. --Value as the state of a system,
       with a stochastic model and a method for re-
       solving value conflicts in decisions proposed.

1979. ___, Walters, Stanley S., Brooks, Franklin C., and
       Blackwell, David H. (1953) The Theory of
       Value and the Science of Decision; A Summary.
       J. Operat. Res. Soc. Amer. 1: 103-113. --A
       value equation and theorem for solution; value
       unit defined and exemplified; the uncertainty
       principle in value theory discussed.

1980. +Stumpers, F. L. (1953) A Bibliography of Infor-
       mation Theory, Communication Theory and
       Cybernetics. Trans. Internatl. Res. Engineers.

1981. Szent-Györgyi, Albert (1957) Science, Ethics and
       Politics. Science 125: 225-226.

1982. +Thrall, Robert M. (1954) Multidimensional Utility
       Theory. IN: Robert M. Thrall, Clyde H.
       Coombs, and Robert L. Davis, eds. Decision
       Processes. New York: Wiley.

1983. ___, Coombs, Clyde H., and Davis, Robert L., eds.
       (1954) Decision Processes. New York: Wiley.

--Proceedings of an eight-week seminar on the Design of Experiments in Decision Processes, including models for analyzing individual and social choice, theory and refinements of utility theory.

1984. +Tucker, A. W. (1950) Contributions to the Theory of Games. Annals of Mathematics Studies, 24: Princeton: Princeton Univ. Press. --Includes contributions by H. F. Bohnenblust, G. W. Brown, M. Dresher, S. Karlin, J. C. C. McKinsey, L. S. Shapley, R. M. Snow, D. Gale, H. W. Kuhn, A. W. Tucker, J. von Neumann, S. Sherman and H. Weyl.

1985. +Vail, Stefan (1954) Alternative Calculi of Subjective Probabilities. IN: Robert M. Thrall, Clyde H. Coombs, and Robert L. Davis, eds. Decision Processes. New York: Wiley. --Contradicts hypothesis that choice is based on a simple psychological "product" of utility and the perception of probability.

1986. +von Bertalanffy, Ludwig (1950) The Theory of Open Systems in Physics and Biology. Science 111: 23-29. --An organismic, teleological approach to human behavior.

1987. +von Neumann, John and Morgenstern, Oskar (1944) Theory of Games and Economic Behavior. Princeton: Princeton Univ. Press. --Mathematical models from the theory of games, applied to problems in economics and sociology, including choice and related phenomena.

1988. Waddington, Conrad H. (1942) Science and Ethics. London: Allen and Unwin. --An objective, normative ethics, interpreted through organic evolutionism, in opposition to the relativism and reductionism of behavioral science theorists.

1989. +Wiener, Norbert (1950) <u>The Human Use of Human Beings</u>. Boston: Houghton, Mifflin. --An extension of concepts from information theory to a social philosophy.

1990. Wigner, Eugene P., ed. (1947) <u>Physical Science and Human Values</u>. Princeton: Princeton Univ. Press. --A symposium.

1991. Young, John Z. (1951) <u>Doubt and Certainty in Science</u>. Oxford: Clarendon Press. --Mainly devoted to technical biology, but contains the suggestion that an ethical system that is not culture-bound might be constructed through considering symbolic communication across space and time, this being the specifically human survival mechanism.

Abel, T. M.   304, 658.
Aberle, D. F.   1-2.
Ackoff, R. L.   1230-31, 1323-25.
Acton, Lord   1830.
Adair, J.   3.
Adams, J.   Appendix.
Adams, J. K.   305.
Adler, A.   306.
Adler, F.   634.
Adler, M.   1232-33.
Adorno, T. W.   307.
Aiken, H. D.   1234-39.
Aiyar, C. P. R.   921.
Aiyar, P. S. S.   1240.
Akzin, B.   1831.
Albert, E. M.   1241-48.
Albrecht, M. C.   635.
Alexander, F.   308.
Alexander, S.   1249-51.
Alisjahbana, T.   1832.
Allen, G. C.   1064.
Allier, R.   4.
Allott, A. N.   5.
Allport, F. H.   309-311.
Allport, G. W.   312-15, 345, 412, 614.
Almond, G. A.   922-23.
Amer. Anthrop. Assn.   6.
Ames, A.   346.
Anderson, A. R.   1252.
Anderson, R. G.   Appendix.
Anderson, Rose G.   316.
Anderson, T. W.   1920.
Andrews, A. L.   387.
Angell, R. C.   636-37, 758.
Anshen, R. N.   1833.
Appleby, P. H.   924-25.
Apter, D.   926.
Arensberg, C. M.   638.
Arnheim, R.   317.

Arnoff, E. L.   1325.
Aron, R.   758.
Arrow, K.   1065-66.
Arsenian, S.   318-19.
Asch, S.   320.
Ashley Montagu, M. F.   7.
Asmus, V.   1253.
Atkinson, J. W.   495.
Aubert, V.   639.
Auerbach, J. G.   321.
Austen, J. L.   1254.
Ayer, A. J.   1255-57.
Ayres, C. E.   1067-70.

Babbitt, I.   1834.
Bagolini, L.   1258.
Baier, K.   1259-60.
Bailey, W. C.   8.
Bain, A.   1261.
Bain, R.   640-41.
Bakan, M.   1262.
Bakke, E. W.   1071.
Balandier, G.   9.
Bales, R. F.   642, 830.
Balint, M.   322.
Balz, A. G. A.   1263-64.
Banfield, E. C.   1013, Appendix.
Baran, P. A.   1072.
Barber, B.   643.
Barbour, I.   1835.
Barker, E.   927.
Barker, R. G.   323.
Barkin, S.   638.
Barkley, K. L.   324.
Barnard, C. I.   1073-74.
Barnes, H. E.   644.
Barnett, H. G.   10, Appendix.
Barrabee, P.   645.
Barth, K.   1836.
Bartlett, E. M.   1265.

Barton, R. F. 11.
Bates, A. 1857.
Bates, J. 1921.
Bateson, G. 12-18, 569.
Bauer, R. A. 325-26.
Bavelas, A. 327.
Bayer, R. 1266.
Bayliff, R. E. 928.
Beaglehole, E. 328-29.
Beard, C. A. 1837.
Beard, M. R. 1837.
Beardslee, D. C. 361.
Beauvoir, S. de 1267.
Becker, H. 644, 646-48.
Bell, E. S. 374.
Bellah, R. N. 649-50.
Bellin, S. 847.
Belo, J. 19.
Bendix, R. 651-53.
Benedict, R. 20-23.
Benne, K. D. 654-55.
Bennett, J. C. 1838.
Bennett, J. W. 24-26.
Bennis, W. G. 330.
Benoit-Smullyan, E. 1075.
Bentley, A. F. 1839.
Berdie, R. F. 570.
Berelson, B. 656-57, 783.
Berenson, B. 1840-41.
Berger, M. 658.
Bergmann, G. 1268.
Bergson, A. 1076-77.
Bergson, H. 1269-70.
Bernard, J. S. 659-61, 758.
Bernard, L. L. 662.
Bertocci, P. A. 1271.
Bhattacharyya, K. 1272.
Bidney, D. 1273-76.
Biebuyck, D. 27.
Bierstedt, R. 663.
Bigelow, J. 1970.
Bills, R. E. 331.
Black, M. 1277.
Blackham, H. J. 1278.
Blackwell, D. 1922, 1979.

Blackwell, G. W. 664.
Blake, R. R. 612.
Blanchard, W. H. 332.
Blanshard, B. 1279.
Blondel, C. 333.
Bloom, C. C. 1078.
Blum, F. H. 1079
Boas, F. 28-31
Boas, G. 1280.
Boder, D. P. 334.
Boggs, J. W. 109.
Bohannan, P. 32.
Bohnert, H. G. 1923-24.
Boisen, A. T. 335.
Bollnow, O. F. 1281.
Bolton, E. B. 336.
Bonar, J. 1080.
Bond, C. M. 1842.
Borgatta, E. F. 337.
Bosanquet, B. 1282-85.
Boucke, O. F. 1081.
Bouglé, C. C. 665.
Boulding, K. E. 1082-85.
Bouwsma, O. K. 1286.
Bovard, E. W. 338.
Bowdery, G. J. 1287.
Bowles, W. 503.
Bowman, C. C. 667-70.
Bradley, F. H. 1288.
Braithwaite, R. B. 1289-91.
Brandt, R. B. 1292-97.
Breasted, J. H. 1843.
Brecht, A. 929.
Bréhier, E. 1298.
Brentano, F. 1299.
Brickner, R. M. 1925.
Bridgman, P. W. 1926-28.
Brightman, E. S. 1300-01.
Brinkmann, C. 1086.
Brinton, C. 1844.
Britton, K. 1302.
Broad, C. D. 1303-06.
Brodbeck, A. J. 854.
Brodbeck, M. 1307.
Brogan, A. P. 1308.

Bronfenbrenner, M. 1087.
Bronowski, J. 1929-30.
Brooks, F. C. 1979.
Brookings Institution 930.
Brown, D. M. 931.
Brown, D. R. Appendix.
Brown, G. G. 201.
Brown, H. C. 1309.
Brown, J. S. 671.
Brubacher, J. S. 1845.
Bruck, H. W. 1044.
Bruner, E. M. 33.
Bruner, J. S. 339-40, 545.
Brunswik, E. 607.
Bryson, L. 34.
Buber, M. 1846.
Buchanan, D. C. 1847.
Buchanan, J. N. 1088-89.
Buchanan, N. S. 1090.
Bunzel, R. L. 35-36.
Burdeau, G. 932.
Burgess, E. W. 672-74.
Burke, K. 1848-51.
Burlingame, R. 1852.
Burrows, E. G. 37.
Burtt, E. A. 1310.
Bush, V. 1931.
Busia, K. A. 38.
Bye, R. T. 1091.

Caiger, G. 675.
Calpin, G. H. 676.
Campbell, C. A. 1311-12.
Canguilhem, G. 1932.
Cantril, H. 341-46.
Capen, S. 1853.
Caponigri, A. R. 1313.
Cardozo, B. N. 1854.
Carritt, E. F. 1314-15.
Carstairs, G. M. 347.
Carter, L. F. 348.
Carter, R. E. 933.
Carter, T. M. 349.
Carver, T. N. 1092.
Case, C. M. 677-78.

Cassirer, E. 1316-17.
Cater, D. 1094.
Cattell, R. B. 350-52.
Catton, W. R. 679-81, 699.
Caudill, W. 39-40.
Cavell, S. 1318.
Cazeneuve, J. 41, 1247.
Centers, R. 353.
Cerf, W. 1319.
Chalmers, W. E. 638.
Chapman, J. J. 1320.
Chapple, E. D. 42, 201.
Chasdi, E. H. 354.
Chase, S. 1093.
Child, I. L. 297, 355.
Childs, M. W. 1094.
Churchman, C. W. 1321-25.
Clapp, J. G. 1326.
Clark, C. 1095.
Clark, G. H. 1327.
Clark, J. M. 1096-99.
Clark, R. A. 495.
Clark, R. E. 901.
Clark, W. H. 356.
Clippinger, J. A. 357.
Cloutier, G. 43.
Cloward, R. A. 875.
Cobb, J. B. 1328.
Cofer, C. N. 358.
Cohen, A. K. 2, 682-83.
Cohen, F. 1855.
Cohen, J. 1856-57.
Cohen, J. B. 359.
Cohen, M. R. 1329.
Cohen, Y. A. 44.
Cole, G. D. H. 934-35.
Coleman, L. 684.
Collier, J. 1858
Collingwood, R. G. 1330.
Collins, J. 685.
Colson, E. 45.
Commager, H. S. 1859.
Committee on Ethics 46.
Commons, J. R. 1100.
Comte, A. 686.

Congress for Cultural Freedom 1860.
Conklin, E. G. 1933.
Cook, T. I. 936-37.
Coombs, C. H. 360-61, 1983.
Coon, C. S. 47.
Copi, I. M. 1331.
Corkey, R. 1332.
Coser, L. A. 687.
Cottrell, W. F. 688-89.
Couch, A. S. 642.
Cowan, T. A. 1861.
Cowles Commission for Res. in Econ. 1101.
Creegan, R. F. 1333.
Crissman, P. 1334.
Crissy, W. J. E. 372.
Croce, B. 1335-39.
Cronin, J. F. 1102.
Cropsey, J. 1103.
Cuber, J. F. 690-91.
Culwick, A. T. 48.
Curtiss, W. E. 49.
Czezowski, T. 1340.

Dahl, R. A. 938-40.
Danhof, C. H. 1104.
Danto, A. C. 1341.
Davidson, D. 1342-43.
Davis, A. 692.
Davis, A. K. 2, 693.
Davis, R. L. 1983.
De Gre, G. 694.
de Laguna, G. A. 1344-45.
De Liz Ferreira, A. J. 362.
Dembo, T. 363.
Demos, R. 1346.
Denise, T. C. 1248.
Dennes, W. R. 1347-49.
Dennis, B. D. 638.
De Selincourt, O. 1862.
Dessoir, M. 1350-51.
Deutsch, K. W. 941-42.
Deutsch, M. 364.

Devas, C. S. 1105.
DeVos, G. 40.
Dewey, J. 1352-59.
Dexter, L. A. 943.
Dickinson, G. L. 1360.
Dicks, H. V. 365.
Dickson, W. J. 845.
Dieterlen, G. 102.
Diggs, B. J. 1361.
Dilthey, W. 1362-63.
DiVesta, F. 366, 630.
Dodd, S. C. 695-99.
Dollard, J. 367.
Doob, L. W. 368-69.
Dorfman, J. 1106.
Dorr, M. 370, 436.
Douglas, M. 50.
Douglas, P. H. 944.
Driberg, J. H. 51.
Driesch, H. 1934.
Dror, Y. 1863.
Drucker, P. F. 945.
Dryer, D. P. 1364.
Dube, S. C. 52.
Dubin, R. 700.
DuBois, C. 53-55.
Ducasse, C. J. 1365-67.
Duclos, P. 946.
Duffy, E. 371-72.
Duguit, L. 947.
Dukes, W. F. 373.
Duncan, H. D. 701-02.
Duncan, O. 1203.
Duncan-Jones, A. E. 1368-69.
Duncker, K. 1370.
Dunham, B. 1371.
Durkheim, E. 703-06.
Duverger, M. 948.
DuWors, R. E. 707.

Eagleson, O. W. 374.
Easton, D. 949-52.
Eaton, H. 1372.
Edel, A. 56, 1373-79.

Edel, M. 56.
Edgerton, F. 1864.
Edman, I. 1380-81.
Edmonson, M. S. 57.
Edwards, P. 1382-83.
Edwards, W. 375.
Eells, K. 292.
Eggan, D. 58.
Eglar, Z. 59.
Ehrenfels, C. 376.
Ehrenfels, U. R. 60.
Eisentadt, S. N. 708-10.
Eisley, L. 269.
Eissler, K. R. 377.
Elbert, S. H. 61.
Eldersveld, S. J. 954.
Elliot, H. S. R. 1384.
Ellis, H. S. 1090, 1107.
Elton, W. 1385.
Elwin, V. 62.
Embree, J. F. 63-66.
Emerson, A. E. 1935-36.
Epstein, A. L. 67.
Erasmus, C. J. 68.
Erikson, E. H. 378-79.
Eulau, H. 953-54.
Evans, G. C. 1937.
Evans, R. I. 380.
Evans-Pritchard, E. E. 69-72.
Ewing, A. C. 1386-88.
Eysenck, H. J. 381.

Faigin, H. 382.
Fainsod, M. 955.
Fairchild, H. P. 711.
Falk, W. D. 1389-90.
Fanfani, A. 1108.
Farber, M. 1391.
Farrell, B. A. 1392.
Fehr, H. D. 1938.
Feibleman, J. K. 1393-96.
Feigl, H. 1397-99.
Feldman, A. S. 893.
Fenichel, O. 383.
Fensterheim, H. 384.

Ferguson, J. M. 1109.
Ferguson, L. W. 385.
Ferm, V. 1400.
Ferrero, G. 956.
Festinger, L. 386.
Fetter, F. A. 1110.
Feuer, L. S. 1401.
Fichter, J. H. 712-14.
Field, G. L. 957.
Findlay, J. N. 1402.
Finer, H. 958.
Fingarette, H. 1403.
Finkelstein, L. 34.
Firth, Raymond 73-77.
Firth, Roderick 1404.
Fischer, R. 387.
Fisher, F. M. 1111, 1135.
Fisher, S. C. 388.
Fiske, D. W. 426.
Fitch, R. E. 1405.
Fletcher, A. C. 78.
Fletcher, J. M. 389.
Flew, A. 1406.
Flewelling, R. T. 1407-09.
Flubacher, J. F. 1112.
Flügel, J. C. 390.
Folsom, J. K. 715-16.
Foote, N. N. 717.
Forde, C. D. 79.
Fortes, M. 80.
Foster, G. M. 81.
Francastel, P. 718.
Francis, E. K. 719.
Frank, L. K. 391-92.
Frank, P. 1939-42.
Frankel, C. 1410-12.
Frankena, W. K. 1413-16.
Frankfurter, F. 1865.
Frazier, E. F. 720.
French, T. M. 393-94.
French, V. V. 395.
Frenkel-Brunswik, E. 307, 396-400.
Freud, S. 401-05.
Fridenburg, E. Z. 406.

327

Fried, J. 82.
Friedman, L. 407.
Friedman, M. 1113-15.
Friedmann, F. G. 1417.
Friedrich, C. J. 959-61.
Fromm, E. 408-11.
Fürer-Haimendorf, C. 83.

Galbraith, J. K. 1116.
Garnett, A. C. 1418-22.
Garth, T. R. 84.
Garvin, L. 1423-24.
Gaudet, H. 783.
Geertz, C. 85-86.
Geertz, H. 87.
Gehlen, A. 1425-26.
Geiger, G. R. 1427-30.
Geiger, T. 721.
Gentile, G. 1431.
Georgescu-Roegen, N. 1117.
Gerard, H. B. 364.
Gerard, R. W. 1943-44.
Gerth, H. 722, 762.
Gewirth, A. 1432.
Gilbert, K. E. 1433-34.
Gillespie, J. M. 412.
Gillin, J. 88-90.
Gilman, E. 1435.
Gilson, E. 1436.
Ginsberg, M. 723-30.
Ginsburg, S. W. 413.
Ginzberg, E. 1118.
Girshick, M. A. 1922, 1945.
Glasser, E. M. 414.
Gloye, E. E. 415.
Gluckman, H. M. 91.
Goffman, E. 731.
Goguel, F. 1026.
Goheen, J. 1437.
Goldberg, S. C. 416.
Goldenweiser, A. 92.
Goldfrank, E. 93.
Goldschmidt, W. 94-96.
Goldsen, R. K. 848, 882.
Goldstein, K. 417-18.

Golightly, C. L. 1438-40.
Gombrich, E. H. 1866.
Gomperz, H. 1441-42.
Goodman, C. C. 339.
Goodman, M. E. 97.
Goodwin, W. F. 1443-44.
Gorer, G. 98-99.
Gotesky, R. 1445.
Gotshalk, D. W. 1446-47.
Grable, P. 487.
Grace, G. L. 419.
Grace, H. A. 419-20.
Grafton, T. H. 732.
Graham, F. D. 1119.
Graham, G. A. 962.
Graham, J. L. 421.
Graham, S. 733.
Grasso, P. G. 422.
Grave, S. A. 1448.
Gray, A. 1120.
Green, A. W. 423.
Greenacre, P. 424.
Greene, T. M. 1449-52.
Grene, M. 1453.
Griaule, M. 100-02.
Grinnell, R. 1454.
Griswold, E. N. 1867.
Gross, E. 734.
Gross, F. 735-37.
Guetzkow, H. 425, 504.
Gulick, L. 963.
Gurvitch, G. 738-40.

Haavelmo, T. 1121.
Hägerström, A. Appendix.
Hahn, L. E. 1455.
Haigh, G. V. 426.
Haldane, J. B. S. 1946.
Hall, E. T. 103-04.
Hall, E. W. 1456-58.
Hall, R. K. 1868.
Hall, R. M. 427.
Halldén, S. 1459.
Hallowell, A. I. 105.
Hallowell, J. H. 964-66.

Hamburg, C. H. 1460.
Hamilton, W. 1122.
Hammond, W. A. 1461.
Hampshire, S. 1462.
Hand, L. 1869.
Handy, R. 1463.
Haney, L. H. 1123.
Harding, D. W. 428.
Harding, L. W. 429-30.
Hare, A. P. 881.
Hare, R. M. 1464.
Haring, D. G. 106-08.
Harper, R. A. 690.
Harris, D. 431.
Harris, S. E. 884.
Harsanyi, J. C. 1124.
Hart, H. 741-44.
Hart, H. L. A. 1465.
Hart, S. L. 1466-67.
Hartman, R. S. 1468-71.
Hartmann, G. W. 432-43.
Hartmann, N. 1472.
Hartung, F. E. 745.
Hastorf, A. H. 346.
Hauser, P. M. 746.
Havice, D. W. 1473.
Havighurst, R. J. 370, 406, 434-37.
Hawkins, D. 1474.
Haworth, L. L. 1475.
Hayek, F. A. 1125-26.
Hayes, E. C. 747.
Heidegger, M. 1476-77.
Heimann, E. 1127-29.
Heinicke, C. 438.
Held, D. 439.
Helper, M. M. 440.
Hempel, C. G. 1478.
Henle, P. 1479.
Hennemann, G. 1480.
Henry, J. 109.
Herman, A. P. 748.
Herrick, C. J. 1947-48.
Herring, P. 967.
Hersch, J. 968.

Herskovits, F. S. Appendix.
Herskovits, M. J. 110-14, Appendix.
Herz, J. H. 969.
Hickman, C. A. 1130.
Hildebrand, D. 1870.
Hill, T. E. 1481.
Hillenbrand, M. J. 970.
Hilliard, A. L. 1482.
Himes, J. S. 749-50.
Hitchcock, J. T. 115.
Hobbs, N. 441.
Hobhouse, L. T. 751-52.
Hobson, J. A. 1131-32.
Hobson, R. 116.
Hockett, C. F. 117.
Hocking, W. E. 1483.
Hodges, D. C. 1484.
Hodson, H. V. 971.
Hoebel, E. A. 118, 179.
Hofstadter, A. 1485-86.
Hofstadter, R. 972-73.
Hogbin, H. I. 119.
Hoijer, H. 120.
Holcombe, A. N. 974.
Holleman, J. F. 121.
Hollingworth, H. L. 442.
Hollister, W. W. 975, 1487.
Holmes, S. J. 1949-50.
Holt, E. B. 443.
Homan, P. T. 1133.
Homans, G. 753.
Honigmann, J. J. 122-24.
Hook, S. 1488.
Hoop, J. H. 1489.
Horney, K. 444.
Horsburgh, H. J. N. 1490.
Horton, M. McA. 1871.
Horton, P. B. 754.
Hospers, J. 1491, 1747.
Hourani, G. F. 1492.
Hovland, C. I. 445.
Howell, P. P. 125.
Howes, D. H. 588.
Hsu, F. L. K. 126-27.

Hu H.-C. 128.
Hughes, J. H. 446.
Huisman, D. 1493.
Hull, C. L. 447-48.
Hulse, F. S. 129.
Human Organization 130.
Hummel, A. W. 1872.
Humphreys, L. G. 385.
Hungerland, H. 1873.
Hungerland, I. 1494.
Hunt, A. McC. 449.
Husserl, E. 1495.
Hutt, M. L. 450, 519.
Huxley, J. S. 1951-52.
Huxley, T. H. 1953.
Hyman, H. 755.

Iino, D. N. 1874.
Ingalls, D. 1875.
Inkeles, A. 756-57.
Innis, H. A. 1134.
International Sociological
  Association 758.
Irving, J. A. 1496.
Ittelson, W. 346.

Jacob, P. E. 451.
Jacobson, N. 976-77.
James, W. 1497-99.
Janis, I. L. 445.
Janowitz, M. 656, 759-61,
  954.
Jaspers, K. 1500-03.
Jaszi, O. 978.
Jeffrey, R. C. 1954.
Jessor, R. 452.
Jessup, B. E. 1504-06.
Joad, C. M. E. 1507-08.
Johns-Heine, P. 762.
Jonassen, C. T. 763.
Jones, A. H. 764.
Jones, L. V. 453, 1626.
Jordan, E. 1509-10.
Jørgensen, C. 1511.
Joseph, H. W. B. 1512.

Josey, C. C. 454.
Jouvenel, B. de 979-81.
Jung, C. G.

Kadish, M. R. 1513.
Kahl, J. A. 765.
Kahn, M. Z. 1876.
Kalhorn, J. 457.
Kallen, H. M. 1514-16.
Kaplan, A. 556, 1000,
  1517-21.
Kaplan, M. M. 1877.
Kardiner, A. 458.
Karpman, B. 459.
Kates, S. L. 460.
Katona, G. 461.
Kattsoff, L. O. 1522.
Katz, J. 1523.
Kaufman, H. 982.
Kaufmann, F. 1524.
Kay, L. W. 462.
Kaysen, K. 884.
Kecskemeti, P. 983.
Keeley, B. J. 766.
Keesing, F. 131-34.
Keesing, M. 134.
Keith, A. 1955.
Kelley, E. L. 464.
Kelley, H. H. 445, 463.
Kelsen, H. 984-88.
Kenen, P. B. 1135.
Kerr, C. 1071.
Ketchum, J. D. 465.
Keynes, J. M. 1136.
Killian, L. M. 589.
Kilpatrick, F. P. 466.
Kimball, S. T. 135.
Kirby, E. S. 1137.
Kirby, J. D. 767-68.
Klapp, O. E. 769.
Klein, G. S. 467.
Klein, M. 468.
Klineberg, O. 469.
Kluckhohn, C. 136-54, 162,
  198, 483, 774, Appendix.

Kluckhohn, F. 154, 220, 770-74.
Knight, F. H. 1138-44.
Knox, Israel 1525.
Kobrin, S. 775.
Koch, A. 1526-27.
Koenig, I. 901.
Koffka, K. 470.
Köhler, W. 471-72.
Koivisto, W. A. 1145-46.
Kolb, W. L. 714, 776-79.
Koppers, W. 155.
Korzybski, A. 1878-79.
Kosa, J. 780.
Kounin, J. S. 323.
Kramrisch, S. 1880.
Krieger, M. 1806.
Krige, E. J. 156.
Krige, J. D. 156.
Kris, E. 473, 1521.
Krishan, D. 781.
Kroeber, A. L. 157-62.
Kropotkin, P. A. 163.
Krusé, C. 1528-29.
Kuhn, H. 1434, 1530.
Kuhn, M. H. 1130.
Kunz, H. 1531-32.
Kurtz, P. W. 1533-34.

LaBarre, W. 164.
Ladd, J. 1535-37.
La Flesche, F. 78.
Lafleur, L. J. 1538-40.
Laidler, H. W. 1147.
Laird, J. 1541.
Lalande, A. 474-75.
Lamb, H. 1148.
Lamont, C. 1542.
Lamont, W. D. 1543-44.
Landis, P. H. 782.
Langer, S. K. 1545.
Langner, T. S. 476.
Lantz, H. R. Appendix.
Lanz, H. 1546.
Laserson, M. M. 1547.

Laski, H. J. 989-92.
Lasswell, H. D. 484, 993-1001.
Lauterbach, A. 1149.
Lavine, T. Z. 1548.
Lazarsfeld, P. F. 657, 783.
Leake, C. D. 1956.
Lechner, R. 1549.
Lecky, P. 477.
Lecky, W. E. H. 1881.
Lee, A. McC. 478-80.
Lee, D. D. 165-170.
Lee, H. N. 1550-52.
Leighton, A. H. 481-82.
Leighton, D. 483.
Lepley, R. 1553-56.
Lerner, A. P. 1150.
Lerner, D. 484, 1001.
Lerner, E. 485.
Lerner, M. 1002-03.
LeSenne, R. 1557.
Leslie, G. R. 754.
Levin, H. J. 1151.
Levine, I. 1558.
Levinson, D. J. 307, 757.
Lévi-Strauss, C. 171.
Levy, M. J. Jr. 2.
Lévy-Bruhl, L. 784.
Lewin, K. 486-87.
Lewis, C. I. 1559-60.
Lewis, J. D. 978.
Lewis, O. 172.
Lewis, W. A. 1152.
Leys, W. A. R. 1561-63.
Li An-Che 173.
Lienhardt, G. 174.
Likert, R. 488.
Lindblom, C. E. 940.
Lindzey, G. 315.
Linton, R. 175-77.
Lipman, M. 1564.
Lippitt, R. 488-89.
Lippmann, W. 1004-06.
Lipps, H. 1565.
Lipps, T. 1566.

331

Lipset, S. M.   653.
Littauer, S. B.   1957.
Little, I. M. D.   1153-54.
Little, K.   178.
Livingston, J.   1007.
Llewellyn, K.   179.
Lo, C. F.   490.
Loewenberg, J.   1567.
London, I. D.   491.
Lowe, W. L.   492.
Lowell, E. L.   495.
Lowenthal, L.   785.
Lowie, R. H.   180-81.
Luce, R. D.   1958.
Lundberg, G. A.   786-92.
Lurie, W. A.   493.
Lyman, E. L.   793.
Lynd, R. S.   794.
Lynes, R.   1882.

McAllester, D. P.   182.
McArthur, C. C.   183.
Macbeath, A.   1568-70.
McClelland, D.   494-96.
McCulloch, W. S.   1959-60.
McCurdy, H. G.   497.
MacCurdy, J. T.   498.
MacDonald, D. V.   499.
MacDonald, M.   1571.
McDougall, W.   500-01.
McFeat, T. F. S.   184.
Macfie, A. L.   1155-56.
McGill, V.   1572-73.
McGilvary, E. B.   1574.
McGinnies, E. M.   502-03,
  545.
McGreal, I.   1575.
MacIver, R. M.   34, 795-98.
McKeachie, W. J.   504.
McKeon, R.   34, 1576-80.
McKinsey, J. C. C.   1342.
McKnight, R. K.   26.
McNair, R.   185.
McPhee, W. N.   657.
McRae, D.   505.

Mabott, J. D.   1581.
Magid, H. M.   1582.
Mahadevan, T. M. P.   1583.
Malinowski, B.   186-87.
Maller, J. B.   414.
Mandelbaum, D. G.   188-89.
Mandelbaum, M. H.   1584.
Mannheim, K.   799-800.
Mannoni, O.   506.
Maquet, J.   190.
Marcel, G.   1585.
March, J. G.   1008.
Marett, R. R.   191-92.
Margenau, H.   1961.
Maritain, J.   1586-89.
Marshak, J.   1157.
Marshall, A.   1158.
Marshall, H. R.   1590.
Martin, R. T.   507.
Martin, W. E.   508.
Marvick, D.   760-61.
Marx, F.   1009.
Maslow, A. H.   509-11.
Mason, E. P.   512.
Mason, E. S.   961
Matthews, W.   193.
Maunier, R.   1010.
Mausner, B.   513.
Mayer, C. L.   514.
Mayer, K. B.   801.
Maynard, A. E.   515.
Mayo, E.   1159.
Mazlish, B.   1883.
Mead, G. H.   1591-94.
Mead, H.   1595.
Mead, M.   18, 194-202,
  204.
Meade, J. E.   1160.
Meeker, M.   292.
Mei, Y. P.   1596.
Meinong, A.   1597.
Meister, D. E.   467.
Melden, A. I.   1598-1600.
Melikian, L. H.   516.
Mendenhall, R. C.   802.

Meng, H. 517.
Menninger, K. A. 518.
Mercier, P. 203.
Merriam, C. E. 1011-12.
Merrill, F. E. 803.
Merton, R. K. 804-05.
Messner, J. 1601-02.
Mesthene, E. G. 1603.
Metraux, R. 202, 204.
Metzger, W. 973.
Meyerhoff, H. 1604.
Meyerson, M. 1013.
Miller, D. R. 450, 519-20.
Miller, D. L. 1605.
Mills, C. W. 521-22, 722.
Mills, G. 205, Appendix.
Minas, J. S. 1475.
Mises, L. von 1161.
Mitchell, E. T. 1606.
Mitchell, W. C. 1162-63.
Money-Kyrle, R. E. 523-26.
Monro, D. H. 1607.
Montagu, A. M. F. 7.
Monypenny, P. 1014.
Moore, A. 1608.
Moore, C. A. 1609-10.
Moore, G. E. 1611-12.
Moore, O. K. 1252.
Moore, W. 1613.
Moore, W. E. 806.
Moos, M. 937.
Moos, S. 1164.
Morgan, C. D. 534.
Morgan, K. W. 1884.
Morgenbesser, S. 1341,
  1614.
Morgenstein, H. 1015-18.
Morgenstern, O. 1987.
Morgenthau, H. J. 1015-18.
Morris, B. 1615-18.
Morris, C. W. 453, 1619-26.
Morris, R. T. 807.
Morrow, G. R. 1165.
Mosca, G. 1019.
Mosier, C. I. 613.

Mosteller, F. 808.
Mothershead, J. L. 1627.
Mounier, E. 1628.
Mukerjee, R. 809-15.
Mullahy, P. 527-28.
Muller, H. J. 1962.
Mumford, L. 1885.
Munch, P. A. 816.
Munro, T. 1629.
Münsterberg, H. 1630.
Murdock, G. P. 206.
Murphy, A. E. 1631-32.
Murphy, G. 529-30.
Murray, H. A. 531-34.
Musgrave, R. A. 1166.
Myint, H. 1167.
Myrdal, G. 1168-70.

Nadel, S. F. 207.
Naegele, K. D. 817-18.
Nahm, M. C. 1633-35.
Nakamura, H. 1636-37.
Narain, D. 819.
Nassar, C. 535.
Naumberg, M. 536.
Negley, G. 1638.
Nelson, J. O. 1639.
Nelson, L. 835, 1640.
Neugarten, B. L. 435.
Neumann, E. 537.
Nichols, C. A. 538.
Nicol, E. 1641.
Niebuhr, H. R. 1886.
Niebuhr, R. 1887.
Nielsen, K. 1642.
Nikam, N. A. 1643.
Nikhilananda, S. 1644.
Nisbet, R. A. 820.
Nissen, H. 1963.
Nogee, P. 808.
Norbeck, E. 208.
Norbeck, M. 208.
Nordskog, J. E. 821.
Northrop, F. S. C. 1645-51.
Nostrand, H. L. 1888.

Nottingham, E. K. 822.
Noüy, P. du L. 1964.
Nowell-Smith, P. 1652-53.
Noyes, C. R. 1171.

Oakeshott, M. 1020.
O'Dea, T. 285, 818, 823-24.
Ofstad, H. 1654, Appendix.
Ogden, C. K. 1889.
Oliver, H. M. 1172-73.
Olson, R. L. 209.
Opler, M. E. 212-17.
Opler, M. K. 210-11.
Oppenheim, F. E. 1021-22.
Oppler, A. C. 1023.
Ornstein, H. 1024.
Osborne, H. 1655-56.
Osgood, C. E. 539.
Osgood, R. E. 1025.
Otto, M. C. 1657.

Padover, S. 1026.
Page, C. H. 658.
Palau Marti, M. 218.
Pap, A. 1383, 1658-59.
Papandreou, A. G. 1174.
Pareto, V. 1175.
Parker, D. H. 1660-65.
Parrington, V. L. 1890.
Parsons, E. C. 219.
Parsons, K. H. 1176.
Parsons, T. 825-32.
Partridge, P. H. 1666.
Pauker, G. 1027.
Peacock, A. T. 1177.
Pear, T. H. 758.
Peirce, C. S. 1667.
Pell, B. 691.
Pelzel, J. C. 220.
Pennock, J. R. 1028-30.
Pepper, S. C. 1668-74.
Perry, C. M. 1675-78.
Perry, R. B. 1679-80.
Peterfreund, S. P. 1248.
Peters, H. N. 540-41.

Petrazycki, L. J. 1891.
Piaget, J. 542.
Pickford, R. W. 543.
Piers, G. 544.
Pigou, A. C. 1178-79.
Pitt-Rivers, J. A. 221.
Pitts, W. 1960.
Plessner, H. 1681-82.
Polak, F. L. 1180.
Polak, J. J. 1214.
Polanyi, M. 833-34.
Polin, R. 1683-84.
Pool, I. de S. 1001, 1031-32.
Pope, A. 1892.
Popper, K. 1685.
Portilla, M. 222.
Portnoy, J. 1686.
Pos, H. J. 1687.
Postman, L. 340, 545-46.
Potter, D. M. 1893.
Pound, R. 1894.
Powdermaker, H. 223-25.
Prall, D. W. 1688-91.
Pratt, J. B. 1692.
Precker, J. A. 547-48.
Prichard, H. A. 1693-94.
Prior, A. N. 1695.
Prothro, E. T. 516, 549.
Pugh, T. J. 550.

Radcliffe-Brown, A. R. 226.
Rader, M. M. 1696.
Radhakrishnan, S. 1697-98.
Radin, P. 227-28.
Raghavan, V. 1895-96.
Raiffa, H. 1958.
Ramirez-Lopez, R. 551.
Ramsey, C. E. 835.
Ranadive, B. T. 1181.
Rand, B. 1699.
Rangeley, W. H. J. 229.
Rapoport, A. 1965-68.
Rapoport, R. N. 230.
Raths, L. 552-53.
Ratner, S. 1897.

Raup, R. B. 554.
Ray, S. 1900.
Read, H. E. 1898.
Read, K. E. 231.
Read, M. 232.
Readio, J. 452.
Reder, M. 1182.
Redfield, R. 233-36.
Reichard, G. A. 237.
Reichenbach, H. 1700.
Reid, I. De A. 836.
Reid, J. R. 555, 1701.
Reininger, R. 1702.
Reiser, O. L. 1703.
Reulet, A. S. 1704.
Rice, P. B. 1705-07.
Richards, A. 238.
Richards, I. A. 1889, 1899.
Rieff, P. 837.
Riemer, N. 1033.
Riemer, S. 838.
Riesman, D. 839-42.
Rioux, M. 843.
Ritchie, B. F. 556.
Robbins, L. 1183-84.
Roberts, J. M. 239-40, 256,
286-87, 774.
Robinson, E. S. 1708.
Robinson, M. Z. 436.
Robson, R. A. H. 1857.
Roethlisberger, F. J. 844-45.
Rogers, C. R. 557-58.
Roheim, G. 559.
Roll, E. 1185.
Romanell, P. 1709-10, 1956.
Rome, S. C. 1711.
Rommetveit, R. 560.
Romney, K. 774.
Rose, A. M. 561-64.
Rosen, B. C. 565.
Rosenberg, B. G. 566.
Rosenberg, M. 846-48.
Rosenblueth, A. 1969-70.
Rosenstock-Franck, L. 1026.
Rosenthal, D. 567.

Rosenzweig, S. 568.
Roshwald, M. 1712.
Ross, A. M. 1186.
Ross, W. D. 1713-14.
Rossi, P. H. 849.
Rossiter, C. 1034.
Rostow, W. W. 1187-88.
Rouse, I. 269.
Roy, E. 1900.
Royce, J. 1715.
Rubin, M. 850.
Ruddle, S. M. 437.
Rudner, R. 1716-18.
Ruesch, J. 569.
Ruml, B. 1189.
Russell, B. 1719-22.
Russell, H. N. 1971.
Russell, L. J. 1723.
Ruyer, R. 1724-25.
Ryan, B. F. 851, 885.
Ryan, J. A. 1190-91.
Ryle, G. 1726.
Rynin, D. 1727-28.

Sabine, G. 1035.
Sacksteder, W. 1729.
Salisbury, W. S. 852.
Samuelson, P. A. 1192.
Sanford, R. N. 307.
Sanjuan, P. 248.
Santayana, G. 1730-33.
Sapin, B. 1044.
Sapir, E. 241.
Saran, A. K. 1734.
Sarbin, T. R. 570.
Sarton, G. 1972.
Sartre, J.-P. 1735.
Saunders, L. 853.
Savage, L. J. 1115.
Sayre, W. S. 1036.
Sayres, W. C. 242.
Schaefer, B. R. 571.
Schanck, R. L. 1736.
Schapera, I. 243-44.
Schapiro, M. 245.

335

Scheffler, I.   1737.
Scheler, M. F.   1738-39.
Schlesinger, H. J.   467.
Schlick, M.   1740.
Schmeidler, G. R.   572.
Schmidt, P. F.   1741.
Schneider, B. H.   546.
Schneider, D. M.   246.
Schneider, L.   854.
Schnier, J.   1901.
Schoeffler, S.   1193.
Schooler, K.   348.
Schrickel, H. G.   573.
Schroedinger, E.   1973.
Schücking, L. L.   855.
Schuetz, A.   1742.
Schumpeter, J. A.   1194-95.
Schuster, C. A.   1743.
Schweitzer, A.   1902-03.
Scitovsky, T.   1196.
Seashore, H. G.   574.
Seeman, M.   856-57.
Segerstedt, T. T.   858.
Selby-Bigge, L. A.   1744.
Selekman, B. M.   1197.
Sellars, R. W.   1745.
Sellars, W. S.   1746-47.
Selsam, H.   1748.
Sesonske, A.   1318, 1749.
Seward, G. H.   575.
Shackle, G. L. S.   1198.
Shah, A. M.   247.
Shand, A. F.   576.
Shapley, H.   1974.
Sharp, F. C.   1750-51.
Sharp, M.   1904.
Sheldon, W. H.   1752.
Shepard, H. A.   859.
Sherif, M.   577.
Sherman, M. H.   578.
Sherrington, C.   1975-76.
Shils, E. A.   830, 831,
   860-62.
Shimkin, D. B.   248.
Shroff, R. G.   247.

Shubik, M.   1037.
Siches, L. R.   1905.
Sidgwick, H.   1753.
Siegel, A.   513.
Siegel, B. J.   249.
Siegel, S.   579, 1343.
Simmel, G.   863-64.
Simon, H. A.   1038-40.
Simons, H. C.   1199.
Simpson, G.   865-66.
Simpson, G. G.   1977.
Sims, N. L.   867.
Singer, E. A.   1754-55.
Singer, M.   250-54, 544.
Singh, B.   1200.
Sington, D.   1041.
Sisson, B.   580.
Sisson, E. D.   580.
Sjoberg, G.   868.
Skinner, B. F.   558, 581.
Slichter, S. N.   1201.
Slotkin, J. S.   255.
Small, A. W.   869.
Smart, W.   1202.
Smith, A. J.   582.
Smith, G. H.   583.
Smith, H. L.   870.
Smith, J. W.   1756.
Smith, M. B.   584-85.
Smith, N. M.   1978-79.
Smith, T. V.   1327, 1757-59.
Smith, W.   256.
Smith, W. B.   1760.
Snyder, R.   1042-44.
Snygg, D.   454, 586-87.
Solomon, R. L.   588.
Sommer, R.   589.
Sontag, F.   1761.
Sorokin, P.   871-72.
Speck, F.   257.
Spencer, H.   873.
Spencer, K.   258, 818.
Spengler, J. J.   1203.
Speroff, B. J.   590.
Spiegelberg, H.   1762.

Spier, L. 259.
Spindler, G. D. 260-62.
Spiro, M. E. 263.
Spoerl, D. T. 591.
Spranger, E. 592.
Sprott, W. J. H. 1763.
Srinivas, M. N. 874.
Srinivasan, N. 1045.
Stace, W. T. 1764-66.
Stagner, R. 593.
Stanley, J. C. 594-95.
Stark, W. 1204.
Stebbing, L. S. 1767.
Steed, G. P. 264.
Stein, H. D. 875.
Steiner, F. 265.
Stevenson, C. L. 1768-72.
Steward, J. 266.
Stigler, G. J. 1205-07.
Stoetzel, J. 267.
Stolnitz, M. J. 1773-75.
Stone, J. 1906.
Storer, T. 1776.
Stouffer, S. A. 876-78.
Stout, A. K. 1777.
Straus, J. H. 879.
Straus, M. A. 851, 879.
Strauss, L. 1046.
Strayer, P. J. 1208.
Strelsky, N. 716.
Strodtbeck, F. L. 774, 880-81.
Strong, F. W. 385.
Studies in Ethical Theory 1778.
Stumpers, F. L. 1980.
Sturr, J. 496.
Suchman, E. A. 848, 882.
Suci, G. J. 539.
Sumner, W. G. 883.
Suppes, P. 1342-43, 1779.
Sutherland, A. 596.
Sutton, F. X. 2, 884.
Suzuki, D. T. 1780.
Swabey, W. C. 1781.
Swanson, G. E. 520, 654-55.

Szent-György, A. 1981.

Taeusch, C. F. 1209.
Tajfel, H. 597.
Tambiah, S. J. 885.
Tanaka, K. 1907.
Tannenbaum, F. 1047.
Taussig, F. W. 1210.
Tax, S. 268-69.
Taylor, O. H. 1211-12.
Taylor, P. W. 1782.
Taylor, R. 1783-84.
Taylor, W. S. 1785-86.
Telling, I. 1908.
Tempels, P. 1909.
ter Haar, B. 270.
Thomas, J. L. 886.
Thomas, W. I. 887-88.
Thompson, G. G. 446.
Thompson, L. 271-77.
Thomson, D. 1048.
Thorndike, E. L. 598-602.
Thrall, R. M. 1982-83.
Thurstone, L. L. 603-04.
Tillich, P. 1787-88.
Tinbergen, J. 1213-14.
Toby, J. 878.
Todd, J. E. 605.
Tolman, E. C. 606-07.
Tomas, V. 1789.
Tomasic, D. 889.
Tonnies, F. 890.
Torrey, J. 386.
Toulmin, S. E. 1790-92.
Trager, G. L. 104.
Tresselt, M. E. 384.
Trilling, L. 1910.
Trimborn, H. 1911.
Trow, W. C. 608.
Trueblood, C. K. 609.
Truman, D. 1049-50.
Tsanoff, R. A. 1793.
Tsurumi, S. 1794.
Tucker, A. W. 1984.
Tufts, J. H. 1359, 1795.

Tumin, M. 891-93,
Appendix.
Turner, R. H. 894-900.
Turner, W. D. 610.

Ugurel-Semin, R. 611.
University of California
Associates 1796.
Untereiner, W. 278.
Urban, W. M. 1797-98.
Ushenko, A. P. 1799.
Uyeda, S. 1800.

Vaihinger, H. 1801.
Vail, S. 1985.
Van der Kroef, J. M. 279.
Vanderplas, J. M. 612.
Van Dusen, A. C. 613.
Vansina, J. 280.
Van Valkenburg, R. F. 281.
Veatch, H. 1802.
Veblen, T. 1215.
Vedder, C. B. 901.
Vernon, P. E. 314, 614.
Vickrey, W. 1216.
Vidich, A. J. 818.
Viner, J. 1217.
Vivas, E. 1803-06.
Voegelin, C. F. 269,
Appendix.
Voegelin, E. 1051.
Voegelin, F. M. Appendix.
Voget, F. W. 282.
Vogt, E. Z. 3, 240, 283-87,
818.
Volkelt, J. 1807.
von Bertalanffy, L. 1986.
von Fritz, K. 1912.
von Mering, O. 288,
Appendix.
von Neumann, J. 1987.
von Wright, G. H. 1808-09.

Waddington, C. H. 1988.
Waggoner, H. H. 1913.

Wagner, D. O. 1218.
Wagner, G. 289.
Wahl, J. 1810.
Waldo, D. 1052-53.
Walker, E. R. 1219.
Wallis, W. D. 290.
Walters, S. S. 1979.
Ward, A. D. 1914.
Warner, W. L. 291-92.
Warren, R. L. 902.
Warren, W. P. 1811.
Wasserman, P. 1220.
Wayne, I. 903.
Webb, B. 1221.
Webb, S. 1221.
Weber, M. 904-06.
Wegrocki, H. 615.
Weidenfeld, A. 1041.
Weil, E. 1026.
Weiss, A. P. 616.
Weiss, P. 1812.
Weisskopf, W. A. 1222-23.
Weitz, M. 1915.
Wells, D. A. 1813.
Wells, H. 1054.
Wendt, H. W. 496.
Werkmeister, W. H. 1814.
Westermarck, E. 293-94.
White, E. E. 1224.
White, L. 295-96.
White, M. G. 1815-16.
White, R. K. 617-19.
White, W. 832.
Whitehead, A. N. 1817-20.
Whitely, P. L. 620.
Whiting, B. 438.
Whiting, J. W. M. 297.
Whorf, B. 298.
Whyte, W. F. 907-09.
Wickert, F. L. 621.
Wieman, H. N. 1821.
Wiener, N. 1969-70, 1989.
Wiese, L. 910.
Wieser, F. 1225.
Wigner, E. P. 1990.

Wild, J. 1822.
Wilensky, H. L. 638.
Wilkening, E. A. 911.
Willerman, B. 386.
Williams, D. C. 1823.
Williams, G. 1824.
Williams, R. M. 822, 912-13.
Williamson, R. de V. 1055-56.
Willie, C. V. 914.
Wilson, G. 299.
Wilson, M. 300.
Wimberly, S. 613.
Wisdom, J. 1825.
Wissler, C. 301.
Wolfe, A. B. 1226.
Wolfenstein, M. 622-23.
Wolff, K. H. 915.
Wolff, W. 624-25.
Wood, L. 1826.
Woodbridge, F. J. E. 1827-28.
Woodruff, A. D. 626-30.
Woods, F. J. 916.
Wooton, B. 917.

Worthy, J. C. 638.
Wortley, B. 1057.
Wright, A. F. 1916-17.
Wright, D. McC. 1227-28.
Wright, H. F. 323.
Wright, Q. 1058-62.
Wright, W. H. 1918.
Wundt, W. 631.
Wyzanski, C. E. 1919.

Yee, C. 1829.
Young, J. Z. 1991.
Young, P. T. 632.
Young, R. 1063.

Zborowski, M. 302.
Zelditch, M. 918-19.
Zilboorg, G. 633.
Zimet, C. N. 566.
Zingg, R. M. 303.
Zinkin, M. 1229.
Znaniecki, F. 888, 920.

APPENDIX

Note: Between the completion of this bibliography in September, 1958 and sending it to press in April, 1959, there came to the attention of the compilers certain items which seemed to have enough interest or importance to add. However, limitations of time made impossible the work that would have been required to incorporate them into the elaborate Guide and to introduce appropriate cross-notations into the body of the bibliography. We have, therefore, compromised by presenting this Appendix and by inserting the names in the Author Index.

1. Anderson, R. G. (1911) Some tribal custons in their relation to medicine and morals of the Nyam-Nyam and Gour peoples inhabiting the Bahr el Ghazal. London: Wellcome Tropical Research Laboratories. —Introduced as an early example of recognition by a medical man of the connection between values and "applied anthropology."

2. Banfield, Edward C. (1958) The Moral Basis of a Backward Society. Glencoe, Ill.: Free Press. — Based on recent field work in Southern Italy. Centers on the concept of "amoral familism."

3. Barnett, H. G. (1953) Innovation, the Basis of Cultural Change. New York: McGraw-Hill Book Co. — The concept of values is used frequently and systematically in the theory. Consult the index to this book.

4. Brown, D. R. and Adams, J. (1954) Word frequency and the measurement of value areas. J. Abnorm. Soc. Psych. 49: 427-434.

5. Hägerström, A. (1952) Moral Psykologi. (The Psychology of Morals). Stockholm.

6. Herskovits, Melville J. and Herskovits, Frances S.
      (1958) <u>Dahomean Narrative</u>. Evanston: North-
      western University Press. --There is a section
      on "the system of values as revealed in narrative
      forms" (mythology and folklore).

7. Kluckhohn, Clyde (1958) Have there been discernible
      shifts in American values during the past
      generation? <u>IN</u>: Elting Morison, ed. <u>The</u>
      <u>American Style</u>. New York: Harper and Bros.
      --This represents the extended study of which
      item 153 in the bibliography is an excerpt.

8. ___ (1958) The scientific study of values and contem-
      porary civilization. <u>Proceedings of the</u>
      <u>American Philosophical Society</u>. 102: 469-476.

9. ___ (In Press) (1959) <u>The Scientific Study of Values</u>.
      Toronto: University of Toronto Press. --In
      spite of the similarity in titles there is little
      overlap in the content of the above two items.
      The last reviews some of the work of the Harvard
      Values Project and also presents a revision
      of portions of item 151.

10. Lantz, Herman R. (1958) <u>People of Coaltown</u>. New
      York: Columbia University Press. --Chapter 11
      deals with the "themes and values" of an
      American town in a somewhat new way.

11. Mills, George (1959) <u>Navaho Art and Culture</u>.
      Colorado Springs: Taylor Museum of the
      Colorado Springs Fine Arts Center.

12. Ofstad, Harald (1958) <u>The Functions of Moral</u>
      <u>Philosophy</u>. Oslo (Norway): Oslo University
      Press. --A recent example of a theory of values
      by a philosopher which takes account of relevant
      work in the social sciences. Seven pages of
      bibliography.

13. Tumin, Melvin, and others (1958) Values in action: A Symposium. Human Organization 17: 2-34. -- Discussion and comments based on the experience of a number of action programs in applied anthropology.

14. Voegelin, Charles F. and Voegelin, Florence M. (1957) Hopi Domains. A Lexical Approach to the Problem of Selection. International Journal of American Linguistics, Memoir 14. --Chapter C deals with "intellectual and emotional expressions and values." It constitutes an innovating technique for approaching cultural values by linguistic means.

15. von Mering, Otto (1959) A Grammar of Human Values. Pittsburgh: University of Pittsburgh Press.